How to Do Things with Narrative

Narratologia

―
Contributions to Narrative Theory

Edited by
Fotis Jannidis, Matías Martínez, John Pier,
Wolf Schmid (executive editor)

Editorial Board
Catherine Emmott, Monika Fludernik, José Ángel García Landa, Inke Gunia,
Peter Hühn, Manfred Jahn, Markus Kuhn, Uri Margolin, Jan Christoph Meister,
Ansgar Nünning, Marie-Laure Ryan, Jean-Marie Schaeffer, Michael Scheffel,
Sabine Schlickers

Volume 60

How to Do Things with Narrative

Cognitive and Diachronic Perspectives

Edited by
Jan Alber and Greta Olson

In collaboration with
Birte Christ

DE GRUYTER

ISBN 978-3-11-065167-6
e-ISBN (PDF) 978-3-11-056995-7
e-ISBN (EPUB) 978-3-11-056846-2
ISSN 1612-8427

Library of Congress Cataloging-in-Publication Data
A CIP catalog record for this book has been applied for at the Library of Congress.

Bibliographic information published by the Deutsche Nationalbibliothek
The Deutsche Nationalbibliothek lists this publication in the Deutsche Nationalbibliografie;
detailed bibliographic data are available on the Internet at http://dnb.dnb.de.

© 2019 Walter de Gruyter GmbH, Berlin/Boston
This volume is text- and page-identical with the hardback published in 2018.
Printing and binding: CPI books GmbH, Leck
♾ Printed on acid-free paper
Printed in Germany

www.degruyter.com

Festschrift for Monika Fludernik
on the occasion of her sixtieth birthday

Tabula Gratulatoria

Sharon Achinstein • Jon Adams • Richard Adelman • Jan Alber • Hans-Jörg Albrecht • Vera Alexander • Heinrich Anz • Christiane Gieseking-Anz • Ronald Asch • Peter Auer • Achim Aurnhammer • Susanne Bach • Anne Bandry • Joachim Bauer • Ricarda Bauschke • Sabina Becker • Catherine Belsey • Jürgen Bengel • Walter Bernhart • Juliane Besters-Dilger • Peter Bierbaumer • Katharina Böhm • Uwe Böker • Dustin Breitenwischer • Ulrich Bröckling • Elisabeth Bronfen • Franz-Josef Brüggemeier • Andreas Buchleitner • Michael Butter • Mara Cambiaghi • Jean-Jacques Chardin • Elisabeth Cheauré • Birte Christ • Robert Clark • Jonathan Culler • William V. Davis • Rudolf & Christel Denk • Ines Detmers • Hans Jürgen Diller • Gregor Dobler • John Drakakis • Michael Draxlbauer • Wolfgang Dressler • Heather Dubrow • Marie-Luise Egbert • Balz & Kristina Engler • Bernd & Lucia Engler • Nicole Falkenhayner • Michel Faure • Astrid Fellner • Elzbieta Foeller-Pituch • Johannes Franzen • Wolfgang Freitag • Tim Freytag • Werner Frick • Hans-Helmuth Gander • Hans-Joachim Gehrke • Andreas Gelz • Christine Gerhardt • Hal Gladfelder • Paul Goetsch • Anja Göritz • Gudrun Grabher • Joachim Grage • Jonas Grethlein • Sabine Griese • Ina Habermann • Ralf Häfner • Brigitte Halford • Craig Hamilton • Burkhard Hasebrink • Peter Haslinger • Nikolina Hatton • Christoph Houswitschka • Rüdiger Heinze • Lena Henningsen • Wolfgang Hochbruck • Maartens Hoenen • Walter Höflechner • Anne Holzmüller • Hans Hubert & Birgit Laschke-Hubert • Marianne Hundt • Haiyan Hu-von Hinüber • Oskar von Hinüber • Daniel Jacob • Wolfgang Jäger • Manfred Jahn • Christa Jansohn • Andrew James Johnston • Thomas Jürgasch • Joseph Jurt • Irene Kacandes • Rolf Kailuweit • Stefan Kaufmann • Martin A. Kayman • Hugo Keiper • Alison Keith • Antje Kellersohn • Till Kinzel • Mario Klarer • Holger Klein • Daniela Kleinschmit • Susanne Klingenstein • Grete Walter-Klingenstein • Thomas Klinkert • Ursula Kluwick • Wolfgang Kofler • Werner Konold • Barbara Korte • Bernd Kortmann • Helga Kotthoff • Hanna Kubowitz • Dorothea Kullmann • Helmut Kury • Henrike Lähnemann • Sieglinde Lemke • Jörn Leonhard • Stephanie & Julian Lethbridge • Veronika Lipphardt • Jakob Lothe • Manfred Löwisch • Gabriele Lucius-Hoene • Sämi Ludwig • Christian Mair • Henrike Manuwald • Amit Marcus • Manfred Markus • Dieter Martin • Matías Martínez • Michael McKeon • Martin Middeke • Jarmila Mildorf • Anja Müller-Wood • Aldo & Lina Nemesio • Dietmar Neutatz • Reingard Nischik • Margot Norris • Gabrielle Oberhänsli-Widmer • Greta Olson • Rahel Orgis • Stephan Packard • David & Miriam Paroissien • Sylvie Patron •

Walter Perron • Marjut & Bo Pettersson • Stefan Pfänder • Jim Phelan • Stefan Pollak • Ferdinand R. Prostmeier • Wolfgang Raible • Maurus & Ljiljana Reinkowski • Brian Richardson • John Richetti • Peter Philipp Riedl • Claudia & Alfons Riehl • Gisela Riescher • Matti Rissanen • Nikolaus Ritt • Stephen Rupp • Andrea Sand • Ursula Schaefer • Frank Schäfer • Markus Schäffauer • Carl Eduard Scheidt • Herbert Schendl • Hans-Jochen Schiewer • Stefan Schmidt • Uwe Eduard Schmidt • Gerhard Schneider • Volker Schupp • Philipp Schweighauser • Stefan Seeber • Barbara Seidlhofer • Roger D. Sell • Elena Semino • Mick Short • Sabine Sielke • Verena & Hans Spada • Uta Störmer-Caysa • Birgit Studt • Yasushi Suzuki • Irma Taavitsainen • Markus Tauschek • Gordon Teskey • Roland Thomaschke • Stefan Tilg • Michael Toolan • Gerald & Birgül Urban • Massimo Vogliotti • Sabine Volk-Birke • Ralf von den Hoff • Richard Walsh • Peter Walter • Robert Weninger • Weertje Willms • Franz Wöhrer • Werner Wolf • Evi Zemanek • Peter V. Zima • Bernhard Zimmermann • Thomas & Gertraud Zotz

Acknowledgements

The completion of this volume would not have been possible without the generous assistance of several individuals. Hence the editors would like particularly to thank Judith Eckenhoff, Lea Gorski, and Karoline Rauschen at the RWTH Aachen; and Lisa Beckmann, Madeline Kienzle, Maren Walinski, and Stefanie Rück at the University of Giessen for their assistance with research, editing, and proofreading. Dr. Birte Christ was an invaluable help in bringing the volume to completion. We would also like to express our gratitude to project editor Stella Diedrich of De Gruyter and 'Narratologia' series editors, Professors John Pier and Wolf Schmid, for their generous support of our project.

Contents

Jan Alber and Greta Olson
Monika Fludernik and the Invitation to Do Things with Narrative —— 1

Marco Caracciolo
Perspectives on Narrative and Mood —— 15

Hilary Duffield
Enigmatic Experientiality in the Films of Alfred Hitchcock —— 29

Wolfgang G. Müller
Irony in Jane Austen: A Cognitive-Narratological Approach —— 43

Wolf Schmid
Fictional Minds in Cognitive Narratology —— 65

Eva von Contzen
Dido's Words: Representing Speech and Consciousness in Ancient and Medieval Narrative —— 79

Miriam Nandi
Narrative Identity and the Early Modern Diary —— 93

Susan Lanser
The Diachronization of *Jane Eyre* —— 109

Philippe Carrard
Historiographic Discourse and Narratology: A Footnote to Fludernik's Work on Factual Narrative —— 125

Dorothee Birke and Robyn Warhol
Multimodal You: Playing with Direct Address in Contemporary Narrative Television —— 141

Vera Nünning and Ansgar Nünning
How to Stay Healthy and Foster Well-Being with Narratives, or: Where Narratology and Salutogenesis Could Meet —— 157

Benjamin Kohlmann
Muße, Work, and Free Time: Nineteenth-Century Visions of the Non-Alienated Life —— 187

Kerstin Fest
The Intermediate State between Good and Bad Company: Managing Leisure in Frances Brooke's *The Excursion* —— 205

Margarete Rubik
Out of the Dungeon, into the World: Aspects of the Prison Novel in Emma Donoghue's *Room* —— 219

Franz K. Stanzel
Epilogue: Notes on a Possible History of Reception – From Stanzel to Fludernik —— 241

Contributors —— 245

Jan Alber and Greta Olson
Monika Fludernik and the Invitation to Do Things with Narrative

This collection of essays seeks to combine narratological analyses with an investigation of the ideological ramifications of the use of narrative strategies.[1] As the anthology's title indicates, the overarching question asked here is how to do things with narrative.[2] The essays that follow this introduction do not posit any intrinsic or stable connection between narrative techniques, on the one hand, and world views, on the other. Instead, the articles collected here demonstrate that world views are always expressed through specific formal strategies. This insight leads to the question of why these particular techniques (rather than others) are utilized. The contributors to this volume operate on the basis of the "Proteus Principle," which assumes "many-to-many correspondences between linguistic form and representational function[s]" (Sternberg 1982, 112).

All of the essays printed here emphasize the relevance of theoretical concepts that were developed by Monika Fludernik, who has been Professor of English Literature at the University of Freiburg in Germany since 1994. They focus either on her contributions to narrative theory or her books and articles that emphasize the extra-textual and political implications of narrative research. While some contributions deal with Fludernik's notion of experientiality (Caracciolo, Duffield) or the resulting development of a cognitive narratology (Müller, Schmid), others relate to her work on you-narratives and address the uses of the second-person singular pronoun in contemporary television series (Birke and Warhol). In addition, some essays respond to Fludernik's call for a diachronization of narratology and look at specific manifestations of narrative in the Middle Ages (von Contzen), the

---

[1] For Wolf Schmid, the ideological perspective of a narrative encompasses factors such as "knowledge, way of thinking, evaluative position and intellectual horizon" (2010, 101). In this anthology, we look at what Seymour Chatman would call the "attitudinal function[s]" or "slant[s]" (1986, 197) of Anglophone narratives. The term 'narrative strategies' cuts across the distinction between story (the *what?* of narrative) and discourse (the *how?* of narrative). The contributions all deal with the purpose or 'point' of the interactions between narrative content and narrative form.
[2] Subsequent to the editors' conceptualization of this volume, Janine Utell's *Engagements with Narrative* (2016) was published, the introduction to which is entitled "How to do things with narrative." We wish to acknowledge the overlap and also to point out the similarly pragmatic spirit of Utell's work in considering how best to use narrative analysis to interpret textual as well as other forms of human activity.

Renaissance (Nandi), and the nineteenth century (Lanser). Philippe Carrard relates to Fludernik's work on factual narratives by zooming in on the specific connections between historiographic discourse and narratology.

Responding to the ideological implications of Fludernik's research, Ansgar and Vera Nünning investigate the overlap between the fields of narrative studies and what has come to be known as 'salutogenesis,' i.e., a focus on factors that support one's health and well-being. Benjamin Kohlmann traces the discursive afterlife of *Muße* (i.e., leisure understood as freedom from economic constraint and as a marker of social distinction) in nineteenth-century prose narratives. While Kerstin Fest investigates the central ambivalence of the concept of leisure in Frances Brooke's eighteenth-century novel *The Excursion* (1777), Margarete Rubik, by contrast, addresses the representation and role of imprisonment in Emma Donoghue's novel *Room* (2010). Collectively, the articles all employ Fludernik's concepts to illustrate how narratives function individually and in relation to their specific form-function strategies. Yet they also attend to the ideological functions of narrative elements by pointing to how narrative techniques shape all manner of human activity and forms of knowledge.

Let us explain the theoretical concepts on which the contributions are based in greater detail. In *Towards a 'Natural' Narratology* (1996), Fludernik rejects all traditional plot-based concepts of narrativity and equates narrativity with experientiality.[3] For her, narrativity is situated in an organic frame of embodied and evaluative experientiality. Fludernik defines experientiality as "the quasi-mimetic evocation of 'real-life experience'" (1996, 12), and argues that it is "established by the reader in the reading process" (1996, 36). She points out that experientiality, like everything else in narrative, reflects a cognitive schema of embodiedness that relates to human existence and human concerns. In Fludernik's model, there can be narratives without plot, but there cannot be any narratives without a human experiencer. The fictional existence of an anthropomorphic experiencer is the *sine qua non* for the constitution of narrativity. Embodiment (or embodiedness) – our physical being in the world – constitutes the most basic feature of experientiality. Everything that happens in fictional narratives has its ultimate roots in someone's embodied experience of the world, which is necessarily situated in a specific time and space frame.

---

3 In 1998, *Towards a 'Natural' Narratology* won the Perkins Prize for the book that makes the most significant contribution to the study of narrative. The prize is awarded by the International Society for the Study of Narrative (ISSN).

Fludernik also argues that readers narrativize texts on the basis of cognitive parameters that are derived from their real-world experiences.[4] They thereby establish experientiality in the reading process. The categories and criteria of 'natural' narratology are summarized in a four-level model. Fludernik's *level I* includes the pretextual real-life schemata of action and experience such as the schema of agency as goal-oriented process or reaction to the unexpected, the configuration of experienced and evaluated occurrence, and the 'natural' comprehension of observed event processes as well as their supposed cause-and-effect explanations (1996, 43). Fludernik's *level II* introduces parameters of narrative mediation that provide access to narratives. On this level she distinguishes between the real-world scripts of TELLING and REFLECTING, the real-world schema of VIEWING, and the access to one's own experiences (EXPERIENCING).[5] Furthermore, Fludernik situates the schema of ACTION or ACTING on *level II*. This schema includes not only understandings of goal-oriented human action, but, in the process of narrativization, additionally invokes the entire processuality of event and action series.

Fludernik's *level III* constitutes a fine-tuning of *level II* through well-known 'naturally' occurring storytelling situations, generic criteria and narratological concepts. Generic models consist of the relationship between the teller and the audience as well as the told, including institutionalization, tradition as a memory trace, performance – as the most important constitutive feature of 'natural' narrative –, and the distinction between elaborated and simple oral storytelling. *Level III* also features generic parameters such as the concept of the Gothic novel (1996, 44–45). Finally, Fludernik's *level IV* is that of narrativization, the level on which the parameters from *levels I* to *III* are utilized in order to grasp, and usually transform textual inconsistencies and oddities into a coherent whole (1996, 46).

Towards a 'Natural' Narratology has played a crucial role in the development of a cognitive narratology, an approach that focusses specifically on "the mental states, capacities, and dispositions that provide grounds for – or conversely, are grounded in – narrative experiences" (Herman 2014, 46; see also Fludernik

---

[4] Frames and schemata are static cognitive parameters, whereas scripts are dynamic. "Frames basically deal with situations such as seeing a room or making a promise while scripts cover standard action sequences such as playing a game of football, going to a birthday party, or eating in a restaurant" (Jahn 2005, 69). Fludernik uses these three terms interchangeably because they all refer to cognitive parameters in which some kind of knowledge is stored.

[5] The idea behind these scripts of narrative mediation is that we know what it is like to tell stories (TELLING), to reflect upon questions and problems (REFLECTING), to observe scenes and give neutral reports of them (VIEWING), and to live through pleasant and unpleasant experiences (EXPERIENCING).

2010c).⁶ Fludernik's model also allows for a reconceptualization of traditional narratological concepts. For example, she argues that fictional first-person narratives have their roots in spontaneous oral stories of personal experience, while fictional third-person narratives go back to oral stories of vicarious experience. Furthermore, Fludernik rethinks classical narratological taxonomies on the basis of cognitive scripts such as TELLING (which plays a role in Stanzel's authorial as well as the first-person narrative situation), VIEWING (which is relevant in cases of what Genette calls external focalization), EXPERIENCING (which plays a role in Stanzel's reflector-mode narratives), and REFLECTING (which is relevant with regard to self-reflexive postmodernist narrators).

The main criticisms of Fludernik's cognitive model concern the universality of the proposed set-up and the diachronic aspect of narrativization, i.e., the interplay of cognitive frames and scripts and the development of new forms of literary fiction (see Fludernik 2003b and 2010d). At the same time, however, 'natural' narratology sparked off new developments such as unnatural narratology (see Alber 2016b) and second-generation cognitive narratology. Narratologists such as Jan Alber, Stefan Iversen, Maria Mäkelä, Henrik Skov Nielsen, and Brian Richardson try to come to terms with unnatural textual phenomena that transcend our real-world experience, but they also all explicitly state that they are "inspired by and indebted to Fludernik's approach" (Alber et al. 2012, 371).⁷ Similarly, Karin Kukkonen and Marco Caracciolo acknowledge that what they call their "second-generation" cognitive work, which emphasizes the "enactive, embedded, embodied, and extended qualities of the mind" (2014, 261), is based on "first-generation" cognitive narratologists like Fludernik (2014, 263). To put this slightly differently, the recent foci on evaluative enactment, the embodied mind, the experiential feel, sensorimotor skills, and practical engagements concerning the question of 'what it is like' to have a certain experience, develop the already existing cognitive groundwork further (see also Caracciolo 2014, 47–48).⁸

Even though Fludernik successfully developed a comprehensive new narratological model by redefining narrativity in terms of experientiality, she has never

---

6 The term *cognitive narratology* was first used by Manfred Jahn (1997). Further representatives of this approach are Jan Alber, Marco Caracciolo, Richard Gerrig, David Herman, Patrick Colm Hogan, Karin Kukkonen, Alan Palmer, Ralf Schneider, Peter Stockwell, Sven Strasen, and Lisa Zunshine.
7 See also the debate about the unnatural in the journal *Narrative* (Fludernik 2012).
8 Fludernik is not entirely happy with the dichotomy between first- and second-generation cognitive narratology. Instead, she argues that Kukkonen and Caracciolo "foreground *one* (original) strand in the cognitive science" (2014a, 406) while there are also many others.

lost sight of the particular and special qualities of specific narratives.⁹ Fludernik maintains a strong interest in odd, weird, or otherwise outstanding narrative phenomena, as her studies on the historical present tense (1991), free indirect discourse (1993a), you-narratives (1993b, 1994a, 1994b, and 2011b), we-narratives (2011b), they-narratives (2017b), metalepsis (2003c), descriptive lists and list descriptions (2016), as well as narratological postmodernisms (1996, 269–310; 2000a; 2001) attest. In this context, we would also like to mention her work on the narrativity of drama (2008b).

Moreover, Fludernik's narratological thinking is outspokenly diachronic. She is interested in the historical development of narrative forms. In her article "The Diachronization of Narratology," for instance, she writes that "a reorientation of narratology in the direction of diachronic inquiry is now on the cards – no longer as a weird antiquarian interest but as a vital and exciting new area of research." Fludernik then goes on to offer her own "programme for diachronic narratological study" by providing "some guidelines for the prospectors keen to participate in this paradigm shift" (2003a, 332). More specifically, she investigates changes in narrative beginnings as well as metafictional commentary and attendant scene shifts from the Middle Ages to the twentieth century (see also Fludernik 2011a, 2011d, 2014b, and 2014c).

A final narratological area of expertise concerns the relationship between factual and fictional narratives. It is not easy to define factual narratives. Thus Jean-Marie Schaeffer proposes the following three ways to distinguish between the two. According to the semantic definition, "factual narrative *is* referential whereas fictional narrative has no reference (at least not in 'our' world)"; according to the syntactic one, "factual narrative and fictional narrative can be distinguished by their logico-linguistic syntax"; and, according to the pragmatic definition, "factual narrative advances *claims* of referential truthfulness whereas fictional narrative advances no such claims" (2014, 179). In contrast to Schaeffer, Fludernik refuses to conceptualize the relationship between fictional and factual narratives in terms of a strict binary opposition. Instead, she proposes a more flexible and sliding-scale range between the two. As she writes: "rather than sending fictionality into narratological exile from factual narratives, the opportunity provided by studying factual storytelling should result in a grasp of the overlaps, continuities, and hybridizations, aligned with the factuality/fictionality continuum" (2013, 134; see also Fludernik et al. 2015). She is primarily

---

9 In terms of overviews of narratological developments, see Fludernik 2005a and 2009 and Alber and Fludernik 2010.

interested in literary factual narratives that involve an aesthetic-stylistic appreciation (such as certain letters, diaries, autobiographies, and histories).

Monika Fludernik is best known for her paradigm-breaking work on 'natural' narratology, her reconceptualization of narrative on the basis of experientiality, and her insistence on understanding narrative within a diachronic framework. Yet we wish to argue that the extra-textual and political trajectories of her scholarship should not be underestimated. Here, her research stands in synecdochically for a larger trend in the humanities and social sciences, in particular, but also to a lesser degree in the natural sciences. This is to understand and analyze the entire range of human activities as well as forms of world-making as governed by processes of narrativization. A narrative-based concept of knowledge formation has led to what has been called the 'narrative turn,' which began in the 1980s and continues until this day. Fludernik's quite substantial work on a narrative conceptualization of law and legal practice, including punishment, is indicative of this trend (Fludernik and Olson 2004a and 2004b, Fludernik 2008a and 2014d). In particular, Fludernik has examined the implications of narrative and metaphorical representations of imprisonment and crime from the medieval period forward in fictional and non-fictional texts (2004a, 2005b, 2005c, 2010, 2017a). This includes not only an interest in written texts but also an investigation of the cultural-political work that televisual texts concerning crime have on attitudes towards punitivity (Fludernik 2004b; Fludernik and Brandenstein 2009). As she demonstrates in *Imagining the Prison: Carceral Metaphorics in Fact, Fiction, and Fantasy* (under review), images of imprisonment in narrative and metaphor play central roles in shaping attitudes relating to punitivity, imprisonment, trust in given legal cultures, and ethnicity/race- and gender-related forms of social confinement.

Taking a closer look at this extensive study and some of the earlier texts that contributed to its development helps to demonstrate how narrative and form-focused analyses such as those performed by Fludernik can contribute to various kinds of social critique. In a central move, Fludernik's *Imagining the Prison* goes beyond the Foucauldian periodization that says that prior to roughly 1800 the emphasis was on punishing the criminalized person's body publically, whereas afterwards the emphasis shifted to forms of imprisonment based on surveillance and self-surveillance. As in Foucault's reading of Bentham's Panopticon, self-surveillance serves as a metaphor for the self-disciplining techniques that individuals now practice on themselves (Foucault 1979 [1975]). In an emphasis on continuity between forms of punishment in the old gaol and new penitentiary types of prison institutions, Fludernik shows that prisons remain effective tools with which the state exercises violent control over the disempowered, and this violence reflects on dominant class structures within a given society.

As in her earlier work on the carceral imaginary (Fludernik 2004a, 2004b, 2004c, 2005b, 2005c), *Imagining the Prison* reveals how images of prison unveil larger attitudes about imprisonment, individual rights, and their legitimacy within a given legal environment. Significantly, the author draws readers' attention to the ideological work of representations of imprisonment in both narrative and metaphor. In another hallmark of her original work, Fludernik's prison study demonstrates overlaps between narrative and metaphorical language use and topoi (see also Fludernik 2010a) to show how the real conditions of imprisonment in various historical settings often stand in radical contradiction to the topoi with which these conditions are presented in fictional and non-fictional literary texts.

Yet it is not only in the fields of critical legal studies, crime, and prison research that Fludernik has shown how narrative analysis has repercussions for critical analyses of unjust power relations. Her work on postcolonial fictions has importantly led to a revision of concepts of hybridity (1998a, 1998b, 2000b, 2002 [1998], Fludernik and Nandi 2001) as well as those surrounding alterity (2003d, 2004a, 2004b, 2004c, 2004d). In general, she has demonstrated how narrative perspective, particularly within colonial scenarios and their aftermaths, reflect, reproduce, and conversely may also challenge prevailing power relations. Thus narrative situatedness bespeaks a speaker's or focalizer's relative state of empowerment or disempowerment within a given communicative system (1999, 2003d, 2011c). In this way Fludernik's work relates to that of Susan Lanser and others, who have pointed out that one's narrative stance may represent an anti-hegemonic response to power (Lanser 1981, 1992). It is not then incidental that Fludernik has called for a better articulation of postcolonial narratology (1996). Further, her work on metaphor as a form of ideological articulation has also been pioneering. Since the editors of this volume are also engaged in using narratological insights to perform social critique (Olson and Copland 2016, Alber 2016a), we assert that the political aspect of Fludernik's work may ultimately have as large an impact on scholarship as her more classic narratological research.

No single volume, no matter how ambitious in scope, could do justice to the breadth of Monika Fludernik's scholarly pursuits. Specifically, Fludernik's research in the fields of linguistics and stylistics is not adequately represented in the contributions to this volume, although her foundation in linguistics forms the backbone of her work on narrative, metaphor, and cognition. Fludernik's attention to the smallest units of language, for instance, her work on pronouns, address, deixis, and discourse markers, has informed her nuanced reexaminations of narratological models in general and her refinement of conceptualizations of focalization and free indirect discourse in particular.

We would like to close this introduction by summarizing the individual articles in this volume. Several of the contributions focus on experientiality or the cognitive project as a whole. This includes Marco Caracciolo who, for instance, extends Fludernik's focus on experientiality by dealing with the question of how narratives can elicit distinct moods. Specifically, he shows how two crucial features of experientiality – namely, evaluative dynamics and embodiment – influence the affective dimension of narrative engagements. For Caracciolo, mood serves as a 'protointerpretation,' an equivalent – in the affective domain – to the more sophisticated interpretations that we produce and exchange through language. Hilary Duffield, in turn, elaborates on Fludernik's notion of experientiality from a different angle. She looks at three films by Hitchcock – *Spellbound* (1945), *Vertigo* (1958), and *Marnie* (1964) – to investigate what she calls 'enigmatic experientiality,' i.e., cases in which we can see the experiential result of somebody's trauma visualized on the screen, but do not know its story-based cause. Wolfgang G. Müller analyzes the uses of irony in Jane Austen's *oeuvre* from a cognitive-narratological perspective to demonstrate how Austen's large-scale use of free indirect discourse is strongly gendered and thereby privileges female consciousness. Finally, Wolf Schmid provides an in-depth discussion of the ways in which cognitive narratologists deal with fictional minds. He argues that they often overemphasize the importance of mental functioning and thus calls for a renewed focus on events and actions.

Other contributors to this volume respond to Fludernik's call for a diachronization of narratology. Eva von Contzen, for example, analyzes speech and consciousness representations in ancient and medieval narratives. She demonstrates that there are hardly any passages that provide insight into the minds of the characters in premodern texts. Von Contzen develops a new model of analysis that also takes the fact into consideration that many characters in premodern narratives are taken from previous literary and cultural traditions. Miriam Nandi deals with the interplay between narrative and identity in early modern diaries by Lady Anne Clifford, Ralph Josselin, and Samuel Pepys. She shows that diaries are not coherent, teleological narratives; rather, they typically construct serial, sequential 'mini-narratives' that are open-ended and lack closure. Yet they still create concordance and durability and bring the disparate elements of life together in a 'synthetic' whole. Susan Lanser, in turn, looks at the diachronization of Charlotte Brontë's *Jane Eyre* (1847). More specifically, she addresses Brontë's creation of a narratee that evokes a "new culture in which telling one's story to strangers becomes the vehicle not only for the novel as an instrument of social change." With references to the interpellation of the reader-figure in *Jane Eyre* and references to her earlier work on the gendering of personal voice in fiction, Lanser makes a case for how diachronic narratology involves an awareness of ideology as well as an intersectional approach to materialist histories of narrative: "In short, we can put into narratological practice the truism that no text, however recent, lives outside history." Concluding this group of essays, Philippe Carrard continues Fludernik's analyses of factual narratives by looking at current scholarly historiography. He attends to the question of which features of classical narratology can be preserved and which ones can be discarded or marginalized in the context of such an analysis.

Rooted in Fludernik's work on you-narratives, Dorothee Birke and Robyn Warhol's essay on the use of direct address in recent television series has implications that go beyond a critical medial reception of narratological insights into second-person address. Their essay demonstrates that direct address is also employed to signal the sophisticated self-referential televisual strategies of what has not unproblematically been categorized as 'quality' television. Ansgar and Vera Nünning show that narratives and storytelling have a number of tangible health benefits; there is a considerable conceptual overlap between the fields of narrative studies and 'salutogenesis.' Benjamin Kohlmann and Kerstin Fest investigate how eighteenth- and nineteenth-century prose narratives negotiate the ambivalent phenomenon of *Muße* (leisure). Margarete Rubik draws on Fludernik's tools for the analysis of prison narratives by looking at Emma Donoghue's novel *Room* (2010). In his epilogue to this volume, Franz K. Stanzel praises the ways in which Fludernik's cognitive narratology further develops tools and concepts of structuralist narratology.

This volume documents Monika Fludernik's work in narratology and in narrative and metaphor analysis as a platform for societal critique. Her work has been central to advancing both cognitive and diachronic trajectories within narratological research. Yet it also intersects with developments in intermedial narratology, narratology and affect, and, for instance, new conceptualizations of fictionality. As the last part of this introduction has argued, we view Fludernik's extensive work on the topoi and narratives of imprisonment and crime to be centrally important to comprehending affective responses to these phenomena. We understand both strands of Monika Fludernik's work to be indicative of the many things one can do with narrative, and we offer this volume as an invitation to our sister and fellow narratologists to consider ever more things worth doing.

References

Alber, Jan. 2016a. "Towards Resilience and Playfulness: The Negotiation of Indigenous Australian Identities in Twentieth-Century Aboriginal Prose." *European Journal of English* 20.3: 292–309.
---. 2016b. *Unnatural Narrative: Impossible Worlds in Fiction and Drama*. Lincoln: University of Nebraska Press.
Alber, Jan, and Monika Fludernik. 2010. "Introduction." In *Postclassical Narratology: Approaches and Analyses*, edited by Jan Alber and Monika Fludernik, 1–31. Columbus: Ohio State University Press.
Alber, Jan, Stefan Iversen, Henrik Skov Nielsen, and Brian Richardson. 2012. "How Unnatural is Unnatural Narratology? A Response to Monika Fludernik." *Narrative* 20.3: 371–382.
Caracciolo, Marco. 2014. *The Experientiality of Narrative: An Enactivist Approach*. Berlin and Boston: De Gruyter.
Chatman, Seymour. 1986. "Characters and Narrators: Filter, Center, Slant, and Interest-Focus." *Poetics Today* 7.2: 189–204.
Fludernik, Monika. 1991. "The Historical Present Tense Yet Again: Tense Switching and Narrative Dynamics in Oral and Quasi-Oral Storytelling." *Text* 11.3: 365–397.
---. 1993a. *The Fictions of Language and the Languages of Fiction: The Linguistic Representation of Speech and Consciousness*. London: Routledge.
---. 1993b. "Second Person Fiction: Narrative You as Addressee and/or Protagonist." *Arbeiten aus Anglistik und Amerikanistik* 18.2: 217–247.
---. 1994a. "Introduction: Second-Person Narrative and Related Issues." *Style* 28.3: 281–311.
---. 1994b. "Second-Person Narrative as a Test Case for Narratology: The Limits of Realism." *Style* 28.3: 445–479.
---. 1996. *Towards a 'Natural' Narratology*. London and New York: Routledge.
---. 1998a. "Colonial vs Cosmopolitan Hybridity." In *Hybridity and Postcolonialism: Twentieth-Century Indian Literature*, edited by Monika Fludernik, 261–290. Tübingen: Stauffenburg.
---. ed. 1998b. *Hybridity and Postcolonialism: Twentieth-Century Indian Literature*. Tübingen: Stauffenburg.
---. 1999. "When the Self is an Other: Vergleichende erzähltheoretische und postkoloniale Überlegungen zur Identitäts(de)konstruktion in der (exil)indischen Gegenwartsliteratur." *Anglia* 117.1: 71–96.
---. 2000a. *Echoes and Mirrorings: Gabriel Josipovici's Creative Oeuvre*. Frankfurt am Main: Peter Lang.
---. 2000b. "The Hybridity of Discourses about Hybridity: Kipling's 'Naboth' as an Allegory of Postcolonial Discourse." In *Crossover: Cultural Hybridity in Ethnicity, Gender, Ethics*, edited by Therese Steffen, 151–168. Tübingen: Stauffenburg.
---. 2001. "New Wine in Old Bottles? Voice, Focalization, and New Writing." *New Literary History* 32.3: 619–638.
---. 2002 [1998]. "The Constitution of Hybridity: Postcolonial Interventions." *Satya Nilayam. Chennai Journal of Intercultural Philosophy* 2: 15–49.
---. 2003a. "The Diachronization of Narratology." *Narrative* 11.3: 331–348.
---. 2003b. "Natural Narratology and Cognitive Parameters." In *Narrative Theory and the Cognitive Sciences*, edited by David Herman, 243–267. Stanford: CSLI Publications.
---. 2003c. "Scene Shift, Metalepsis and the Metaleptic Mode." *Style* 37.4: 382–400.

---. 2003d. "Selbst- und Fremdbestimmung: Literarische Texte und die Thematisierung von Aus- und Abgrenzungsmechanismen." In *Zwischen Ausgrenzung und Hybridisierung. Zur Konstruktion von Identitäten aus kulturwissenschaftlicher Perspektive. Tagungsband zur vierten Jahrestagung des SFB 541 der Universität Freiburg, April 2001*, edited by Elisabeth Vogel, Wolfram Lutterer, and Antonia Napp. Identitäten und Alteritäten, 14. 123–143. Würzburg: Ergon.

---. 2004a. "Fiction vs. Reality: What is the Function of Prisons in Literary Texts?" In *Images of Crime II*, edited by Hans-Jörg Albrecht, Telemach Serassis, and Harald Kania, 279–297. Freiburg: edition iuscrim.

---. 2004b. "Literarische Funktionen von Kriminalität." In *Alltagsvorstellungen von Kriminalität. Individuelle und gesellschaftliche Bedeutung von Kriminalitätsbildern für die Lebensgestaltung*, edited by Michael Walter, Harald Kania, and Hans-Jörg Albrecht. Kölner Schriften zur Kriminalität und Kriminalpolitik, 5. 59–76. Münster: LIT Verlag.

---. 2005a. "Histories of Narrative Theory (II): From Structuralism to the Present." In *A Companion to Narrative Theory*, edited by James Phelan and Peter J. Rabinowitz, 36–59. Malden: Blackwell.

---. 2005b. "Metaphoric (Im)Prison(ment) and the Constitution of a Carceral Imaginary." *Anglia* 123: 1–25.

---. 2005c. "'Stone Walls Do Not a Prison Make': Rhetorical Strategies and Sentimentalism in the Representation of the Victorian Prison Experience." In *Captivating Subjects: Writing Confinement, Citizenship and Nationhood in the Nineteenth Century*, edited by Julia Wright and Jason Haslam, 144–174. Toronto: University of Toronto Press.

---. 2008a. "Ethik des Strafens – Literarische Perspektiven." In *Bausteine zu einer Ethik des Strafens. Philosophische, juristische und literaturwissenschaftliche Perspektiven*, 213–231. Würzburg: Ergon.

---. 2008b. "Narrative and Drama." In *Theorizing Narrativity*, edited by John Pier and José Ángel García Landa, 355–383. Berlin and New York: De Gruyter.

---. 2009. *An Introduction to Narratology*. London and New York: Routledge.

---. 2010a. "Das Gefängnis als Empathieraum: Sympathielenkung und Identifikation mit dem inhaftierten Subjekt an der Wende zum 19. Jahrhundert." In *Empathie und Erzählung*, edited by Claudia Breger and Fritz Breithaupt, 151–172. Freiburg: Rombach.

---. 2010b. "Narrative and Metaphor." In *Language and Style. In Honour of Mick Short*, edited by Dan McIntyre and Beatrix Busse, 347–363. Basingstoke: Palgrave.

---. 2010c. "Narratology in the 21st Century: The Cognitive Approach to Narrative:" *PMLA* 125.4: 924–930.

---. 2010d. "Naturalizing the Unnatural: A View from Blending Theory." *Journal of Literary Semantics* 39.1: 1–27.

---. 2011a. "1050–1500: Through a Glass Darkly; or, The Emergence of Mind in Medieval Narrative." In *The Emergence of Mind: Representations of Consciousness in Narrative Discourse in English*, edited by David Herman, 69–100. Lincoln: University of Nebraska Press.

---. 2011b. "The Category of 'Person' in Fiction: You and We Narrative-Multiplicity and Indeterminacy of Reference." In *Current Trends in Narratology*, edited by Greta Olson, 101–141. Berlin and New York: De Gruyter.

---. 2011c. "The Narrative Forms of Postcolonial Fiction." In *The Cambridge History of Postcolonial Literature*, edited by Ato Quayson, 903–937. Cambridge: Cambridge University Press.

---. 2011d. "The Representation of Mind from Chaucer to Aphra Behn." In *Narrative Development from Chaucer to Defoe*, edited by Gerd Bayer and Ebbe Klitgård, 40–59. New York and London: Routledge.
---. 2012. "How Natural is 'Unnatural Narratology'; or, What is Unnatural about Unnatural Narratology?" *Narrative* 20.3: 357–370.
---. 2013. "Factual Narrative: A Missing Narratological Paradigm." *Germanisch-Romanische Monatsschrift* 63.1: 117–134.
---. 2014a. "Afterword." *Style* 48.3: 404–410.
---. 2014b. "Collective Minds in Fact and Fiction: Intermental Thought and Plural Consciousness in Early Modern Narrative." *Poetics Today* 35.4: 685–726.
---. 2014c. "Description and Perspective: The Representation of Interiors." *Style* 48.4: 46–78.
---. 2014d. "A Narratology of the Law? Narratives in Legal Discourse." *CAL: Analysis of Law: An International & Interdisciplinary Law Review* 1.1: 87–109.
---. 2016. "Descriptive Lists and List Descriptions." *Style* 50.3: 309–326.
---. 2017a. "Panopticisms: From Fantasy to Metaphor to Reality." *Textual Practice* 31.1: 1–26.
---. 2017b. "The Many in Action and Thought: Towards a Poetics of the Collective in Narrative." *Narrative* 25.2: 139–163.
---. under review. *Imagining the Prison: Carceral Metaphorics in Fact, Fiction, and Fantasy*.
Fludernik, Monika, and Martin Brandenstein. 2009. "Images of Crime and the German Justice System in German Trial Soaps." In *Images of Crime III: Representations of Crime and the Criminal*, edited by Telemach Serassis, Harald Kania and Hans-Jörg Albrecht, 165–182. Berlin: Duncker & Humblot.
Fludernik, Monika, Nicole Falkenhayner, and Julia Steiner, eds. 2015. *Faktuales und Fiktionales Erzählen*. Würzburg: Ergon.
Fludernik, Monika, and Miriam Nandi. 2001. "Hybridität – Theorie und Praxis." *Polylog* 8: 7–24.
Fludernik, Monika, and Greta Olson, eds. 2004a. *In the Grip of the Law: Prisons, Trials and the Space Between*. Frankfurt am Main: Peter Lang.
---. 2004b. "Prison Metaphors: The Carceral Imaginary?" In *In the Grip of the Law: Prisons, Trials and the Space Between*, 145–167. Frankfurt am Main: Peter Lang.
Foucault, Michel. 1979 [1975]. *Discipline and Punish. The Birth of the Prison*. Translated by Alan Sheridan. New York: Vintage Books.
Herman, David. 2014. "Cognitive Narratology." In *The Handbook of Narratology: Vol. II*, edited by Peter Hühn, John Pier, Wolf Schmid, and Jörg Schönert, 46–64. Berlin and Boston: De Gruyter.
Jahn, Manfred. 1997. "Frames, Preferences, and the Reading of Third-Person Narratives: Towards a Cognitive Narratology." *Poetics Today* 18.4: 441–468.
---. 2005. "Cognitive Narratology." In *Routledge Encyclopedia of Narrative Theory*, edited by David Herman, Manfred Jahn, and Marie-Laure Ryan, 67–71. London: Routledge.
Kukkonen, Karin, and Marco Caracciolo. 2014. "Introduction: What is the 'Second Generation'?" *Style* 48.3: 261–274.
Lanser, Susan Snaider. 1981. *The Narrative Act: Point of View in Prose Fiction*. Princeton: Princeton University Press.
---. 1992. *Fictions of Authority: Women Writers and Narrative Voice*. Ithaca: Cornell University Press.
Olson, Greta, and Sarah Copland. 2016. "Towards a Politics of Form." *EJES* 20.3: 207–221.

Schaeffer, Jean-Marie. 2014. "Fictional vs. Factual Narration." In *Handbook of Narratology: Vol. I*, edited by Peter Hühn, John Pier, Wolf Schmid, and Jörg Schönert, 179–196. Berlin and Boston: De Gruyter.
Schmid, Wolf. 2010. *Narratology: An Introduction*. Berlin and New York: De Gruyter.
Sternberg, Meir. 1982. "Proteus in Quotation-Land: Mimesis and the Forms of Reported Discourse." *Poetics Today* 3.2: 107–156.
Utell, Janine. 2016. *Engagements with Narrative*. Abingdon: Routledge.

Marco Caracciolo
Perspectives on Narrative and Mood

1 Introduction

In *Towards a 'Natural' Narratology*, Monika Fludernik defines the experientiality of narrative as "the quasi-mimetic evocation of 'real-life experience'" (1996, 9). The term "evocation" is less clear-cut than 'representation,' and subtly shifts the emphasis from the narrative itself (where "real-life experience" would be represented) to the narrative's effects on its readers (or viewers, listeners, etc.). When something is represented, we know what it is and where to pinpoint it; when something is evoked, it hovers intangibly between the evoker, the evoked object, and the audience of the evocation. That intangibility is one of the defining traits of mood – my topic in this chapter – and a phenomenon that, I will argue, plays a significant role in our encounters with narrative.[1]

Two further features of experientiality, both articulated in the introduction to *Towards a 'Natural' Narratology*, pave the way for the approach to mood that I will offer in the following pages. Experientiality, we read, "*includes* this sense of moving with time, of the *now* of experience, but this almost static level of temporal experience is supplemented by more dynamic and evaluative factors" (1996, 21). The "sense of moving with time" is more than a matter of narrative representation: it arises in the interaction between the text itself and the audience, whose experience is temporally patterned via "dynamic and evaluative factors." Finally, experientiality goes hand in hand with the embodiment of our cognitive makeup: "Embodiedness evokes all the parameters of a real-life schema of existence which always has to be situated in a specific time and space frame, and the motivational and experiential aspects of human actionality likewise relate to the knowledge about one's physical presence in the world" (Fludernik 1996, 22). We have, again, the evocation of the "parameters of a real-life schema of existence," which reflect the inextricable link between human cognition and the physical structure of our bodies.

---

[1] I discuss mood as a psychological phenomenon and not in the sense of Gérard Genette's category of "narrative mood" (1980, Ch. 4). In broad strokes, I will be defining mood as a relatively stable emotional tone that has no clear-cut intentional object (see below).

That last point about embodiment, in a book from 1996, is a remarkable insight into what would become one of the main areas of research in the mind sciences in the space of a few years (Gibbs 2005; Gallagher 2005). The emphasis on embodiment goes hand in hand with Fludernik's implicit shift away from the notion of representation in her definition of narrative experientiality. That shift contains, in nuce, a wholly new paradigm for research in narrative theory. Surely, narrative represents things: human or anthropomorphic characters, their actions and interactions, and other events such as natural processes. In the sentence 'He stood up and left the room,' for instance, the entities 'he' and 'room' and the actions 'standing up' and 'leaving' are represented insofar as they are picked out from the flux of experience and made clear-cut, almost object-like, in their verbal existence. This is what concepts do, after all: they break down the "buzzing confusion" of our experience – to lift William James's famous characterization of consciousness (1890, 488) – into mental units that can be moved around, replicated, and traded at will. Narrative does the same, but at a higher level: it strings concepts together, using *other* concepts as a glue, mainly concepts of temporal sequentiality (he stood up before leaving the room), causality (he stood up in order to leave the room), and, in some cases, thematic coherence (for instance, if this sentence appears in a story about a man's bad temper). In my work, which builds on Fludernik's account of experientiality, I have called this representational aspect of narrative *abstractive* (Caracciolo 2014b, 200–205). The abstraction has to do with the fact that, in representing things and happenings through concepts, narrative inevitably – and, in most cases, helpfully – abstracts from the details of experience and focuses only on what is felt to be relevant in a given context: surely, the man 'stood up' in a certain way, and had a certain facial expression while doing so, but here we know only that he 'stood up.'

However, narrative is not limited to this conceptual abstraction. This is where Fludernik's evocation comes into play. At the same time as it picks out certain characters and actions, narrative can evoke affective stances that are *not* representational in nature, because they emerge in the audience's experience without having a direct semiotic equivalent in the text. This is the level of narrative that Fludernik's notion of experientiality discloses and allows us to grasp. Crucially, the two features of experientiality discussed above – namely, evaluative dynamics and embodiment – feed into this affective dimension of narrative engagements.

The deep connection between narrative and affect has attracted some attention in postclassical narratology. Meir Sternberg's account of the three *narrative universals* of suspense, curiosity, and surprise is an important precedent: as emotional effects of storytelling, these universals are a manifestation of the evaluative, affective dynamics that underlie narrative engagements (1978, 2001). More recently, Patrick Colm Hogan's (2011) *affective narratology* and a double special issue of *Poetics Today* on narrative and the emotions (Keen 2011) have gone further in that direction. Still, in these contributions, the issue of how narratives can elicit specific moods is never addressed. This is the focus of the present chapter. I single out mood because this affective phenomenon is particularly difficult to theorize from within a representationalist conception of narrative – that is, one that reduces narrative to the abstractive dimension of representation. By contrast, an emphasis on experientiality gives us much more leeway in understanding how stories may trigger feelings at this level.

2 Preliminaries on Mood

Research in psychology and neuroscience often uses narrative – typically in the form of short film clips – to evoke certain moods in participants (Philippot 1993). The mood-inducing or at least mood-affecting power of narrative is thus implicitly acknowledged. But the reasons for this capacity are unclear. Narratives may evoke a wide gamut of moods that are not represented at the diegetic level. For instance, a story does not have to deal with a depressed character to come across as depressing. How is this possible? My approach in this chapter is informed by the contemporary philosophy of mind and, more specifically, by the movement of 'embodied cognition' – though, as we will see, my interest lies more in the phenomenology of narrative than in cognitive processing per se.

I begin by considering the distinction between emotions and moods. Emotions are intentional mental states in the philosophical sense of the word 'intentional': they are directed towards specific objects or situations; as such, they tend to be circumscribed and episodic (Solomon 1993, 112). Being nervous about missing a flight or frustrated after making a careless mistake in chess are examples of emotions, since they are intentionally directed at two states of affair (the missed flight, the chess blunder). Moods, by contrast, are diffuse and tend to lack a distinct intentional object. When I wake up 'in a good mood,' for instance, everything looks somewhat different and I approach my daily tasks with energy and optimism. These feelings are not directed at anything in particular, but they pervade all my thoughts and interactions. One should not draw too sharp a line between emotions and moods, though. We can be dejected or elated about something that happened to us, but when those emotions tinge one's attitude towards life as a whole, they become moods.

The same can happen during audiences' encounters with narrative. In an essay on "Art and Mood" (2003, 539–545), Noël Carroll argues that artworks can evoke moods via emotional responses: an accumulation of emotions can tip our affective balance one way or another, leading to moods. In the following section I will focus on this link between emotional responses and the mood that emerges from a narrative. I will then complicate this account by turning to two additional factors. First, mood is not just a function of narrative contents – the situations and characters represented by a text, and the circumscribed emotions they elicit – but of style and narrative structure as well. Second, I will argue that mood should be theorized in terms of bodily feelings, as a shift in the audience's embodied orientation towards the world. In the last part of this chapter, I will illustrate these claims through a case study. I will discuss a corpus of online reviews of Christopher Nolan's film *Memento* (2000), focusing on how mood and related notions become a vehicle for audiences' interpretive negotiations of the plot. This corpus is a subset of the over 2,000 online reviews published in the "Internet Movie Database" (IMDb) from the film's release in 2000 to March 2015.[2]

3 Mood, Atmosphere, and Emotional Responses

Consider a well-known short story by Ernest Hemingway, "Hills Like White Elephants" (2003 [1927]). The story is based on the dialogue between an American man and a girl at a Spanish railway station: the two characters discuss – without ever mentioning it – the possibility of the girl having an abortion. As we read, we may develop an emotional connection to the characters and their predicament, resulting in emotional responses such as sympathy for the girl, distrust for the man, or curiosity about their past. The exact emotions involved will vary from reader to reader, but these appear particularly likely.

This engagement with the characters may be mediated by what scholars in the field of human geography would call "sense of place" (Foote and Azaryahu 2009). The physical landscape is made palpable and unique by its affective qualities: its barrenness, the whiteness of the sunlit hills (which are compared to "white elephants"), the symbolic nature of the railway junction, which suggests

---

[2] These reviews were collected on 12 March 2015. The use of online materials as data on readers' (or, in this case, viewers') responses has distinct advantages and disadvantages, which I have discussed extensively elsewhere, see Caracciolo 2016, 26–27. In this context, it will suffice to say that this method should be regarded as a heuristic tool in support of theoretical hypotheses, not as providing 'hard' empirical evidence.

two different directions and, therefore, a choice between keeping the child and having the abortion. These features of the landscape enrich our understanding of the characters' situation by giving rise to a distinctive atmosphere.[3] If the dialogue between Hemingway's characters occurred in a dark motel room and not at a sunlit railroad crossing, the projected atmosphere – and therefore our evaluation of the characters – would be different: less expectant perhaps, and far bleaker. In this way, we have an interaction between three affective phenomena: we respond emotionally to the characters and their situation; we become attuned to the atmosphere evoked by the text through the affective qualities of the spatial setting; and we enter a certain mood as our emotional engagement with both characters and place 'tinge' our overall reading experience. Mood is thus always evaluative insofar as it contains, no matter how implicitly, a global perspective on a story's emotional stakes.

Note how the evoked atmosphere bridges the divide between emotions directed at the represented characters and location and the seemingly more impalpable mood created in the audience. This is because atmosphere is an experiential category that emerges from readers' interests and sensitivities; it is thus closely related to the seemingly more subjective notion of mood. In narrative experientiality, textual features and the audience's responses tend to blend into one another. This in-betweenness is part of the very nature of mood, which pervades our engagement with a story even as it is triggered by responses to specific aspects of the text.

4 Mood and Narrative Patterns

It is not only through representation that narrative may create moods: stylistic strategies and narrative patterns play an equally important role. To understand this point, we need to consider another aspect of Carroll's argument in his essay "Art and Mood" (2003). Instrumental music, Carroll points out, is capable of evoking moods without representing states of affair (such as characters or locations) that may elicit circumscribed emotions. How does this happen? Carroll's answer turns on music's capacity to move our bodies imaginatively:

> Instrumental music, in virtue of changing tempi and volume, can be felt as speeding up and slowing down, rising and falling [...]. These terms, and a variety of others, may not only describe the musical text, but also how the music sounds or feels in our bodies [...]. At the

---

[3] For more on narrative and sense of place, see Easterlin 2012, Ch. 3 and Caracciolo 2013.

minimum, it seems fair to say that the impression of movement in music, with non-random frequency, engenders feelings that in one way or another *bring to mind* certain kinds of movement. And if this is true, then we have successfully isolated *one* way in which pure instrumental music can, and often does, elicit mood states in listeners. (2003, 548–549)

According to Carroll, pace and rhythm can thus explain the mood-affecting power of instrumental music. Through its non-representational features and patterns, music taps into bodily feelings that are associated with specific moods. For example, a slow, stately piece may create a calm, meditative mood; a fast-paced piece will convey a sense of dynamism; and so on. Hence the questions: can narrative work in a similar way? Can it influence mood not just through the emotional dynamics of characters and situations, but through its overall shape and structure? Intuitively, the answer is yes: an action film or a thriller can be fast-paced, an arthouse film or a novel in the *nouveau roman* tradition can seem to move much more slowly. It is easy to see how these variations in narrative speed, see Hume (2005), translate into different moods – anxious and hectic for the former, contemplative for the latter. Style can have similar effects: in Hemingway's short story, for instance, the clipped dialogue between the two protagonists, with its frequent repetitions and ellipses, contributes to setting the text's rhythm. The characters' rapid and ambivalent back-and-forths play a role in shaping the audience's mood. The same can be said about the story's suspenseful ending, which leaves readers pensive and hesitant about the meaning of the exchange they have just witnessed.

In other instances, as my case study will illustrate, it is not so much the pace or style of narrative, but the discrepancy between story and discourse that becomes associated with a certain mood. The suggestion is that narrative may possess a sense of rhythmicity not unlike that of music; narrative and music may even have shared underpinnings in evolutionary history and psychological development, as scholars have argued, see Dissanayake (2011); Walsh (2011). This rhythm depends on the 'how' of narrative – that is, on the way in which its events and existents are arranged in a formal pattern of discourse, which offers variations on the "sense of moving with time" that defines Fludernik's experientiality (1996, 22). To the specifically somatic nature of this sense of movement we turn in the next section.

5 Mood and Bodily Feelings

In *Feelings of Being* (2008), Matthew Ratcliffe explores the question of mood from the perspective of an embodied phenomenology. Ratcliffe prefers the term 'existential feelings' over 'mood' because the affective phenomenon he wants to theorize is broader than the everyday usage of 'mood' would suggest. Here I will keep the term 'mood' while capitalizing on two important aspects of Ratcliffe's account of existential feelings. First, mood is something that involves us in the sense that it is a matter of existential orientation; from the perspective of Martin Heidegger's phenomenology of being, moods "are spaces of possibility, which determine the various ways in which things can be experienced" (Ratcliffe 2008, 38). When narrative evokes certain kinds of moods, it invites the audience to try on a whole evaluative and existential outlook at this deep level. Second, Ratcliffe persuasively argues that existential feelings are grounded in the body. He draws a parallel between mood and touch, suggesting that in moods we experience bodily sensations that are not just sensations *of* the body but a certain way of relating ourselves to the world. Put otherwise: in moods as in tactile experience, the distinction between subjective and objective, inner and outer, breaks down.

This idea about the centrality of the body in mood ties in with Carroll's approach: as we have seen above, the sensation of our bodies moving (actually or imaginatively) in response to an instrumental piece favors the creation of a certain mood in the audience. Likewise, one may hypothesize that the rhythm and pace of narrative can give rise to bodily feelings, which are responsible for the shifts in mood brought about by narrative engagements. It is because our bodies respond in certain ways to stylistic and narrative patterns that stories may encourage us to temporarily change our existential orientation. Obviously, this hypothesis would have to be evaluated experimentally. I speculate about this possibility in Caracciolo (2014a), where I use Edgar Allan Poe's "The Tell-Tale Heart" (1843) and Tom Tykwer's film *Run Lola Run* (1998) as case studies. In both narratives, the audience's engagement is keyed to a rhythmic movement at the diegetic level: the heartbeat in Poe's short story and the protagonist's multiple runs through Berlin in the film. Our experience is further modulated by stylistic qualities, which reflect the affordances of different media (the prosody of Poe's sentences, the editing and soundtrack of Tykwer's film). This combination of diegetic (representational) and stylistic features of the narrative may result in bodily feelings that are imagined and, at least potentially, re-enacted by the audience. These feelings contribute to our absorption in the story and coincide with a palpable mood: dark and sinister in "The Tell-Tale Heart," frenetic and upbeat in

Run Lola Run. Not all narratives are equal in this respect, however: some appear to exploit the link between somatic experience and mood in particularly salient ways.

6 Narrative Strategies, Mood, and Psychiatric Illness in *Memento*

One of the arguments advanced by Ratcliffe in *Feelings of Being* is that changes in existential feelings are at the heart of the experience of psychiatric illness. This idea appears particularly relevant to Christopher Nolan's *Memento* (2000) – a film whose protagonist, Leonard, suffers from anterograde amnesia: he remembers his past up to the moment when he received a severe blow to the head, but he has been unable to form new memories ever since. The last thing he recalls is the violent rape and murder of his wife. Avenging that murder is Leonard's obsession, but his quest is complicated by the fact that he cannot keep track of any progress he makes in the investigation: unless he writes things down, he is bound to forget everything. Leonard's psychological condition is conveyed to the viewer through an elaborate narrative structure, which has been taken as a prototypical example of narrative complexity in contemporary film, see Buckland (2009); Kiss and Willemsen (2017). Leonard's story is broken down into two parts, which are interwoven rather than shown chronologically; further, one of the two parts – in black and white – follows the chronology, whereas the other is displayed in color and unfolds in reverse order.

This complexity gives rise to a distinctive mood, which is often remarked upon by reviewers in the Internet Movie Database. What emerges is a sense of mystery and suspense as the spectators try to reconstruct the film's story. This is shown by the high frequency of words like 'mystery,' 'confusing,' 'confused,' 'intriguing,' and 'suspense' in the reviews – and by the relatively high frequency of the term 'mood' itself (see Table 1).

Term	In 2,009 reviews of *Memento* (from IMDb)	In reference corpus (COCA)[4]
Mystery	5.82	0.28
Confusing	5.28	0.09
Confused	4.80	0.23
Gimmick	3.57	0.02
Intriguing	2.73	0.09
Suspense	2.49	0.03
Trick	1.20	0.19
Mood	0.58	0.30

Tab. 1: Word frequencies. Ratio per 10,000 words.

Admittedly, these findings are not particularly surprising, but a closer look at the online reviews reveals a few more interesting phenomena. The reviewers are split between those who find Nolan's narrative structure convincing and those who feel cheated, considering the film's scrambled temporality a mere trick: one that flaunts a sense of mystery, but is ultimately shallow and unwarranted. This is confirmed by the unusually high frequency of words like 'gimmick' and 'trick.' Among those who liked Nolan's film, many comment on the match between the feelings evoked by the narrative and the mental state of the protagonist, as if the non-linear presentation of the story yielded insight into Leonard's psychiatric condition. In some cases this interpretation results in an explicit appeal to the notion of mood: "Story and acting are outstanding but a mention also has to go to the cinematography and soundtrack that both helped greatly to create the oppressive mood that pervaded throughout [sic] film and is [sic] essential to generate the sense of fragility that exists in Leonard's connection to the world" (ismay03 2005).

In other cases, the term mood is not used, but the reviewer still comments on global feelings reminiscent of what I have called mood so far: "I don't think I have ever seen a movie do such a good job of making the audience feel like they couldn't remember anything either" (ashleysheffer786 2013). Other reviewers interpret the mood evoked by the film in even more general terms, as an existential feeling that extends beyond psychiatric illness: "At the end of the movie, you may

---

[4] Corpus of Contemporary American English (COCA; http://corpus.byu.edu/coca/). It consists of 520 million words collected from various sources between 1990 and 2015.

feel vulnerable as a human being. You may feel like an imperfect creation of nature and marvel at how flawed you are, or how flawed you can possibly be; an almost helpless feeling" (cinematicvision 2004). The narrative structure of Nolan's film may or may not be associated with the character's psychiatric condition, but in either case it appears to create a distinctive mood in the audience.

The involvement of viewers' bodily experience is more difficult to detect in online reviews, most likely because the embodied nature of mood tends to pass unnoticed if viewers are not explicitly invited to pay attention to it, see Caracciolo (2014a, 60–61). Still, a number of embodied metaphors seem to suggest that the audience's engagement with *Memento* took on somatic qualities. Here are two examples of this figurative language: "Seeing [the story] backwards made me feel as if I were putting a puzzle together without having use of my hands" (mccrew17 2001); "We feel cut loose from our mental moorings and find ourselves adrift in a world bereft of the rules of chronological reasoning" (Zwick 2001). Obviously, these metaphorical scenarios cannot prove anything about the bodily nature of mood; yet – when combined with Ratcliffe's phenomenological arguments – the reviewers' references to embodied gestures such as "putting a puzzle together" and being "cut loose" from a stable position are at least suggestive of an embodied involvement.

7 Conclusion

I have suggested in this chapter that mood is a site of negotiation of narrative's meanings and values: even more than individual emotional responses, the moods evoked by narrative can be viewed as attempts at articulating a story's relevance. In this sense, mood serves as a 'protointerpretation,' an equivalent – in the affective domain – to the more sophisticated interpretations that we produce and exchange through language. Just like interpretation, mood is an overall response that can be shaped both by story-level events and existents and by discursive strategies such as pace (e.g., the fast pace of an action film), style (the clipped dialogue of Hemingway's short story), and non-linear storytelling (the reverse chronology of Nolan's film). As cognitive narratology engages with the embodied dimension of narrative, the seemingly abstract patterns of discourse should not be left on the sidelines, for these patterns are – in themselves – shaped by the embodied schemata that make up Fludernik's experientiality.

Defined, following Ratcliffe, as a shift in existential orientation, mood can also explain the impact of narrative on our lifeworld: in engaging with stories we open ourselves to affective qualities and patterns that can alter our attitude towards reality. This alteration tends to be only temporary, of course, as is the case with the unease that we may feel after watching *Memento*. More long-term effects are possible, though perhaps also subtler. For instance, narrative may prove valuable in conveying and exploring existential outlooks typical of pathological conditions. Many reviewers of *Memento* find value in the film's approach to amnesia: the mood-inducing power of narrative holds considerable promise as a tool for probing and communicating the experience of mental illness. All of this would deserve being studied more systematically and empirically, as part of a broader effort to understand the real-world, psychological effects of engaging with stories, see, e.g., Kuiken, Miall, and Sikora (2004).

Fludernik's key concept of experientiality helps bring into focus these experiential transactions because of how it opens up narrative theory to non-representational aspects of storytelling – particularly the temporal and evaluative dynamics that underlie the audience's engagement. Ultimately, it may well be the case, as Walsh suggests, that "much of the power of narratives, even very simple ones, to move and persuade is not specific to whatever those narratives are about; it is the affective potential intrinsic in the permutations of narrative form itself" (2011, 63). This shift from the 'aboutness' of narrative (its representational and conceptual dimension) to its 'affective potential' raises exciting possibilities for narrative theory. These possibilities resonate with Fludernik's model insofar as the emotional effects of narrative are shared between conversational storytelling and other narrative practices. Perhaps grasping the analogy between the rhythm of music (or poetry) and narrative can defuse the objections that have been voiced against another aspect of Fludernik's conception of narrative experientiality – namely, its reliance on the notion of mimesis, see Alber et al. (2010). This is another lead worth pursuing in future research in narratology: if one builds a theory of narrative more based on the affective, evaluative, and embodied 'how' than on the 'what' of mimetic representation, then there is less of a need for an alternative model geared towards antimimetic texts.

References

Alber, Jan, Stefan Iversen, Henrik Skov Nielsen, and Brian Richardson. 2010. "Unnatural Narratives, Unnatural Narratology: Beyond Mimetic Models." *Narrative* 18.2: 113–136.
ashleysheffer786. 2013. "Memory." *IMDb: Memento Reviews & Ratings*. Accessed 22 May 2016. Web.
Buckland, Warren, ed. 2009. *Puzzle Films: Complex Storytelling in Contemporary Cinema*. Chichester: Wiley-Blackwell.

Caracciolo, Marco. 2013. "Narrative Space and Readers' Responses to Stories: A Phenomenological Account." *Style* 47.4: 425–444.
---. 2014a. "Tell-Tale Rhythms: Embodiment and Narrative Discourse." *Storyworlds* 6.2: 49–73.
---. 2014b. *The Experientiality of Narrative: An Enactivist Approach*. Berlin and Boston: De Gruyter.
---. 2016. *Strange Narrators in Contemporary Fiction: Explorations in Readers' Engagement with Characters*. Lincoln: University of Nebraska Press.
Carroll, Noël. 2003. "Art and Mood: Preliminary Notes and Conjectures." *Monist* 86.4: 521–555.
cinematicvision. 2004. "Truthful Review—You May Not Like It Because It Can Confuse." *IMDb*: Memento *Reviews & Ratings*. Accessed 22 May 2016. Web.
Dissanayake, Ellen. 2011. "Prelinguistic and Preliterate Substrates of Poetic Narrative." *Poetics Today* 32.1: 55–79.
Easterlin, Nancy. 2012. *A Biocultural Approach to Literary Theory and Interpretation*. Baltimore: The Johns Hopkins University Press.
Fludernik, Monika. 1996. *Towards a 'Natural' Narratology*. London: Routledge.
Foote, Kenneth E., and Maoz Azaryahu. 2009. "Sense of Place." In *International Encyclopedia of Human Geography*, edited by Rob Kitchin and Nigel Thrift, 96–100. Amsterdam: Elsevier.
Gallagher, Shaun. 2005. *How the Body Shapes the Mind*. Oxford: Clarendon Press.
Genette, Gérard. 1980. *Narrative Discourse: An Essay in Method*. Translated by J. E. Lewin. Ithaca: Cornell University Press.
Gibbs, Raymond W. 2005. *Embodiment and Cognitive Science*. Cambridge: Cambridge University Press.
Hemingway, Ernest. 2003 [1927]. "Hills Like White Elephants." In *The Complete Short Stories of Ernest Hemingway: The Finca Vigía Edition*, 211–214. New York: Scribner.
Hogan, Patrick Colm. 2011. *Affective Narratology: The Emotional Structure of Stories*. Lincoln: University of Nebraska Press.
Hume, Kathryn. 2005. "Narrative Speed in Contemporary Fiction." *Narrative* 13.2: 105–124.
ismay03. 2005. "Some Memories Are Best Forgotten." *IMDb*: Memento *Reviews & Ratings*. Accessed 22 May 2016. Web.
James, William. 1890. *The Principles of Psychology: Volume I*. New York: Holt.
Keen, Suzanne, ed. 2011. "Narrative and the Emotions." Special Issue. *Poetics Today* 32: 1–2.
Kiss, Miklós, and Steven Willemsen. 2017. *Impossible Puzzle Films: A Cognitive Approach to Contemporary Complex Cinema*. Edinburgh: Edinburgh University Press.
Kuiken, Don, David S. Miall, and Shelley Sikora. 2004. "Forms of Self-Implication in Literary Reading." *Poetics Today* 25.2: 171–203.
mccrew17. 2001. "Just Give It the Oscar Already… (SPOILERS!!)." *IMDb*: Memento *Reviews & Ratings*. Accessed 22 May 2016. Web.
Memento. Directed by Christopher Nolan. 2000. Los Angeles: Newmarket, September 5. DVD/Blu-ray.
Philippot, Pierre. 1993. "Inducing and Assessing Differentiated Emotion-Feeling States in the Laboratory." *Cognition and Emotion* 7.2: 171–193.
Ratcliffe, Matthew. 2008. *Feelings of Being: Phenomenology, Psychiatry and the Sense of Reality*. Oxford: Oxford University Press.
Solomon, Robert C. 1993. *The Passions: Emotions and the Meaning of Life*. Indianapolis: Hackett Publishing.

Sternberg, Meir. 1978. *Expositional Modes and Temporal Ordering in Fiction*. Baltimore: Johns Hopkins University Press.
---. 2001. "How Narrativity Makes a Difference." *Narrative* 9.2: 115–122.
Walsh, Richard. 2011. "The Common Basis of Narrative and Music: Somatic, Social, and Affective Foundations." *Storyworlds* 3: 50–71.
Zwick, Roland E. 2001. "Ingenious Tour de Force." *IMDb:* Memento *Reviews & Ratings*. Accessed 22 May 2016. Web.

Hilary Duffield
Enigmatic Experientiality in the Films of Alfred Hitchcock

1 Introduction

In the long-standing debate concerning whether character or plot is more important in narrative, there is a tendency to formulate the argument in binary terms and prioritize one aspect over the other. Aristotle's foregrounding of plot in the *Poetics* can be seen as an early example of one element of narrative being privileged over another. However, if we look at the work of more recent scholars, they formulate models which acknowledge the inseparable interaction of narrative elements. Marie-Laure Ryan's study of plot in tandem with an investigation of its interaction with private character worlds is a key example of this (1991). Moreover, Monika Fludernik's groundbreaking work on the theory and historical scope of experientiality in narrative discourse demonstrates that even in periods and genres prior to the rise of psychological realism (where we might expect plot to dominate), experientiality – i.e. "the quasi-mimetic evocation of 'real-life experience'" (1996, 12) – is a key component of narrative. Thus not only in theory, but most certainly in practice, narrative does not involve an either/or process regarding the experientiality of internal character worlds and plot. Certain authors may prioritize one over the other – for example in Dickens, plot is more dominant and experientiality often absent or covert, while in Austen the reverse is the case.

There are, however, creators of narrative worlds who demonstrate the interactive nature of plot and character by adeptly and intricately combining experientiality and plot. The films of Alfred Hitchcock are a key example. Many of Hitchcock's films are depictions of traumatized minds and thus complex cinematic representations of experientiality. Hitchcock's films offer so much material for the study of experientiality in narrative, of which this paper can only highlight a small part. Hitchcock created a whole cinematic style characterized by the depiction of intense human reaction on the screen and in turn the stimulation of response in the viewer. Indeed, as Robin Wood stresses, Hitchcock's film art is a far more direct evocation of human experience for the viewer than that offered in the pages of a novel. Discussing a short scene from *Marnie*, he observes: "A novelist [...] couldn't make us react in this direct, immediate way, as image succeeds image – he couldn't control our reactions so precisely in time [...]. The novelist can analyze and explain; Hitchcock can make us experience directly" (2002, 56).

This paper aims to show the key parameters involved in Hitchcock's sophisticated interconnection of experientiality and plot – most particularly in a phenomenon I call *enigmatic experientiality;* this is at the core of the three films which are representative of Hitchcock's creative output over three central decades of his career as a director in the USA: *Spellbound* (1945), *Vertigo* (1958), and *Marnie* (1964).

2 The Key Components in the Construction of Enigmatic Experientiality in Hitchcock

The following key elements, which are configured in different ways in Hitchcock's films, are at the heart of his technique of narrative representation.

2.1 Cognitive Stratification

Hitchcock's description of the bomb-under-the-table scenario in a discussion of how to create narrative suspense with François Truffaut indicates how keenly he was conscious of the crucial role of different knowledge levels for dramatic narrative effect:

> The bomb is underneath the table and the public *knows* it, probably because they have seen an anarchist place it there. The public *is aware* that the bomb is going to explode at one o'clock and there is a clock in the décor. The public can see that it is a quarter to one. [...] The audience is longing to warn the characters on the screen: "You shouldn't be talking about such trivial matters. There's a bomb beneath you and it's about to explode!" (1967, 52; see also the discussion in Brewer 1996, 110–114 and Dannenberg 2008, 36–42)

The overpowering experience of suspense by the audience in the scenario described here lies in their superior knowledge combined with their inability to intervene in the precarious situation because they occupy a separate ontological level. What Hitchcock is describing here is one form of cognitive stratification – "different possible combinations of knowledge imbalance on the part of characters and the reader" (Dannenberg 2008, 40). We can see here how experientiality on the fictional level of the story world and the viewer's own emotional response both play a role in this interaction of different knowledge levels. In his films, Hitchcock uses cognitive stratification in a variety of different combinations. *Vertigo* is of particular interest in this respect because of a key shift in its use of cognitive stratification in connection with plot and character experientiality in comparison with both *Spellbound* and *Marnie*.

Regarding the above terms, it should also be noted that two allied concepts formulated by narrative and film theorists respectively are a further indication of the pivotal nature of knowledge worlds in narrative. Ryan's 'principle of diversification' (1991) asserts that tellable narrative is created by complex systems consisting of divergent character wishes, knowledge, obligations, and intentions; in film studies, Bordwell defined the terms restricted and unrestricted narration with reference to the "*range* of knowledge" (2008, 57) that can be depicted in different scenes of a film: restricted narration refers to a scene limited to a particular character's knowledge.

In film, therefore, shifts between unrestricted and restricted narration are a key component of one variation of cognitive stratification. However, there are already multiple possibilities in a scene of restricted narration concerning the use of cognitive stratification: the viewer may only know as much as the character, or alternatively s/he may know more than he does; moreover, on the level of the story, an additional character may be present who also knows more than the character whose knowledge is restricted. Cognitive stratification thus refers to all possible combinations of knowledge imbalance embraced by the interaction of the levels of character experientiality and readerly engagement with the narrative. Strategic shifts in the balance of cognitive stratification concerning ignorance and knowledge – and also the interplay of starkly contrasting character worlds of innocence/ignorance vs. knowledge – give rise to a range of representational techniques across Hitchcock's films.

A major expressional mode for the construction of experientiality in Hitchcock is the depiction of emotional experience; this is closely connected to Hitchcock's recurrent use of stories of trauma and of traumatized characters. However, experientiality denoted by rational-deductive thought processes is also a decisive component in his films, and this is primarily articulated via a recurrent investigator figure. The construction of enigmatic experientiality in conjunction with cognitive stratification can therefore be studied by isolating certain key character roles (in the Proppian sense), as listed below, and pinpointing how they relate to each other and to the level of the viewer.[1]

---

[1] Walker's study of Hitchcock's motifs across his films sees the three major characters as the hero, heroine, and the villain, viewed in terms of their interaction with the motif of the corpse (2005, 123–141). In the three films selected for this paper, however, the figure of the corpse does not play a role.

2.2 Key Character Roles Involved in the Construction of Enigmatic Experientiality and Cognitive Stratification in Hitchcock's Films

The Traumatized Character: This figure is at the heart of Hitchcock's use and creation of experientiality. Very often the cause of the trauma is the source of mystification, creating the enigmatic experientiality. Thus a traumatized mind is depicted which stimulates curiosity in the viewer concerning what events occurred to create this mental condition in the character. Particular filmic focalization techniques, such as dreams, reaction shots, point-of-view shots, and special visual effects intensify the depiction – or implication – of the character's inner world, making it the subject of attention but without revealing the cause.[2] In Hitchcock, therefore, experientiality tends to be constructed around an intense emotional state so that the viewer can see the experiential *result* of the trauma visualized on the screen, but does not know its story-based *cause*.

The Investigator Figure: This is a character role which can be taken on in various ways according to the specific film. Thus in *Vertigo*, the investigator figure – Scottie (James Stewart) – is also the subject of trauma himself as well as being employed to investigate the apparent mental possession of Madeleine Elster (Kim Novak), whilst in *Spellbound* this role is played by a separate figure, Dr. Constance Petersen (Ingrid Bergman), who tries to get to the bottom of John Ballantyne's (Gregory Peck) trauma. The investigator figure is thus generally the surrogate for the viewer's own sense of curiosity concerning the enigmatic trauma.

The Murderer/Villain: This character can play a relatively major or also a minimal role in terms of the level of actual representation in the narrative discourse, but notwithstanding any lack of visibility in the film's discourse, s/he is always important for the dynamics of the plot. In terms of the representation of experientiality this figure can also be of note concerning Hitchcock's filmic use of focalization, as can be seen, notably, in *Spellbound*.

---

[2] The film-analytical terminology in this paper largely follows the work of David Bordwell and Kristin Thompson (Bordwell 2008; Bordwell and Thompson 2010), particularly chapter 6 of Bordwell and Thompson (2010, 223–268), whilst also being indebted to further clarification and discussions offered by Manfred Jahn on film narratology as well as Bordwell and Thompson's own online elaboration of their terminology (Thompson and Bordwell 2008). For a discussion of key forms of the reaction shot and point-of-view editing in Hitchcock as a variation on the term "the look" see also Walker 2005, 171–177.

3 Enigmatic Experientiality in Three Hitchcock Films

The following sections take the key elements discussed above and investigate their varying configuration in Hitchcock's films, revealing both variations in his strategy and certain aspects of progression in his development as a director.

3.1 *Spellbound*

In *Spellbound* John Ballantyne is the enigmatic traumatized figure and Dr. Constance Petersen is the investigator figure. Since the film is initially set in a psychiatric institution, the reflection on the human psyche and foregrounding of the experientiality of mental illness and trauma is particularly strong: the film is largely populated by psychiatrists or would-be psychiatrists (as in the case of John Ballantyne, who, in his traumatized state, believes himself to be Dr. Anthony Edwardes, whose murder he is accused of). Not only Ingrid Bergman's character, but also her former teacher, Dr. Alex Brulov, play the role of investigator in the film.

Hitchcock intensifies the cinematic representation of enigmatic experientiality in the character of John Ballantyne using multiple visual cues. Ballantyne is depicted as being mentally overwhelmed by the visual image of dark lines on a white surface and this becomes the central motif to evoke his enigmatic trauma. A particularly intense representation of this motif comes in a scene in which, after Ballantyne and Petersen have arrived at Brulov's house, Ballantyne looks at his reflection in a bathroom mirror while Petersen sleeps. The viewer may initially be able to fully decode Ballantyne's state of mind as simply having decided to take a shave after examining his face in the mirror, because he picks up the razor and prepares the shaving soap. Shortly afterwards, however, all decipherability vanishes as Ballantyne becomes transfixed by the image of the thin dark hairs of the shaving brush against the white foam of the soap. His mental response is demonstrated by reaction shots of his face interlaced with a crescendo of point-of-view shots of the white foam on the shaving brush, the white washbasin, the white bathroom tiles, and the white bath, culminating in the white bedspread with a darker linear pattern. Ballantyne now approaches the figure of Petersen asleep on the bed, the razor in his hand – an image which is constructed to suggest to the viewer that he might possibly really be a deranged murderer. Hitchcock thus creates an impression of extreme experientiality in terms of the depiction of the character's emotional world via the reaction shots, but withholds the context, triggering a desire on the part of the viewer to know the circumstances that have led to the mental condition. This sequence thus demonstrates how Hitchcock manipulates the viewer so that s/he is unable to satisfactorily apply 'Theory of Mind' (Zunshine 2011) to 'mind read' and create a satisfactory explanation of the details of a character's emotional state using the information offered by facial expression. The viewer can see the response of the mind in the visual details of Ballantyne's face, but cannot apply any interpretative model to successfully decode what the depicted mind/character is thinking and experiencing.

Next to these key scenes of enigmatic facial response, a dream sequence which is narrated by Ballantyne and visualized by an embedded film sequence as he reports the details of the dream, is another notable realization of enigmatic experientiality in *Spellbound*. The sequence is noteworthy for its surreal images (designed by Salvadore Dali) which play out in a nightclub and then on a rooftop which, to a first-time viewer of the film, seem absolutely incomprehensible and thus the articulation of pure dream-time experientiality. These bizarre dream images only develop into a coherent narrative towards the end of the film when Ballantyne, Petersen, and Brulov discover the truth behind the former's amnesia and trauma, in which it emerges that Ballantyne has unwittingly assumed the identity of the doctor whose murder he witnessed. This information is revealed in a key scene towards the end of the film, in which Petersen accuses the actual murderer, Dr. Murchison, of the crime and he admits his guilt. Since the key revelation only comes towards the end, only one single and consistent form of cognitive stratification is used in this film – for with the exception of Murchison, all characters and the viewer are unaware of Ballantyne's identity and innocence until Petersen makes a key deduction and accuses Murchison; thus the knowledge deficit across the characters and for the viewer continues until the film's final revelation without any shift or further change.

Nevertheless, the discovery scene does contain an interesting and radically unexpected point-of-view shot, which rather overturns the previous dynamics of the film's knowledge worlds. When Murchison is accused by Petersen, his final act is not to kill her but to turn the gun on himself once she has left the room. Hitchcock now finally chooses – having kept the contents of Murchison's mind and key role in events completely hidden until now – to radically reverse this at the moment when he turns the gun on himself and pulls the trigger, compelling the audience to experience his suicide from his visual perspective. The point-of-view shot of Murchison's suicide – as well as being an interesting example of Hitchcock's tendency to play with radical and unexpected camera perspectives – also demonstrates how focalization does not have to involve actual experientiality in terms of an inner emotional world: at the moment of Murchison's suicide, there is visual proximity and thus immediacy of experience, but no inkling or explanation of the deeper emotional level of this character's experientiality at the moment he ends his life.

3.2 *Vertigo*

Vertigo has not one but two (apparently) traumatized or mentally unstable characters: the retired police officer John (Scottie) Ferguson, who suffers from acrophobia (fear of heights), and the woman who is introduced to him as 'Madeleine Elster.' The film's action is initiated when Madeleine's husband, Gavin Elster, asks Scottie to keep his wife under surveillance because of fears that she is dangerously possessed by Carlotta Valdes, a female ancestor who committed suicide.

To some extent, therefore, Scottie combines both the role of investigator and traumatized figure – but not in terms of the generation of mystery in the pattern of *Spellbound*, since the cause of Scottie's trauma (his failure to prevent a colleague from falling to his death) is already made clear in the film's expository sequence. It is the figure of Madeleine Elster who is the central enigma in this phase of the film's narrative: the use of cognitive stratification – both the viewer and Scottie are mystified by her behavior – gives rise to a sequence of investigative scenes in which Scottie follows Madeleine, observes her, tries to make sense of her behavior, and becomes increasingly fascinated by her. The richness and variation of the scenes of Scottie's observation and later accompaniment of Madeleine – from the scenes following her car around the streets of San Francisco, to a scene near the Bay in which she apparently attempts suicide, through to a scene in the depths of a forest in which she mysteriously seems to disappear behind a large tree – make the sustainment of the mystery very powerful in this phase of the film, which then culminates in Madeleine's apparent suicide when she jumps from a tower before Scottie can reach her.

In terms of the use of cognitive stratification and the representation of experientiality, it is after Madeleine's fall from the tower that *Vertigo* undergoes further decisive shifts which mark it out as more complex than either *Spellbound* or *Marnie*. After Madeleine's (apparent) death, Scottie suffers a nervous breakdown. The representation of his own traumatized experientiality is marked by various cinematic means: facial reaction shots depicting, variously, terror, emotional loss, and the descent into depression (but unlike Ballantyne in *Spellbound*, these expressions are not the subject of mystery but can easily be decoded because the viewer knows the cause of his emotional state). A key part of this phase in the film is a sequence of dream images which signals the onset of Scottie's nervous breakdown. Here, multiple reaction shots of Scottie's face (one in-dream, another post-dream) and flashing color changes enclose a sequence of dream images, culminating in a vertiginous falling sequence. This dream sequence is more intensely emotionally experiential than the cooler surreal compositions of Ballantyne's dream in *Spellbound*; nevertheless, certain images also function on the level of unconscious cognitive-detective activity, since they seem to contain hidden information – particularly the image of Carlotta Valdez's empty grave and the focus on her pendant (which later becomes the means for a key discovery by Scottie). The dream sequence of *Vertigo* is thus more varied a composition than that of *Spellbound*, working on multiple visual and cognitive levels, both emotional and deductive. Thus while the dream sequence of *Spellbound* presents material from Ballantyne's past trauma in defamiliarized form, the dream sequence of *Vertigo* also anticipates developments discovered by Scottie in the future of the story world.

The most significant cognitive shift in the film's discourse, however, comes after Scottie has recovered from his breakdown. Here the film enters a completely new phase in terms of cognitive stratification with a dramatic double shift in the film's knowledge landscape. After Scottie observes a girl on the street who reminds him of Madeleine, the knowledge world of the viewer is transformed. Scottie asks the girl out to dinner, and after they say goodnight, the viewer abruptly leaves the sphere of Scottie's knowledge for the first time. A subjective analepsis from Judy's consciousness then reveals to the viewer that she is the same woman that Scottie knew as 'Madeleine,' and that she imitated Elster's wife as part of his successful plan to murder her by making it look like suicide (substituting the real wife's body for Madeleine before pushing her from the tower). Judy is therefore real and 'Madeleine' is "a creation of male fantasy" (Hollinger 1987, 22).

From the moment when for the viewer (but not for Scottie) 'Madeleine' is revealed to be a fiction and Judy steps into her place, the knowledge dynamics of the film are completely transformed. The narrative interest is no longer one primarily driven by mystery and Scottie's inquiry.[3] Above all, the viewer's and Scottie's knowledge worlds no longer have parity, so that the narrative interest is now dominated by the viewer's suspense concerning *when* and *how* Scottie will discover that Madeleine and Judy are the same person, and above all *how* he will

---

[3] Laura Mulvey's incisive comments on *Vertigo*'s visual power dynamics concerning Scottie's voyeurism and the male gaze in *Vertigo* understate the impact of this radical shift in the knowledge configuration of the film: "Apart from one flash-back from Judy's point of view, the narrative is woven round what Scottie sees or fails to see" (2016, 23). Hollinger substantially extends Mulvey's brief analysis of *Vertigo* by analysing both its "narrative and visual design" (1987, 27); she also concludes that after "the spectator is [...] allowed to enter Judy's consciousness [...] [t]he break from Scottie's perspective is complete" (24).

react to the knowledge. This break in connection between the viewer and Scottie means that the narrative dynamics is now driven by a state of *staggered recognition* on the level of the characters (Judy knows more than Scottie and dreads the moment when he will discover what she knows and who she is). Both the viewer and Judy therefore anticipate Scottie's future moment of anagnorisis.[4] In the final phase of the film, the viewer's knowledge of character experientiality and the back story is therefore complete: the scenario thus becomes an emotional bomb-under-the-table scenario with the viewer knowing more than either of the characters, but particularly more than Scottie. Because the viewer now knows both the characters' back stories and their current emotional states – that Scottie loved Madeleine and that Judy loves Scottie – the suspense centers on whether the revelation of Judy's identity can bring a positive conclusion to the relationship and Scottie can accept Judy as not being Madeleine – a scenario which becomes increasingly unlikely as he systematically tries to get her to transform her appearance back to that of Madeleine, and culminates in his discovery of a pendant amongst her things which triggers his recognition that Judy *is* Madeleine and that effectively the latter never existed.

Notably, at the conclusion of the film, after Judy has plunged to her death in the same way as the real Madeleine Elster did, we are only given brief glimpses of Scottie's reaction before the film closes. The shift in cognitive stratification that takes place after Judy's analeptic memory is revealed to the viewer also transfers the viewer's sympathy to Judy and away from Scottie – especially as from this point onwards he becomes more and more obsessed with forcing Judy to visually become Madeleine. Thus when, ironically, she undergoes the same fate as Madeleine – death by falling from the tower – it is indicative of the film's changed empathetic experientiality that we are no longer given access to Scottie's emotional world beyond a glimpse of his face after Judy falls.[5]

3.3 *Marnie*

In *Marnie* the investigative role is taken on by Mark Rutland (played by Sean Connery), and the enigmatic traumatized figure is the kleptomaniac Marnie

---

[4] For a more detailed exploration of the role of Aristotle's concept of anagnorisis in the narrative dynamics of recognition and cognitive stratification, see Dannenberg 2008, 98—102.
[5] Walker remarks on the parallels between the male protagonists of *Spellbound* and *Vertigo*, notably the fact that their "traumatic incidents [...] are connected by the experience of falling." However, "*Spellbound*, unlike *Vertigo*, allows the hero to work through his fears to a happy ending" (2005, 243).

Edgar (played by Tippi Hedren). Unlike in *Vertigo*, however, there is no internal shift in knowledge levels during the film's discourse and the viewer remains fully in the dark about the nature of the trauma that Marnie has suffered until the revelation at the end of the film of the circumstances of her childhood. Indeed, in *Marnie*, the mystifying details and progression of the discovery plot are much reduced in comparison with both *Spellbound* and *Vertigo*. While Hitchcock backgrounds plot, he increases but at the same time visually simplifies the representation of traumatic experientiality. In terms of focus, Marnie's enigmatic experientiality is even more at the center of the film than John Ballantyne's was in *Spellbound*, but it does not receive the more complex pictorial visual treatment of either of the earlier two films in terms of intricately visual dream sequences. Instead, the representation of Marnie's enigmatic experientiality is limited to her kleptomaniac behavior and a plethora of facial reaction shots in which the reader is invited to 'read' her mind without being given sufficient information to do so. In contrast to the complex use of dreams in the two earlier films, and the use of changing color in the dream sequence of *Vertigo*, *Marnie* employs a much more sparing and fleeting use of the single color red: repeatedly, when Marnie sees a red object, a reaction shot underlines her (unexplained) emotional response to this trigger, and the reaction shot of her face briefly pulses with the color red to visually amplify her internal experience. This strategy is used at key points to signal a moment of connection to her unknown trauma. As a repeated motif, the color red thus plays a similar role to John Ballantyne's response to the motif of the black lines on white surface used as the enigmatic indicator of hidden information from the character's past world; however, in *Spellbound* the black-on-white motif and Ballantyne's response to it is an intradiegetic feature perceived and discussed by characters in order to foreground the enigmatic experience for the viewer, whereas the red screen in *Marnie* operates differently; while the red motif does occur within the story world in the form of an object (a bunch of gladioli, a huntsman's red jacket), the red screen overlay effect is a narrative orchestration of her experiential world on the level of the discourse and thus cannot be thematized in the same way in the characters' dialogue.

The facial reaction shots used to depict Marnie's enigmatic internal world usually indicate a mixture of horror and confusion. One key scene in which red is used is the hunting scene, in which Marnie becomes upset in response to the vision of the dogs killing a fox, and in this state she is then fully triggered by the sight of a huntsman's red jacket. Again, the brief overlaying of her reaction shot with a red screen indicates that Marnie is experiencing a significant emotional trigger. Nevertheless, whilst the viewer can decode the signals indicating the emotional acuteness of Marnie's response, s/he is incapable of constructing any coherent plot concerning events in Marnie's past to which the color red is apparently referring. The fox-hunting scene is particularly interesting in terms of cinematic empathy orchestration: the viewer can successfully decode Marnie's empathy with the hunted fox – particularly as the scene cuts between reaction shots of Marnie's distraught face and point-of-view shots showing Marnie's view of other characters engaged in the hunt laughing in a cruel and slightly exaggerated way at the death of the fox. Nevertheless, although the immediate context of the fox hunt as a trigger of Marnie's reaction is clear, there is no indication of the ultimate significance of the emotional state signified by the red screen. The depiction of Marnie's experientiality is therefore intensely constructed in the film's actional present rather than more systematically working to direct the viewer's attention to gaps in the past. Highlighting Hitchcock's cinematic ability to communicate his characters' experience to the viewer, Wood emphasizes how in *Marnie* Hitchcock gets the viewer to "share" her mental state (2002, 56) – but this is a sharing without depth of *comprehension* of a mental state. Accordingly, the film has no complex and drawn-out plotting of a developmental trajectory of discovery in the manner of both *Spellbound* and *Vertigo*: Marnie's trauma and the significance of the red screen are not in any way connected coherently to the past until the very last minutes of the film. *Marnie* is thus a further development in Hitchcock's representation of trauma, in which plot is downgraded and the evocation of pure enigmatic experientiality is heightened.

4 Conclusion

This paper has shown how, over the course of three decades, as represented by three films, the coordination of experientiality, plot, and the depiction of trauma in Hitchcock's film art is constructed around a number of key elements which nevertheless differ significantly across the films in terms of their execution. *Spellbound* is characterized by the key components of enigmatic trauma, investigation, and final revelation leading to a positive conclusion. The traumatized character's mental state is underlined by key visual effects – facial reaction shots, dream sequences with hidden meanings, and finally clarified by the revelation of the cause of trauma and the true culprit. *Vertigo* intensifies the role of the traumatized or emotionally unstable character by putting two different figures in this role – but only one is the actual source of mystery (Madeleine). The decisive shift in cognitive stratification through which the viewer must realign his or her emotional and visual connection away from Scottie towards Judy is further transformed in the film's dramatic ending, which severs the connection of both Scottie and the viewer to Judy. Paradoxically, Judy truly dies the death she only simulated when playing 'Madeleine' and this irony represents a final complexification in a film that is particularly rich in enigma and emotional and perspectival transformations. Finally in *Marnie*, the balance between experientiality and plot is substantially reconfigured; plot is downgraded in favor of a purer, less visually ornamental and more rawly expressionistic experientiality of trauma characterized by the sparing use of the color red in conjunction with Marnie's facial depiction of enigmatic experientiality.

References

Aristotle. 1987. Poetics *I with the* Tractatus Coislinianus: *A Hypothetical Reconstruction of* Poetics *II; the Fragments of the* On Poets. Translated by Richard Janko. Indianapolis: Hackett Publishing.
Bordwell, David. 2008. *Narration in the Fiction Film*. London: Routledge.
Bordwell, David, and Kristin Thompson. 2010. *Film Art: An Introduction*. 9th Edition. New York: McGraw-Hill.
Brewer, William F. 1996. "The Nature of Narrative Suspense and the Problem of Rereading." In *Suspense: Conceptualisations, Theoretical Analyses, and Empirical Explorations*, edited by Peter Vorderer, Hans J. Wulff, and Mike Friedrichsen, 107–127. Mahwah: Lawrence Erlbaum.
Dannenberg, Hilary P. 2008. *Coincidence and Counterfactuality: Plotting Time and Space in Narrative Fiction*. Lincoln: University of Nebraska Press.
Fludernik, Monika. 1996. *Towards a 'Natural' Narratology*. London: Routledge.
Hollinger, Karen. 1987. "'The Look,' Narrativity, and the Female Spectator in *Vertigo*." *Journal of Film and Video* 39.4: 18–27.
Jahn, Manfred. 2003. "A Guide to Narratological Film Analysis." *English Department, University of Cologne*. Accessed 31 December 2016. Web.
Marnie. Directed by Alfred Hitchcock. 1964. Np: Universal, 2001. DVD.
Mulvey, Laura. 2016. *'Visual Pleasure and Narrative Cinema' 1975. Rachel Rose*. London: Afterall.
Ryan, Marie-Laure. 1991. *Possible Worlds, Artificial Intelligence and Narrative Theory*. Bloomington: Indiana UP.
Spellbound. Directed by Alfred Hitchcock. 1945. N.p.: Eurovideo, n.d. DVD.
Thompson, Kristin, and David Bordwell. 2008. "Observations on Film Art." Accessed 31 December 2016. Web.
Truffaut, François, with the collaboration of Helen G. Scott. 1967. *Hitchcock*. New York: Simon & Schuster.
Vertigo. Directed by Alfred Hitchcock. 1958. UK: Columbia Tristar Home Video, 1996. DVD.
Walker, Michael. 2005. *Hitchcock's Motifs*. Amsterdam: Amsterdam UP.
Wood, Robin. 2002. *Hitchcock's Films Revisited*. Revised edition. New York: Columbia University Press.

Zunshine, Lisa. 2011. "1700–1775. Theory of Mind, Social Hierarchy, and the Emergence of Narrative Subjectivity." In *The Emergence of Mind: Representations of Consciousness in Narrative Discourse in English*, edited by David Herman, 161–186. Lincoln: University of Nebraska Press.

Wolfgang G. Müller
Irony in Jane Austen: A Cognitive-Narratological Approach

1 The Problem

Monika Fludernik concludes her lucid article "Interfaces of Language: The Case of Irony" with the following possibly self-ironic words: "Trying to define irony or humour is, perhaps, laughable – ironists and comedians will always be two steps ahead of any plodding interpreters and literary theorists" (2007, 26). Jane Austen, from whose novels Fludernik draws many examples, is a case in point. Austen's use of irony is so multi-faceted and sophisticated and constantly surprising that it can hardly be captured within the compass of a definition or theory of irony. Yet Fludernik's critical survey of the advantages and limitations of extant concepts of irony – including classical definitions, speech act theory, relevance theory, echoic mention theory, unreliability theory, situational irony etc. – represents an important step towards a more adequate appreciation of an apparently elusive phenomenon, which still belongs to the most intriguing assets of literature. In what follows, I will try out a cognitive-narratological approach in order to elucidate aspects of Austen's use of irony. Echoic mention theory and pretence theory will be foregrounded amongst other extant cognitive theories.

The narratological aspect of this study will be constituted by examining Austen's use of irony within their various narrative contexts, for no adequate study of irony in her work is possible without considering narrative technique. Special emphasis will be given to the two forms of free indirect discourse, the free indirect representation of thoughts and the free indirect representation of (spoken) speech. These two forms of free indirect discourse are used for different purposes in Austen's work, as it is evident in the varying representations of major and minor, and male and female characters. This is an aspect of the novelist's art which has thus far been neglected.

It is curious that secondary criticism of Jane Austen tends to praise her irony without going more deeply into this aspect of her art. Thus, referring to Austen, Robert Polhemus correctly maintains that "irony depends on its audience to detect and complete meanings extending beyond the literal sense of the language," but ends by saying that "for Austen, life itself is the principal ironist" (1986, 66; 67). To my knowledge, there is only one comprehensive study of Austen's irony, Kühnel's monograph (1969), a solid piece of work that has nonetheless become somewhat out-dated after four decades of irony theory and progress in narratological research. As to irony theory, I will concentrate on what is useful for my research purposes. After a few general observations on the definition of irony, I will briefly characterize some modern approaches to irony, focusing in particular on cognitive research. Before commencing textual analysis, I will deal with a narrative aspect of Austen's art which is most important to understanding her use of irony, namely the fact that in her work free indirect speech is as central as free indirect thought. This fact has been neglected in narratological research, which has concentrated on Austen's creation of point-of-view narration and the psychological novel and in doing so has emphasized representation of thought at the cost of representation of speech.

2 The Rhetorical Definition of Irony

Classical definitions of irony understand it to be a trope.[1] As a trope, irony represents a use of language that expresses the intended meaning through its opposite, for instance, praise through blame, or blame through praise. More specifically, in its rhetorical sense, irony substitutes a semantically opposed figurative term (*verbum improprium*) for the proper term (*verbum proprium*) in such a way that the substituted term can be recognized. It is the function of so-called irony signals to ensure the comprehension of irony as such. This is what is nowadays called verbal irony. This understanding of irony can also be applied to propositions. An ironic proposition can be interpreted in a literal sense and in a sense contradictory to the literal one.

Since classical times, there have been two different definitions of verbal irony. First, according to Quintilian's narrower definition, irony wants us to understand the opposite of what has just been stated: "Contrarium ei quod dicitur intelligendum est [the opposite of what is said is to be understood]" (*Institutio oratoria* IX.2.44); and, second, according to Cicero's wider definition, irony says something other than what was meant: "Cum alia dicuntur ac sentias [when you say something different from what you mean]" (*De Oratore* II.67.269). Litotes (ironic understatement) is another trope related to irony. Litotes affirms something by the negation of its contrary, for instance, when we refer to a misshaped man with the words, "He is no Adonis." The ironic equivalent of this proposition

---

[1] For a wider definition of irony that is particularly relevant to the performance of drama on stage, see Greiner 2007.

would be "He is an Adonis." The semantic contradiction evoked in litotes is created by negation, while in cases of irony the contradiction forms the essence of the expression. For this reason Linda Hutcheon (1995) appropriately refers to *Irony's Edge* in her study. Due to the periphrastic nature of litotes, this trope can be expanded almost *ad libitum*. I can, for instance, say "This is by no means what I may be tempted to call an Adonis." Such verbosity would be impossible or out of place in an ironic utterance. Verbal irony derives its effect from the incisiveness of the formulation. Emphatic reductions as in "What an Adonis!" can result in the sharp or bitter tone of sarcasm, which is a subcategory of irony.[2] Verbal irony is of a too limited scope to account for the multiple complex forms of irony in literature. But some passages in Jane Austen can be explained in terms of ironia verborum or litotes, for instance the following comments of Mr. Bennet in Austen's *Pride and Prejudice* (1813) on the conceited, domineering Lady Catherine and the insolent good-for-nothing Wickham:

> She [Lady Catherine de Bourgh] is a very fine-looking woman! and her calling here was prodigiously civil! for she only came, I suppose, to tell us the Collinses were well. (1973, 359)[3]

> He [Mr. Wickham] is as fine a fellow [...] as ever I saw. He simpers, and smirks, and makes love to us all. I am prodigiously proud of him. (1973, 330)

The context of the two passages makes it obvious that Mr. Bennet intends his utterances not to be taken literally. He makes his point by stating the opposite of what he purports to convey. His comment on the two characters is a transparent misrepresentation. Using this form of verbal irony is his way of showing his wit and of passing a negative judgment on others. Mr. Bennet's ironic statements also have the function of correcting the effusive evaluation of the same persons by his wife, which in contrast to his remarks constitute non-ironic misrepresentations of the reality of things and persons that are derived from wishful thinking.

3 Communication Models

An important step in the development of a theory and criticism of irony is marked by the advent of communication theory. To describe communicative situations in

---

[2] On sarcasm and its relation to irony, see Rockwell 2006.
[3] Quotations are taken from *The Novels of Jane Austen*, edited by Chapman (1973). The numbers of the volumes and pages are given in brackets in the text.

which irony is directed at one recipient who is expected to understand the utterance the simple bipartite model of sender and receiver is sufficient. Yet to describe more complex situations in which the ironic utterance is directed at different recipients who receive it in different ways, an expansion from a bipartite to a tripartite communicative model is necessary: such a model consists of a sender, a recipient, and a third person as the object or the intended victim of the ironic utterance.[4] An explicit description of this model is offered by Fowler:

> Irony is a form of utterance that postulates a double audience, consisting of one party that hearing shall hear & shall not understand, & another party that, when more is meant than meets the ear, is aware of both that more & of the outsiders' incomprehension. (1984, 295)

In the evaluation of Austen, the communication situation – in which ironic speech-acts are performed – always has to be considered. It is specifically the narrative organization of the text – the use of voice, the number and kind of hearers, the deployed perspective, and the narrative structure – that has to be taken into account.

4 Cognitive Approaches to Irony

For cognitivists, irony is of great interest because the prerequisite for the accurate appreciation of irony requires a cognitive act, in which there is always the possibility of a misunderstanding to be accounted for. Since it is impossible to refer to all of the recent cognitive approaches to irony, I will concentrate on two theories that are especially relevant to this study's topic.[5] The first of these two approaches is the echoic mention theory devised by Dan Sperber and Deirdre Wilson (1981). This theory assumes that a speech act is ironic, when and if the speaker mentions or echoes an earlier utterance in order to express an attitude of contempt or ridicule towards it. The cognitive performance required by the recipient is to recognize the utterance as familiar and to reinterpret it in terms of the new meaning the speaker intends to convey.

The status of "echoic mention" requires clarification in relation to relevance theory. We have to be more explicit here since this is an issue of high importance with regard to the reception of ironic speech-acts. Being an alternative to the clas-

---

[4] A clear account of the triadic communication model of irony can be found in Wolf 2007.
[5] For a more explicit account, see the theoretical part of Müller 2011.

sical code model, relevance theory elaborates on an inferential model of communication, whose foundation was laid by Herbert P. Grice. Relevance theory is concerned with the search of meaning in communication which fits the recipient's expectation of relevance. It is based on the idea that human cognition tends to be geared to the maximization of relevance. In this context, inferential communication – called "ostensive-inferential communication" by relevance theory (Müller 2011, 199) – is of paramount importance. Now irony, which conveys the opposite of the literal meaning of an utterance, is a supreme example of the fact that there are forms of communication that cannot be explained on the basis of a straightforward code model. Verbal irony conveyed by an echoic utterance involves "the expression of a tacitly dissociative attitude [...] to an attributed utterance of thought" (Sperber and Wilson 2006, 622). The concept of cognition differs manifestly in Grice's understanding of irony from that in relevance theory. For Grice, irony is an overt violation of the maxim of truthfulness, which necessitates a process in which literal meaning is first understood and, in a second step, the intended meaning is recognized, so that the co-operative principle of communication is ultimately not violated. According to relevance theory, the recipient immediately seizes upon the ironic meaning as the relevant meaning in a cognitive act that is induced by an "ostensive stimulus" (Müller 2011, 199). This stimulus is what is, in traditional terminology, called the irony signal.

The second cognitive theory that needs to be discussed here is the pretence theory of irony (Clerk and Gerrig 1984). According to the pretence theory, the ironic speaker pretends to be an injudicious person speaking to an uninitiated audience; in doing so, the speaker intends the addressee of the ironic utterance to discover the pretence. The role of pretence was already referred to by Grice who said that "[t]o be ironical is, among other things, to pretend [...], and while one wants the pretense to be recognized as such, to announce it as a pretense would spoil the effect" (1978, 125). This theory is, among other things, useful in accounting for the expansions of irony into larger fictionalization strategies as in Swift's *A Modest Proposal* (1729), whose textual strategy has been called "impersonation irony" (Wilson 2006, 1741).

5 Narratorial (Authorial) Irony

A form of irony that may seem a little problematic in the case of Austen is narratorial irony, a kind of irony for which the narrator is overtly responsible. In avoiding the term "authorial" I follow Holger Klein, who insists on making a sharp distinction between the author and the narrator (2007, 192). This terminological differentiation may be the result of overscrupulousness, as Stanzel's term "auktorial" has come to be rendered in English as "authorial" without implying any reference to the author as a historical person. In his translation of *Theorie des Erzählens* (1979) into English (1984), Stanzel renders "auctorial" as "authorial." It is well known that Jane Austen is one of the most important early practitioners of point-of-view fiction or figural narration, i.e. narratives in the third person that are written in the reflector-mode, and the narrator of her novels very rarely refers to herself in the first person. Yet there are a considerable number of instances in which Austen's narrator makes comments, many of them of an ironic character. And these are usually subtler than those of Henry Fielding, for instance, who has been generally viewed as the much-acclaimed paradigm of the ironic omniscient narrator. Fielding has a predilection for rhetorical irony, the substitution of the proper term with its opposite, most markedly in the novel *The Life and Death of Jonathan Wild, the Great* (1743), in whose title the principle of irony is already markedly evident. The infamous gang leader and highwayman is called "the great." Coming back to Austen's fiction, I will begin with two rather straightforward examples from the context of Mr. Collins's marital projects in *Pride and Prejudice*. The first of these concerns the description of Mr. Collins proposing marriage to Charlotte Lucas a few short days after Elizabeth Bennet rejected his marriage proposal: "But here, she did injustice to *the fire and independence of his character*, for it led him to escape out of Longbourn House the next morning with admirable slyness, and hasten to Lucas Lodge *to throw himself at her feet*" (1973, 121).[6] The irony in this passage results from the substitution of the proper terms with their opposites. The reader is all too aware that "fire" and "independence" are not qualities of Mr. Collins's character, and that a physical action like throwing himself at a woman's feet is completely impossible for such a self-important and heavy-handed person. The irony is an instrument for ridiculing the character of Collins, whose marriage proposal to Elizabeth was rejected and who hastens to make another one to another person posthaste. The understanding of the irony is here, as I would argue, not accomplished by a two-step process of first taking in the literal meaning and then grasping the figurative one. I would like to argue that, in accordance with linguistic relevance theory, which posits that the recipient immediately seizes upon the ironic meaning as the relevant meaning in a cognitive act caused by an "ostensive stimulus," the contradiction between what we know about the character and what is told about him in the situation in question is recognized in a single cognitive act. Of course, such an irony-saturated

---

[6] Emphasis in this and all further examples from Austen's works by W. G. M.

narrative requires a perceptive reader. Engaging the reader strongly and stimulating his or her mental activity, Austen's novels produce intellectual and aesthetic delight.

A similar, yet somewhat more intricate example from the same chapter is the representation of Charlotte Lucas's consciousness as she eagerly waits for the arrival of Mr. Collins: "Miss Lucas perceived him from an upper window as he walked towards the house, and instantly set out to meet him *accidentally* in the lane" (1973, 121). Here, the use of the adverb "accidentally" does not fit its context. Again, the reader is more than aware of the situation, namely that Charlotte Lucas, in intending to 'catch' Mr. Collins, is making a show of acting in an unpremeditated way. Irony is here a device of exposing and criticizing a character's hypocrisy. This type of irony is to be appreciated as narratorial irony. While the whole sentence is written in the form of a factual narrative report, the narrator inserts the adverb "accidentally" in reference to the impression that Charlotte Lucas desires to create. The insertion of this word can also be seen as a glimpse of the figural character's point of view. We can here observe that Austen is more sophisticated than run-of-the-mill ironists. Austen's irony emerges also in narratorial (authorial) comment, which, at times, assumes an aphoristic character.

Here is a comment from *Emma* (1815) which belongs to a similar context to that of the previous example. It refers to the vicar Mr. Elton, who, sometime after his failure to win the hand of Emma Woodhouse, comes back to the village of Highbury, now engaged to another woman: "Human nature is so well disposed towards those who are in interesting situations, that a young person, who either marries or dies, is sure of being kindly spoken of" (1973, 181). This ironic comment is so intricate that the classical definition of irony does not suffice to explain it. In apparently referring to human nature in general, the comment appears to be like an aphorism. Yet the literal statement is subverted by bringing together such absolutely contrasting events as the marriage and death of young people and by referring to them as "interesting situations," that are "sure to be spoken kindly of." The echoic mention theory of irony could be applied to this passage, since one of the issues referred to is the tradition of speaking kindly of deceased people (*de mortuis nil nisi bene*). But by lumping marriage together with death, matrimony is mocked. If the narratorial comment were to be taken as a general truth, or an aphorism, it would betray a callous or cynical attitude on the narrator's part, but in the specific context of the novel a concrete fact is referred to, the upcoming marriage of the vain upstart Elton. Even in this context, narratorial irony does not lose its vitriolic character, which is hidden under apparently innocuous words.

The most famous and at the same time perhaps the most complex instance of Austen's narratorial irony is the aphoristic sentence that opens *Pride and Prejudice*: "It is a truth universally acknowledged, that a single man in possession of a good fortune, must be in want of a wife" (1973, 3). Many critics maintain that the irony of this statement is established via the context, i.e. the dialogue of Mr. and Mrs. Bennet that follows on this sentence. There can hardly be an objection to this position, but I would like to argue that the statement is in itself ironic.[7] In Jane Austen's opening sentence there is only one proposition that contains a contradiction. The aphorism, or rather, maxim is heralded as a universal truth, yet the proposition is narrowed down to a very concrete case, namely that a rich unmarried man must be looking for a wife. What is introduced as a *quaestio infinita*, an infinite question, turns out to be a *quaestio finita*, a finite question. The way Austen deals with the form of the maxim is ironic, and the reader must perform a cognitive act to understand the irony. He or she must understand that what Austen presents as a maxim is only apparently a maxim. It is a maxim that does not express a universal truth but refers to a very concrete situation. To apply the echoic mention theory to this example, the sentence refers to a preformed genre, that of the maxim, which it ironically subverts. A maxim is a concise, pointed, and easily remembered statement that purports to reveal a general truth or principle. Austen explicitly refers to this rhetorical device by echoing the verbal form of the genre in "a truth universally acknowledged." Yet she limits its general applicability to a very specific situation, thus ironizing it. Additionally, the irony of the maxim is intensified by the volition attributed to the rich unmarried man – "must be in want of." This introduces something of a bias to the maxim. Who in fact knows that a wealthy man is in want of a wife? Rich men may have other interests. Austen's ironic maxim provides a key to the novel's plot, which is concerned with the need for the daughters of a genteel family to find well-off husbands. The irony of the opening of the novel sets the tone for some of the ironies of the whole. In this case the irony could be understood without looking at the novel's context, but the subsequent dialogue of Mr. and Mrs. Bennet confirms its meaning. It introduces an essential dimension of the novel's thematic concerns.

Another instance of authorial irony that I wish to discuss is to be found in the marriage proposal at the end of Austen's *Emma*. This is the novel's emotional climax, the moment when Knightley, who has had his emotions so much under control all through the novel, calls Emma "my dearest, most beloved Emma," and she is "almost ready to sink under the agitation of this moment" (1973, 430). Let

---

[7] For an excellent analysis of this aphorism, which comes to the same conclusion as the present writer, see Fludernik 2007, 16.

us see how Austen describes Emma's reply to what realizes her "happiest dream" (1973, 430): "She spoke then, on being so entreated. – What did she say? – Just what she ought, of course. A lady always does. – She said enough to shew there need not be despair – and to invite him to say more himself (1973, 431). In what the reader might expect to be the emotional core of the episode, the narrator takes on an astonishing position/attitude of distance to the lovers. She suggests that Emma reacts to Knightley's proposal by saying what any lady would be saying under the circumstances. The prominent position of the lovers among the characters of *Emma* is thus ironically undermined for the moment. Why does Austen destroy the text's illusion at this particular point? I am not convinced, as some critics argue, that Jane Austen's restraint is to be attributed to her coyness. Nor do I believe that her language skepticism, i.e. the belief that emotions can hardly ever be expressed adequately, is responsible for her restrained dealing with emotions at this point. It is true that a little later the narrator declares that "Seldom, very seldom, does complete truth belong to any human disclosure" (1973, 431). Yet the discrepancy between the overall emotionality of the scene and the surprising dryness at its climax is too great to be explained other than as an ironic intervention.

What might be the reason for this ironic disillusionment, which is to be found in all of Austen's proposal scenes except for her last completed novel *Persuasion* (1818)? I believe that with her ironic presentation of love declarations and marriage proposals she attempts to take a distance from run-of-the-mill sentimental romances, which tend to be targeted to a happy ending which is intended to overwhelm the feelings of the readers. Thus Austen refers to or, if you wish, echoes comparable episodes from fiction and at the same time ironically deviates from them or, rather, refutes them. The passage from *Emma* illustrates the enormous power which even a covert third-person narrator – this is not an omniscient (authorial) one – can have over the characters of the novel. He or she can, for artistic reasons, deny the protagonists a fully-fledged happy ending, or she can grant them extreme emotional fulfillment, as is the case in Austen's revision of the ending of *Persuasion*, which was in the first version subverted by a comic design. At this point the question may be tentatively posed as to whether we should really attribute such decisions to the narrator, who is, contrary to Fielding's narrator, a covert narrator, and hardly manifest in the text. Or, should we instead refer these narrational decisions to the author, not, to be sure, to the author as a biographical person, but the author as an artist.[8]

---

8 From another perspective, the return of the category of the author in narratology has been called for by Korthals Altes (2014). Richard Walsh suggests eradicating extra- and heterodiegetic

A case could be made for the argument that, in Austen's novels, the narrator is not the artist. The narrator is a textual instance introduced by the author for artistic purposes. The author qua artist is responsible for artistic decisions. This is what Henry James meant when in his review of Flaubert's correspondence he included the French novelist's famous quotation, "the artist must be present in his work like God in Creation, invisible and almighty, everywhere felt but nowhere seen" (Chapman 1989, 2). Be that as it may, irony has a sharp edge, even in an apparently highly controlled novelist like Austen.

6 Irony and Free Indirect Representation of Speech and Thought

I will now come to one of the most important and innovative forms of irony in Jane Austen, i.e., her use of irony in free indirect discourse. Before looking at the texts, some basic observations must be made.[9] Free indirect style occurs both as a means of representing speech and thought. Charles Bally, one of the pioneers in this field of research, said: "Le style indirect libre, sert à reproduire les pensées ou les paroles [the free indirect style serves to represent thought or speech]" (1912, 555). In the discussion of Austen's narrative art and her use of irony, a distinction must be drawn between the representation of spoken language and interior language. It is highly interesting – though hardly ever recognized by critics – that Jane Austen avoids rendering the spoken words of her protagonists, who are invariably female, in free indirect discourse, while their thoughts are frequently conveyed in free indirect form. Conversely, the thoughts of her minor characters and practically all of the male characters are, if they are represented at all, usually rendered not in free indirect discourse, while their spoken words are frequently conveyed in the free indirect form. There is no room to go into the intricacies of this important aspect of Austen's narrative art more explicitly, but one point has to be emphasized, namely that the consequence of Austen's artistic decision is to privilege female consciousness. Austen hardly ever gives us insight

---

narrators in narrative fiction: "Extradiegetic and heterodiegetic narrators (that is, 'impersonal' and 'authorial' narrators), who cannot be represented without thereby being rendered homodiegetic or intradiegetic, are in no way distinguishable from authors." He therefore concludes that "the narrator is always either a character who narrates, or the author" (2007, 84; 78). See also Dawson 2013.

9 For a more detailed discussion of this problem, see Müller 1984.

into male consciousness. Her innovation in the field of narrative art is thus strongly gendered.

Her decision to distribute the two forms of representation in relation to gender and to the major-minor distinction of characters also has consequences for her use of irony. Here is an example of the ironic use of spoken speech in free indirect form. Its context is the attempt of Mrs. Dashwood in *Sense and Sensibility* (1811) to dissuade her wealthy husband from fulfilling his father's last wish to support his stepmother and his three half-sisters:

> To take three thousand pounds from the fortune of their dear little boy, would be impoverishing him to the most dreadful degree. [...] How could he answer it to himself to rob his child, and his only child too, of so large a sum? And what possible claim could the Miss Dashwoods, who were related to him only by half blood, which she considered as no relationship at all, have on his generosity to so large an amount? It was very well known that no affection was ever supposed to exist between children of any man by different marriages; and why was he to ruin himself, and their poor little Harry, by giving away all his money to his half sisters? (1973, 8)

The utterances of Mrs. Dashwood are represented here in a hysterically expressive and simultaneously ironized form. Austen makes use of the possibilities of free indirect discourse to present the utterances of Mrs. Dashwood in a more pointed way and to make her arguments follow more rapidly than would be the case in dialogue. Within a paragraph, Mrs. Dashwood's words are unmasked as a mixture of exaggerations and perversions. She reinterprets the active charity her husband wants to offer his impoverished relatives as robbing his only son, i.e. the sole heir of a big inheritance, of his heritage. The illogicality of her argument comes out most clearly in the sentence, "How could he answer it to himself to rob his child, and his only child too, of so large a sum?" The parenthetic phrase "and his only child too," which is to reinforce her argument, weakens it from the angle of logic. One single son would be much less harmed by a little deduction from a huge inheritance than would be the case if he had brothers. The love for her child, which is so eloquently uttered, is in fact used to conceal egotism and avarice. Mrs. Dashwood's overstated argument that the – relatively small – benefit granted to the poor relatives would impoverish her son "to the most dreadful degree" and would ruin her husband and their "poor little Harry" grossly contrasts with the wealth of the family, a fact of which the reader is quite aware. This passage drastically illustrates just how much irony Austen may pack into free indirect speech without any comment on the part of the narrator. This is then showing and not telling.

The following passage from *Mansfield Park* (1814) exemplifies Austen's non-ironical use of free indirect thought. It conveys the inner turmoil in the protagonist Fanny Price, who has to learn that her confidant, Edmund Bertram, has, contrary to his declared intention, decided to take part in a theatre performance about which she feels grave doubts:

> To be acting! After all his objections – objections so just and public! After all that she had heard him say, and seen him look and known him to be feeling. Could it be possible? Edmund so inconsistent. Was he not deceiving himself? Was he not wrong? Alas! It was all Miss Crawford's doing. (1973, 156)

The protagonist's moral indignation is indicated here by expressive stylistic devices such as ellipses, exclamations, and questions, which do not belong to the language of the narrator, but to the inner language of the character, whose words are, however, not quoted directly. The free indirect representation of thought is designed to take the reader as close as possible to the consciousness of the character. It excludes irony, at least in this passage.

The examples above illustrate the two extreme positions between which Austen's use of free discourse is suspended: the first of these consists of the ironic representation of speech and; the second, of the non-ironic representation of thought. Austen is usually praised for her innovative creation of point-of-view fiction, the basis of which is free indirect thought. She is also admired for her use of irony, the basis of which is, to a great extent, free indirect speech. Since the narrative significance of the latter aspect has not been appreciated adequately, at least one more example of irony in free indirect speech bears mentioning, before the thorny question of the irony in free indirect thought in Austen's novels is tackled. This example comes from *Emma*. The novel's protagonist and her protégée Harriet Smith are on their way back from a charitable visit to a poor family, when they meet the village parson Mr. Elton, who is on the way to this very family. They start talking about the need and distress of this family:

> The wants and sufferings of the poor family, however, were the first subject on meeting. *He had been going to call on them. His visit he would now defer*; but they had a very interesting parley about what could be done and should be done. (1973, 87)

There are two sentences inserted in the narrative report that refer to the parson, who declares that he will postpone his visit to the family in distress. On the one hand, these sentences are, through their free indirect form, marked stylistically in the narrative context. On the other hand, they appear to be thrown in in passing, which may allow the reader to easily overlook them. The casual form of their insertion suggests the ease with which Mr. Elton postpones his visit, only to talk about his pastoral care, rather than to practice it. It is Austen's narrative technique – and not any censorious comment – which makes it clear that Mr. Elton does not take his office as parson and his duty to care for the poor seriously. This example shows the subtlety with which Austen handles narrative technique in order to convey moral judgement in an entirely unobtrusive, yet effective way, a technique that demands a perceptive reader to appreciate it. In this case, the change from narrative report to free indirect speech and back to report, even though it is almost imperceptible, is used to pass a moral judgment on a character. The reader, who perceives the irony, goes through a cognitive process of gradual comprehension. The density of such an experience of the text is one reason for the pleasure Austen's novels afford, a pleasure which is composed of deep esthetical, intellectual, and moral satisfaction.

7 Irony in the Free Indirect Representation of Thought

Since free indirect thought tends to minimize the narrator's presence and to favor experiences of empathy with characters, the emergence of irony in passages written in free indirect style is an intriguing phenomenon. At this point the fact is to be recalled that free indirect style is, putting it very simply, the result of a confluence between two voices, the narrator's and the character's. For this reason, free indirect style has been related to the idea of a dual voice (Pascal 1977; Bray 2007). The term "dual voice" is perhaps not a happy one, because in this amalgamation the two constituents lose their respective identities. The constituent related to the narrator is no longer a textual instance telling a story and addressing a reader (narratee), and the constituent related to the character, whose thoughts (or speech) are represented, is no longer the subject of an utterance in any communicative sense. The result of this amalgamation is a form sui generis, in which the constituents of the narrator's and character's voice still loom large. This duality of two contrary possibilities inherent in free indirect style, this polarity contained within one entity is not a static phenomenon. One of the two possibilities may be stronger than the other one. In non-ironic discourse, empathy with the character is stronger. Conversely, ironic discourse creates a distance to the character, and the impact of the narrator's position is felt more strongly.

Since the empathic force of free indirect thought had been emphasized in scholarship for a long time, critics turned to the issue of irony in this form of representing consciousness. A pioneer in this field of research was Dorrit Cohn, who made a distinction between ironic and empathic thought report and discussed many examples of the latter type (1978, 117; see also Fludernik 2009, 95). Cohn states that

> Narrated monologues [her term for free indirect style/discourse] tend to commit the narrator to attitudes of sympathy or irony. Precisely because they cast the language of a subjective mind into the grammar of objective narration, they amplify emotional notes, but also throw into ironic relief all false notes struck by a figural mind. (1981, 117)

In Jane Austen the situation seems to be quite clear. As a rule, free indirect speech, which is not dealt with by Cohn, is ironic in her novels, and free indirect thought tends to be non-ironic or empathic. As far as free indirect thought is concerned, exceptions to this rule can be found in the presentation of the consciousness of female protagonists, who are either naive (such as Catherine Morland in *Northanger Abbey* [1817]) or morally dubious (such as Emma Woodhouse in *Emma*).

The emergence of irony in free indirect thought will be examined by looking at an example from *Emma*. The passage belongs in the context of the representation of the thoughts which go through Emma's head, after she has made the acquaintance of Harriet Smith. It is her project to make Harriet her protégée and to shape her into a woman fit for a respectable husband. In view of this project, she feels it her duty to prevent an alliance of Harriet and Mr. Martin, a farmer who is in love with the young woman. Here is just a part of a much longer passage:

> But they [the Martins] must be coarse and unpolished, and very unfit to be the intimates of a girl [Harriet] who wanted only a little more knowledge and elegance to be quite perfect. *She* would notice her; she would improve her; she would detach her from her bad acquaintance, and introduce her into good society; she would form her opinions and her manners. It would be an interesting, and certainly a very kind undertaking; highly becoming her own situation in life, her leisure, and powers. (1973, 23–24)

This passage takes the reader very close to the mind of the protagonist. The processes going on in her head are represented quite 'authentically,' i.e. in a way fitted to the mental set-up of the character represented; this is particularly evident in the choice of words, which correspond to Emma's way of thinking and are determined by her social arrogance. Words such as "coarse," "unpolished," "unfit," "elegance," "bad acquaintance," "good society," and the use of adverbs such as "very," "highly," and "certainly": all indicate her hypertrophic judgment and almost make us hear Emma's thoughts, although she never actually speaks. However, our proximity to her mental process does not really lead to a sense of empathy or even sympathy on the reader's part, because the representation of Emma's mind is unmistakably marked by ironic distance. It is an astonishing fact, however, that irony is here not produced by any explicit intervention on the part of the narrator. At no moment in this passage does Jane Austen deviate from Emma's thoughts and feelings. She uses not a single word or expression that does not correspond with Emma's way of thinking, a pure example of mind-style.[10] She avoids the technique of including in free indirect style words alien to the mind-set of the represented character, which other novelists employ to convey distance and irony.[11] But she structures free indirect style so as to enact ironic subversion. This is shown most clearly in the following sequence of sentences, each of which is introduced by the anaphoric "she": "*She* would notice her; she would improve her; she would detach her from her bad acquaintance, and introduce her into good society; she would form her opinions and her manners" (1973, 23–24). The self-centeredness of the character is iconically marked by the repeated first pronoun "she." The first "she" is emphasized through italics, which is clearly an authorial marking. The passage, then, confronts us with a character, who wants to reshape or recreate another person according to her own ideas.

Finally, the question needs to be addressed of how irony that is realized in free indirect style is recognized. Critics tend to believe that the irony in such passages is perceived or produced through contextualization. In my opinion this is obvious, but too simple. I concede that it is all too clear that the irony of such passages becomes unmistakable when they are seen in the context of the whole plot and the failures of Emma's match-making projects. However, my argument is that the irony of the passage under discussion and many more passages is the result of Austen's subtle interplay between closeness and distance in the use of free indirect style. The ironic use of free indirect style in the representation of inner processes going on in Emma reveals a fascinating interdependence of nearness and detachment which is the hallmark of Austen's art of characterization in this novel, while free indirect thought appears in Austen's last completed novel, *Persuasion*, in a non-ironic or pure form, because this work's protagonist Anne Elliot, from whose viewpoint most of the events are represented, is beyond any moral doubt. But as we know, purity may not be always very exciting. Issues of empathy and sympathy on the reader's part and of ethics in general emerge in the context of narrative technique and the specific uses of language in character representation. An extreme example of the power of free indirect thought to absorb the recipient's mind is represented by the crime fiction of Patricia Highsmith

---

10 Greta Olson, one of the editors of the present volume, suggests the term "mental lexis" (personal communication). Fludernik is specific about such linguistic phenomena (1996; see also 2006, 85).
11 See Cohn 1981.

which, as it were, forces the reader to enter into the consciousness of psychopathic murderers and thus produces singular aesthetic and ethical experiences.[12] To return to Austen, the interdependence of empathy and irony that is evident in *Emma* may be esthetically and cognitively more intriguing than the dominance of the reader's empathy with a morally perfect protagonist such as Anne Elliot in *Persuasion*. At any rate, it is remarkable that Jane Austen as the inventor of point-of-view fiction produces both, pure empathy and empathy cum irony, in the representation of her protagonists.

8 Irony in Dialogue

Since Austen's use of irony in dialogue is an important dimension of her art, it is necessary to have at least a brief look at it. It is in dialogue that her irony can best be analyzed with the aid of modern linguistic theory. Here is one part of an exchange of words from the first chapter of *Pride and Prejudice*. Mrs. Bennet complains that her husband is annoying her, and he defends himself in an unperturbed way:

> 'You take delight in vexing me. You have no compassion for my poor nerves.'
> 'You mistake me, my dear. I have a high respect for your nerves. They are my old friends. I have heard you mention them with consideration these last twenty years at least.' (1973, 5)

The irony is here realized by a resumption and modification of the interlocutor's original formulation. Mr. Bennet echoes his wife's statement, taking up her personification of her nerves and extending it into a little allegory. There is also pretence at work in his ironical comment. He pretends that what has for a very long time been a nuisance to him, his wife's continual concern with her nerves, is actually something he respects and cherishes. This is irony verging on sarcasm. Cognitive approaches such as the echo and the pretence theory can be helpful for an analysis of such a passage. Who is the recipient of the irony in this instance? It is obviously the reader, but possibly also the ironist himself, who may enjoy treating his wife ironically, with irony being a kind of survival strategy for a husband who has to live with a wife of "mean understanding" (1973, 5).

---

12 For the question of empathy and sympathy for dubious characters, resulting from the use of free indirect discourse, see Müller 2015a. For a new concept of an ethical narratology, see Müller 2015b.

The sparkling passages of dialogue between Elizabeth Bennet and Mr. Darcy in the first half of the novel reveal an extraordinary capacity for irony in the heroine. Here is an example, in which female wit and male heavy-handedness are juxtaposed. Elizabeth mockingly establishes a common basis of understanding with her tongue-tied interlocutor: "'Both,' replied Elizabeth archly; 'for I have always seen a great similarity in the turn of our minds. We are each of an unsocial, taciturn disposition, unwilling to speak [...]'" (1973, 91). Elizabeth's ironic utterance can be understood as a kind of pretence. She establishes a temporary form of identification between Mr. Darcy and herself by characterizing both as unsocial and taciturn. The irony is constituted by the use of the grammatical plural "we," which is used to drive Darcy's singularity home to him, namely that it he alone is taciturn and unsocial. To comprehend the utterance Darcy has to perform a cognitive act, he has to understand that Elizabeth's use of the plural is an instance of pretence and to realize that he, Darcy, is being mocked. The irony is all too obvious, considering the fact that Elizabeth is the wittiest and most eloquent character in the novel. Since Austen has been called the "Prose Shakespeare" (Pollack-Pelzner 2013), it is, perhaps, noteworthy that in *Hamlet* the plural pronoun "we" is, in a similar way, used for ironic purposes. The tragedy's protagonist mocks his enemy, King Claudius, by pretending that there is a community between himself and his murderous uncle. With reference to the murder performed in the play within the play, he says: "Your majesty, and we that have free souls, it touches us not" (2005, 263).

As a somewhat more complex example of irony based on an assumed community between two persons, a passage from *Emma* will now be examined. It comes from a dialogue between the protagonist and her protégée, Harriet Smith. Emma is filling Harriet's ears with hopes for a great match, which she is arranging for her. These plans are completely illusory and shall fail miserably, as the reader learns later in the novel:

> 'This is an alliance which, whoever – whatever your friends may be, must be agreeable to them, provided at least they have common sense; and we are not to be addressing our conduct to fools. [...]'
> 'Yes, very true. How nicely you talk; I love to hear you. You understand everything. You and Mr Elton are one as clever as the other.' (1973, 75–76)

In this passage, the irony is turned against Emma herself in her exaggerated expression of self-righteousness and arrogance. And there are two ironic aspects in Harriet's reply, without her being aware of them, first, the idea that Emma understands everything, when she in fact understands nothing, and, second, the opinion that Emma and Mr. Elton are intellectually equal, which suggests a relationship between the two, which Elton aspires to unbeknownst to Emma. There is a double irony in this exchange of words, an irony that is directed against Emma's intellectual pride and her match-making plans, and an irony directed against Harriet, who allows herself to be manipulated by Emma. The whole passage illustrates the effect that involuntary irony can have. The ironies in this passage show the whole intricate tangle of the three characters in a nutshell – Emma, the self-congratulatory matchmaker; Harriet, the victim of her manipulation; and Mr. Elton, the would-be social climber. The dialogue represents one of the many examples of the pleasure of cognitive processing that Austen's novels afford the reader.

9 Conclusion

This article has provided a comparative investigation of Jane Austen's use of irony in the two basic forms of free indirect discourse, i.e., the free indirect presentation of speech and, of thought. On the basis of our analysis it can be concluded that Austen tends to restrict her use of free indirect thought to female characters and, more specifically, to the protagonists of her novels, while free indirect speech is restricted to minor characters, regardless of whether they are male or female. It is an astonishing phenomenon – one hardly ever recognized by critics – that in her novels the speech of the (female) protagonists is usually exempted from free indirect representation. Therefore, what can be noticed is that Austen's large-scale use of free indirect style is strongly gendered, privileging female consciousness. The article's second result is that, as far as the emergence of irony in free indirect discourse is concerned, the ironic mode tends to be employed for the most part in passages involving free indirect speech, while the use of irony in passages involving free indirect thought is comparatively rare, with the significant exception of *Emma* and, perhaps, *Northanger Abbey*. These are important linguistic and narrative facts that have to be taken into account in any study of Austen's narrative art. To generalize, it is irony, which usually can be explained by using cognitive approaches, that affords the reader an incomparable cognitive delight in processing Austen's novels.

A third result of the examination of Austen's use of irony is to be seen in the fact that it enables a more general appreciation of her art. With the exception of linguistically-oriented critics like Norman Page (1972), narratologists have chiefly been interested in Jane Austen's manipulation of perspective, the basic tool of which is free indirect thought. Two traditions of narrative art have derived out of her innovation; the first consists of point-of-view fiction, rendered with a non-ironic use of free indirect style, as exemplified in *Persuasion*. This tradition finds prominent later representatives in James Joyce's *A Portrait of the Artist as a Young Man* (1916), Virginia Woolf's *Mrs Dalloway* (1925), and Ford Madox Ford's *Parade's End* (1924–1928). The second strand of point-of-view fiction is characterized by the ironic use of free indirect style: it begins with Jane Austen's *Northanger Abbey* and *Emma* and continues with Flaubert's *Madame Bovary* (1856), and Henry James's *The Ambassadors* (1903). There are, of course, many transitions between these two lines of development. While narratologists have never stopped paying tribute to Austen's great innovation in the realm of perspectival narration, readers, by contrast, have never become tired of reading her novels because of their use of irony outside of the realm of point-of-view, that is to say in the sphere of dialogue. The massive emergence of dialogue in Austen's work represents another form of showing rather than telling; it exemplifies the other side of the retreat from omniscient narration. In this way Austen brings a technique to fruition that began in the eighteenth century with Richardson's *Pamela* (1740) and Charlotte Lennox' *The Female Quixote* (1752). Her art of dialogue is almost as important in the composition of her novels as is the discovery of point-of-view, even though this feature of her fiction does not play the same pioneering role for the future of narrative art. Irony is, perhaps, more at home in Austen's dialogues than in her use of free indirect discourse. But here, again, the difference between the free indirect representation of thought and free indirect speech must be kept in mind, for in the latter form irony is used more frequently and in a more explicitly comical way. Irony is, as we have seen, the key to Austen's art.

Finally, the question as to a greater coherence between linguistic and literary studies of irony needs to be raised. As we have seen, it is obvious that cognitive linguistics can help us greatly to provide insights into the use of irony in Austen's dialogues and to some extent into her use of irony in authorial comment. By contrast, I cannot at present name irony research in linguistics that would be helpful to explicating irony as a result of narrative strategies of focalization. Might then linguists, conversely, profit from looking at irony in literature and especially in the work of Jane Austen? A shining example of a researcher taking a linguistically-based approach to the analysis of literary texts is Monika Fludernik in practically all of her works.[13] It may be argued that for a linguist it may indeed be of

---

[13] Another researcher who is as much at home in linguistics as in literary studies and successfully combines the two disciplines is Jarmila Mildorf. See, for instance, Mildorf 2014 and Müller 1984, 2011.

interest to realize the enormous possibilities that emerge in the representation of irony in literary texts. The study of Austen's works may alert the linguist to complexities of the phenomenon of irony, complexities that may also emerge in normal speech situations, which, as we know, are frequently highly intricate. In particular, examples of irony misfiring or misunderstood or irony that is intended to be received differently by various groups of hearers could be an excellent subject for linguistic investigation. Generally the search for maxims for the formation of successful speech acts and communication and, specifically, the exposition of the rules for producing and the principles of understanding irony is important. Yet in view of the richness and inventiveness of an ironist like Jane Austen, such maxims are ultimately of limited usefulness. Moreover, literary examples of irony may shed light on borderline cases, in which irony imperceptibly merges with larger strategies of pretence and deception. Be this as it may, there is no doubt that the phenomenon of irony opens up a field of investigation in which linguists and literary critics may fruitfully cooperate.[14]

References

Austen, Jane. 1973. *The Novels of Jane Austen*. 5 vols. Edited by R. W. Chapman. London, New York, and Toronto: Oxford University Press.
Bally, Charles. 1912. "Le style indirect libre en français moderne." *Germanisch-Romanische Monatsschrift* 4: 549–606.
Bray, Joe. 2007. "The 'Dual Voice' in Free Indirect Discourse: A Reading Experiment." *Language and Literature* 16: 37–52.
Chapman, Sara S. 1989. *Henry James's Portrait of the Writer as Hero*. New York: St. Martin's.
Clerk, Herbert H., and Richard J. Gerrig. 1984. "On the Pretense Theory of Irony." *Journal of Experimental Psychology General* 113: 121–126.
Cohn, Dorrit. 1981. *Transparent Minds: Narrative Modes for Presenting Consciousness in Fiction*. Princeton: Princeton University Press.
Dawson, Paul. 2013. *The Return of the Omniscient Narrator: Authorship and Authority in Twenty-First Century Fiction*. Columbus: Ohio State University Press.
Fludernik, Monika.1996. *Towards a 'Natural' Narratology*. London/New York: Routledge.
---. 2007. "Interfaces of Language: The Case of Irony." In *Irony Revisited: Spurensuche in der englischsprachigen Literatur*, edited by Thomas Honegger, Eva-Maria Orth, and Sandra Schwabe, 11–26. Würzburg: Königshausen & Neumann.
---. 2009. *An Introduction to Narratology*. London and New York: Routledge.

---

14 Such a cooperation has been practiced and called for by Monika Fludernik all through her career as a scholar.

Greiner, Norbert. 2007. "Szenische Ironie in Shakespeares Historien." In *Irony Revisited: Spurensuche in der englischsprachigen Literatur*, edited by Thomas Honegger, Eva-Maria Orth, and Sandra Schwabe, 135–150. Würzburg: Königshausen & Neumann.
Fowler, Henry W. 1984. *A Dictionary of Modern English Usage*. Ware: Omega Books.
Grice, Herbert P. 1978. "Further Notes on Logic and Conversation." In *Syntax and Semantics*. Vol. 9: Pragmatics, edited by Peter Cole, 113–128. New York: Academic Press.
Honegger, Thomas, Eva-Maria Orth, Sandra Schwabe, eds. 2007. *Irony Revisited: Spurensuche in der englischsprachigen Literatur*. Würzburg: Königshausen & Neumann.
Hutcheon, Linda. 1995. *Irony's Edge: The Theory and Politics of Irony*. London: Routledge.
Klein, Holger. 2007. "Narratorial Irony in Fielding and Austen." In *Irony Revisited: Spurensuche in der englischsprachigen Literatur*, edited by Thomas Honegger, Eva-Maria Orth, and Sandra Schwabe, 187–206. Würzburg: Königshausen & Neumann.
Korthals Altes, Liesbeth. 2014. *Ethos and Narrative Interpretation: The Negotiation of Values in Fiction*. Lincoln and London: University of Nebraska Press.
Kühnel, Walter. 1969. *Formen der Ironie und ihre Funktionalisierung bei Jane Austen*. Unpublished Doctoral Dissertation. Frankfurt am Main.
Mildorf, Jarmila. 2014. "Figurenrede im Roman aus kognitionslinguistischer und narratologischer Perspektive am Beispiel von Jean Rhys' Roman *Good Morning Midnight*." *Germanisch-Romanische Monatsschrift* 64: 447–467.
Müller, Wolfgang G. 1984. "Der freie indirekte Stil bei Jane Austen als Mittel der Rede-und Gedankenwiedergabe." *Poetica* 16: 206–236.
---. 2011. "Verbal Irony in Shakespeare's Dramatic Works." In *Bi-Directionality in the Cognitive Sciences*, edited by Marcus Callies, Wolfram R. Keller, and Astrid Lohöfer, 195–210. Amsterdam and Philadelphia: Benjamins.
---. 2015a. "Sympathie für Psychopathen, Ehebrecher, Kuppler & Co? Ein Beitrag zur Verwendung des freien indirekten Stils (erlebte Rede) in der Erzählkunst." In *Empathie, Sympathie und Narration*, edited by Caroline Lusin, 59–72. Heidelberg: Winter.
---. 2015b. "From Homer's *Odyssey* to Joyce's *Ulysses*: Theory and Practice of an Ethical Narratology." *Arcadia* 50: 9–36.
Page, Norman. 1972. *The Language of Jane Austen*. Oxford: Blackwell. Republished in Routledge Revivals 2013. London: Routledge.
Pascal, Roy. 1977. *The Dual Voice*. Manchester: Manchester University Press.
Polhemus, Robert M. 1986. "Jane Austen's Comedy." In *The Jane Austen Handbook*, edited by J. David Grey, 60–71. London: Athlone Press.
Pollack-Pelzner, Daniel. 2013. "Jane Austen, the Prose Shakespeare." *Studies in English Literature 1500–1900* 53: 763–792.
Rockwell, Patricia Ann. 2006. *Sarcasm and other Mixed Messages: The Ambiguous Ways People Use Language*. Lewiston: Edwin Mellen.
Shakespeare, William. 2005. *Hamlet*. Übersetzung mit Anmerkungen von Norbert Greiner. Einleitung und Kommentar von Wolfgang G. Müller. Englisch-deutsche Studienausgabe. Tübingen: Stauffenburg Verlag.
Sperber, Dan, and Deirdre Wilson. 1981. "Irony and the Use-Mention Distinction." In *Radical Pragmatics*, edited by Peter Cole, 295–318. New York: Academic Press.
---. 2006. "Relevance Theory." In *Handbook of Pragmatics*, edited by Lawrence Horne, and Gregory Ward, 607–631. Oxford: Blackwell.
Stanzel, Franz K. 1979. *Theorie des Erzählens*. Göttingen: Vandenhoeck.
---. 1984. *A Theory of Narrative*. Cambridge: Cambridge University Press.

Walsh, Richard. 2007. *The Rhetoric of Fictionality: Narrative Theory and the Idea of Fiction*. Columbus: Ohio State University Press.

Wilson, Deirdre. 2006. "The Pragmatics of Verbal Irony: Echo or Pretence?" *Lingua* 116: 1722–1743.

Wolf, Werner. 2007. "'Schutzironie' als Akzeptanzstrategie für problematische Diskurse: zu einer vernachlässigten Nähe erzeugenden Funktion von Ironie." In *Irony Revisited: Spurensuche in der englischsprachigen Literatur*, edited by Thomas Honegger, Eva-Maria Orth, and Sandra Schwabe, 27–50. Würzburg: Königshausen & Neumann.

Wolf Schmid
Fictional Minds in Cognitive Narratology

1

Characters' consciousness is one of the central factors of every narrative. A narrative is usually defined as a representation of a change of a state of affairs. Since the end of the eighteenth century, events portrayed in literature have essentially been mental ones. This does not mean that the representation of the mind began only then. In Medieval European literatures we find elaborate representations of characters' feelings and thoughts; these are rendered not solely in thought report but also in free indirect speech (e. g. in Chrétien's de Troyes *Yvain ou Le Chevalier au lion* [1177–1181], see Hübner 2003, 149–151; Woledge 1988, 158), or in interior monologues that, in the case of Gottfried von Strassburg's verse novel *Tristan*, take the form of interior dialogues that express the extremely contradictory movements of the hero's soul (see Schmid 2017). Monika Fludernik (2011) examines various forms of mind representation in Middle English narrative. She explains narratology's common underestimation of medieval representations of consciousness due to its exclusive interest in narratives originating with the beginnings of the novel in eighteenth century. The narratological underexploredness of medieval literatures may, however, also have been caused by medievalists' disaffirmation of questions and approaches that seemed anachronistic. Also in ancient (Hebrew and Greek) literatures we find cases of extended mind representation and even elaborate interior monologues (see Dinkler 2015).

Any external or internal action is related to a specific internal movement, conscious or unconscious. The relationship between action and consciousness exists, regardless of whether it is explicitly mentioned by the narrator or inferred by the reader. Consciousness may be rendered appreciable/apprehensible in the narrative in two ways: either as a matter of direct presentation by the narrator or the characters, or as something implied that motivates the characters' actions and about which the reader then has to draw his or her conclusions. In either case, the characters' consciousness is constitutive of the narration.

Now the cognitivist takes the stage. His or her role is to consider what in English is called the *mind*. This concept covers all internal states and actions: speech, thought, perception, desire, emotion – in a word, the whole inner world (Palmer 2002, 2004). Cognitive narratology (which, for the sake of ease rather than of accuracy, is given this term[1]) is primarily interested in two questions that go in opposite directions: 1. "How do stories [...] interlock with interpreters' mental states and processes, thus giving rise to narrative experiences?" (Herman 2014, 46). 2. How do narratives contribute to the discovery of meaning in the experiences that are caused by them? How do narratives help people to orientate themselves in the world, to understand the meanings of their own behavior and the behavior of others (see Herman 2014, 46)? (This second approach relates to the ability of narratives to expand our knowledge of people and their consciousness.)

2

Among the cognitivists, Monika Fludernik (1996) takes a special, fundamental approach. According to her, narrativity is based not on events and their causal concatenation but rather on the subject's experience of these events. This means that the classical concept of narrativity – the representation of changes of state – is replaced by what Fludernik calls experientiality. The experientiality approach proves extremely fruitful. However one may ask whether it makes the classical concept completely superfluous. In the analysis of experience Fludernik demonstrates the whole set of cognitivist tools in practice – particularly 'frames' and 'scripts,' i.e. the schemata by which we recognize situations and processes. There is no doubt that representing subjective experience is one of the seminal anthropological reasons for the overwhelming role of narrative since the modern age.

But let us now turn to questions of mind representation and to one of the representatives of this field of research. "Novel reading is mind reading" (2007, 217) – this is the slogan of the well-known cognitive narratologist Alan Palmer. The independent British scholar is the author of two seminal books: *Fictional Minds* (2004) and *Social Minds in the Novel* (2010). In the first book the cited initial hypothesis is formulated with an orientation to the act of creation: "Narrative is in essence the presentation of fictional mental functioning" (Palmer 2004, 12).

The key concepts of narratological cognitivism are *mind reading* or the *theory of mind*. The latter was introduced into the discussion by Lisa Zunshine's *Why We Read Fiction* (2006). Both concepts refer to the creation of hypotheses about what is going on in someone else's mind. *Mind reading* and the *theory of mind* are based on the interpretation of the observed person's verbal and practical behavior as

---

[1] This branch of narratology itself is not cognitive in the strict sense, but rather cognitivist. Cognitive are the actions and processes which are the subject of cognitivist narratology.

well as of his or her appearance, gestures, and facial expressions. Actually, *mind reading* and the *theory of mind* are not a form of 'reading' or of 'theory' but rather constitute assumptions about human observation.

Cognitive narratologists tend to overestimate the cognitive performance of mind reading and to reduce the difference between the understanding of the real and the fictional mind. Balancing the fundamental difference between real and fictional minds, cognitivism contests one of the central axioms in traditional narrative criticism. In the classical theory of narrative it was generally agreed that fictional narrative differs from factual narrative in that the former represents characters' inner worlds authentically, whereas in real life representing the mind of another would constitute a form of guesswork. Moreover, the fictional narrative was seen as the only genre in which the representation of mind could be carried out unconditionally, and did not need to be justified by sources.

The first narratologist to formulate a hypothesis about this specific trait of fictional narrative was the English novelist Edward Morgan Forster in his famous *Aspects of the Novel*:

> People in a novel can be understood completely [...]. And this is why they often seem more definite than characters in history, or even our own friends; we have been told all about them that can be told; even if they are imperfect or unreal they do not contain any secrets, whereas our friends do and must, mutual secrecy being one of the conditions of life upon this globe. [...] We cannot understand each other, except in a rough and ready way; we cannot reveal ourselves even when we want to; what we call intimacy is only a makeshift; perfect knowledge is an illusion. But in the novel we can know people perfectly, and, apart from the general pleasure of reading, we can find here a compensation for their dimness in life. In this direction fiction is truer than history, because it goes beyond the evidence. (1927, 46–47, 61)

Thirty years later, the German theoretician Käte Hamburger sharpened Foster's thesis about the exclusive role of fictional literature in her *Die Logik der Dichtung* (1957), without referring to him: "Epic fiction is the sole epistemological instance where the I-originarity (or subjectivity) of a third-person qua third-person can be portrayed" (1973, 83).

Hamburger's thesis that someone else's subjectivity can be displayed authentically only in fictional narrative was subsequently endorsed by the Austrian narratologist Franz Stanzel (1959; 1979, 31; 2002) and then strongly affirmed by Dorrit Cohn. Cohn reiterates Hamburger's conclusion in a somewhat less complicated way: "narrative fiction is the only literary genre, as well as the only kind of narrative, in which the unspoken thoughts, feelings, perceptions of a person other than the speaker can be portrayed" (1978, 7).

As a test case, let us now examine a brief extract, in which the omniscient narrator of Leo Tolstoy's novel *War and Peace* (1968/69) presents Napoleon's innermost feelings during the Battle of Borodino without any explanation or foundation:

> Napoleon was experiencing a bitter feeling [...]. In his former battles he had only considered the possibilities of success, now an immense number of unlucky chances presented themselves, and he expected them all. Yes, it was like a nightmare, when a man dreams that an assailant is attacking him, and in his dream he lifts up his arm and deals a blow with a force at his assailant that he knows must crush him, and feels that his arm falls limp and powerless as a rag, and the horror of inevitable death comes upon him in his helplessness. (Tolstoy n. d., 757–759)

In a factual, historical text, presenting the inner life of a statesman in this way would be unthinkable and would not be accepted as scholarly. There are no sources even imaginable that would allow the historian to employ speculations similar to those rendered above.

What Hamburger regarded as a 'symptom' of fiction – the unconditioned, immediate view of the inner life of third persons – also sometimes seems to occur in non-fictional texts, a point that was repeatedly made against Hamburger's thesis. However, in such cases we have to do merely with conjectures and conclusions. A mere conjecture must be either clearly signaled to, or an authentic source of this knowledge (letter, diary, communication) must be provided (see Genette 1990, 762–763). But, like all self-attestations, such sources are subject to the possible lack of self-knowledge as well as distorting self-stylizations. In a factual context such as historiography, the representation of the inner world of third parties – where it occurs at all – is far less authentic than, for example, in Tolstoy's *War and Peace*, where it is used quite naively. The authenticity of the inner lives of Tolstoy's characters is of course bought with their fictiveness and is also dependent on the author's knowledge of the world and life experience and his psychological imagination.

The natural staging of someone else's inner world is certainly one of the reasons for the anthropological and cultural significance of fiction. The reader can step outside of himself or herself and not only lead someone else's life but slip into someone else's subjectivity and tentatively play out someone else's perceptions and ambitions. No conversation and no psychological document can offer such intense experiences of alterity. We can say even more about this: the immersion in the inner world of the fictional other gives a reader the possibility of forming a notion of his or her own identity. The price for playing out this foreign subjectivity is that everything has been conceived of by the author and remains oriented towards him or her, his or her knowledge of the world, and the power of his or her imagination.

3

From the standpoint of actual cognitive narratology, Forster's, Hamburger's, and Cohn's "exceptionality thesis," as it is called by David Herman (2011a, 8–18), was sharply criticized. Herman contests the Cartesian dualism implicit in the assumption of an internal and external world, which in his view is the underlying basis of this "exceptionality thesis." Herman claims to call into question not the specifics of fictional representation but rather the dichotomy between fictional and factual representations and the assumption that only fictional narratives can provide insight into characters' minds. Herman presents two arguments against this presumption: First, the *mediation argument*: "Making sense of fictional minds requires readers to use the same sorts of heuristics that they rely on to interpret others' minds in the world at large" (Herman 2011a, 15). The second one, the *accessibility argument*, boils down to the assumption that the accessibility of another's subjectivity is not limited to fictional narrative. In everyday situations people are dependent on the heuristics acquired from so-called "folk psychology" to draw conclusions about another's soul that are based on appearance, facial expression, gestures, and the given situation. "Everyday minds are not transparent, but they are accessible" (Herman 2011a, 11). This is why for Herman accessibility cannot serve as a criterion of the exceptionality of fictional minds.

Herman assumes that his two arguments are leant support by the articles in the collection *The Emergence of the Mind* (2011) which relate to the emergence of representation of consciousness in English literature. Yet Herman's arguments do not refute Hamburger's and Cohn's positions. Of course, we must note that the author's omniscience is not knowledge, but free invention. In this regard, Gérard Genette states – not without irony: "One's guesses are unerring only in the case of something that one is in the process of *inventing*" (1993 [1990], 65).

Alan Palmer also rejects the idea "that, whereas novels can give us direct access to the minds of characters, by contrast, in reality, we can never really know what other people are thinking" (2011, 197). Palmer calls this opposition "a cliché of literary studies." Referring to the "theory of folk psychology" he states: "All of us, every day, know for a lot of the time what other people are thinking. This is especially true of our loved ones, close friends, family, and work colleagues" (2011, 197).

The following question arises with regard to this statement. If, in real life, we were essentially aware of what is happening in people close to us, how can we explain that husbands are so often unaware of the desires of their wives, even to the extent that a wife's mentioned desire for a divorce may take her husband completely off-guard? What Palmer takes for knowledge is not actual knowledge but the sensation of having knowledge, a sensation that is not infrequently misleading.

Rejecting the 'literary cliché' about the fundamental inaccessibility of real individuals and the transparency of fictional characters, Palmer recognizes that we in real life "sometimes" do not know what is going on in other people, even though they are trying to tell us (2011, 197). An objection to Palmer's concession is that a third-person narrator is as a rule engaged not in mind reading – i.e. in guessing what is going on in one character or another – but rather in giving an accurate representation penetrating the inside of another soul. The complex and badly jointed landscapes of the souls in a realistic novel, say by Tolstoy or Dostoevsky, would not be open to any mind reading by characters in the fictional world, nor to the reader's theory of mind, if the narrator – and through the narrator the author – did not explicitly depict them.

4

Palmer's postulates have been challenged from several positions. Empirical scholars, like Marisa Bortolussi, who study the reception of literature, notice that Palmer "borrowed" from the "soft" cognitive sciences a "limited collection of basic, universal processes associated with everyday social experiences. [...] This exclusive focus on very broad, universal processes has led Palmer (and other narratologists of the cognitive persuasion) to draw some questionable conclusions" (Bortolussi 2011, 284).

Palmer's conviction that we read fictional characters just like real people is, according to Bortolussi, not confirmed by experience:

> A fundamental difference between real people and literary characters is that we deal with the former directly and with the latter only through the intermediary of authorial or narratorial direction [...]. Rather than form a theory of mind for fictional characters, readers may simply construct a representation of what the narrator might intend for us to understand. (2011, 285)

According to Bortolussi, the theory of mind focus is generally overestimated by cognitive narratologists. Palmer's assumption is not supported by experience that readers of the novel are focused less on the events than on characters' reactions to those events – i.e. what they are thinking and feeling; this thesis is refuted by the convincing results of empirical psychological experiments (Bortolussi 2011, 286).

In a similar vein Daniel Hutto criticizes mind reading. The title of his contribution is telling: *Understanding Fictional Minds without Theory of Mind!* (2011). According to him, in the cases discussed by Palmer, no mind reading but rather *mind guessing* is involved. The American narratologist Emma Kafalenos, in turn, accuses Palmer of too rapidly rejecting the epistemological difference between fiction and nonfiction (2011, 254). She also considers problematic his notion of knowing. In the novel, the narrator 'knows' what in the real world is impossible to know. Not distinguishing between what we know as a fact – because the narrator has told us this – and that which a character guesses about is the very mistake Palmer himself commits, according to Kafalenos, in not distinguishing between what we can know about the fictional world and what we know in our own world (2011, 256). In a similar way Palmer's concept of knowing is criticized by the American cognitivist Patrick Colm Hogan (2011), the author of *Cognitive Science, Literature, and the Arts: A Guide for Humanists* (2003).

Drawing an interim balance, we can surmise that Forster's, Hamburger's, and Cohn's theses about the representation of another's inner world as a distinctive feature of fictional narrative has not been shaken by the objections that have been named. But let us have a look at another possible counterargument. The direct representation of another's mind, it would seem, sometimes occurs also in factual texts. But such cases always concern only assumptions and conclusions, the presumptive nature of which is directly stated or is clearly implied through context: *Napoleon apparently thought…*; *From Napoleon's statements we can conclude that he thought…*. More specifically, an historian cannot characterize Napoleon's inner world. Statements of the type *Napoleon thought…* are not admissible in factual texts.[2]

Let us emphasize this point once more: the authenticity of a fictional representation of another's mind is not based on mind reading, but on a rendering that

---

[2] In a recent empirical comparison of factual and fictional biographies, Frederike Lagoni (2016) shows that the examined factual texts contain no fewer instances of mind representation than the fictional ones. The difference is 1) in the type of representation, with a preponderance of thought report occurring in factual texts and of more figural types of representation, such as free indirect discourse, in fictional ones; and 2) the necessity of factual narrators to justify knowledge wherever they go beyond the evidence.

is dependent on the author's knowledge of the world, on his or her life experience, capacity for empathy; and, last but not least, on his or her psychological imagination. Exploring the most secret corners of a woman's soul, for example, through the pen of a 'macho' like Tolstoy, is a marvel of empathy and imagination.

5

Alan Palmer has also raised the question of the ideological and social determination of fictional minds (2004, 2010, 2011). Palmer chides classical narratology for, from an *intraspective* point of view, one-sidedly focusing on closed, private, *intramental* consciousness. He calls on narratology to take an external point of view to consider what he calls the *social mind* and *intermental thought*, "which is joint, group, shared, or collective thought, as opposed to intramental, or private, individual thought" (Palmer 2011, 196). It is not surprising that this concept has caused more than a little debate. One part of this debate was conducted in the journal *Style* in 2011. There we find Palmer's target essay *Social Minds in Fiction and Criticism*, twenty-seven responses to Palmer's thesis by specialists in the field, and Palmer's rejoinders.

The admissibility and feasibility of Palmer's dichotomy of internal and external point of view on consciousness has also been questioned from various positions. Patrick Colm Hogan criticizes that Palmer uses classical narratology as a "straw man" (2011, 244). David Herman questions the parallelization of the oppositions *social* vs. *individual*, *intermental* vs. *intramental*, and *externalist* vs. *internalist* (2011b). Critics have also expressed skepticism about the constructs *social mind* and *intermental thought* (Hutto 2011), which, according to Manfred Jahn, can be called *mind* or *thought* only metaphorically (2011).

The Israeli scholar Shlomit Rimmon-Kenan raises the question of whether traditional literary studies have not engaged in the social and ideological determination of fictional minds, and she sees in Palmer's approach a neglect of the artistic design (2011). Marie-Laure Ryan, in turn, asks the same question, criticizing the fact that Palmer insufficiently defines the mode of existence of social mind, its relationship with the individual consciousness, and its role in the narrative (2011). A common criticism of splitting the mind into an individual and a social part resounds in this chorus of respondents. Inspired by the work of Lev Vygotsky (1934), Charles Fernyhough states that "even, 'internalist' minds are social" (2011), thereby refuting the splitting of mind conducted by Palmer.

It is not by chance then that some of the critical respondents comment on social minds through reference to Russian theoreticians of the 1920s–1930s, including Lev Vygotsky, Mikhail Bakhtin, and Valentin Voloshinov. Palmer himself, who was obviously influenced by the American psychologist of Vygotskian orientation James Wertsch (1991), who pays tribute to his Russian predecessors as well as to the neuropsychologist Alexander Luria. Palmer describes in detail the approaches to social and ideological parameters of speech and mind, which were discovered by Russian theorists (2004, 141–169).

6

At this point it may be helpful to weigh the considerations discussed thus far. Cognitive narratology, which appears in very diverse shapes, opens new horizons for literary criticism. It asks questions of anthropological significance, linking literary studies – a hermeneutical discipline – with empirical sciences. Cognitive narratology's main merit is the analysis of the relationship between narrative and consciousness, i.e. the minds of characters as well as of readers. But not infrequently, highly interesting hypotheses based on mere speculation have to be reined in through empirical analysis and its sobering results.

According to its representatives, cognitive narratology is only in the initial phase of its development. Yet it should now pay attention to some of its shortcomings. Let us mention just two of them.

First, in today's cognitive narratology there is a strong tendency to equate fictional minds with real ones.[3] There is no doubt, psychology has a great deal to learn from the novel. However, Anna Karenina is not our patient, nor is it our task to overcome the narrow norms of the society in which the heroine of the novel lives. We see the heroine on the one hand as a woman with certain traumata that render her undeniably tempting to the therapist's diagnosing eye. Yet on the other hand, we view her as an artifact, as an expression of the artistic design. This artistic factor is not accessible for the psychologist as psychologist, nor for the cognitivist as cognitivist.

Let us now have a look at an example from Leo Tolstoy's famous novel. In his first amorous encounter with Anna, Vronsky's covering her body with kisses is

---

[3] Palmer's originally strong identification (in 2004) gave way to a more cautious approach: "it seems obvious to me that fictional minds are similar to real minds in some ways but profoundly different from them in other ways" (2011, 207).

compared to a killer who cuts his victim into pieces: "And with fury, as it were with passion, the murderer falls on the body and drags it and hacks at it; so [Vronsky] covered her face and shoulders with kisses. She held his hand, and did not stir" (Tolstoy 1965, 158–159). This comparison is given, as it seems at first glance, from the narrator's viewpoint. Yet on further consideration we may conclude that it actually is given from the perceptual and ideological point of view of Anna herself. For the cognitivist as well as for the psychologist, the comparison of the lover with a murderer is, of course, of great significance, and both will draw their interpretive conclusions. The literary scholar, however, in considering the novel's entire artistic design, focuses on the fact that the motif of the body cut into pieces occurs three times in the novel. The first occurrence is in the scene at Moscow's railway station after the meeting with Vronsky, when Anna learns that an accident has occurred: the wheel of the train has cut the body of a railway worker into two pieces. Anna is severely shaken and interprets the accident as an 'evil omen.' The second time the slicing up of a body occurs is in the above-mentioned erotic scene with Vronsky, and the third time is Anna's death under the slicing wheel of the train. This concatenation of motifs causes Anna's death to appear as the fulfillment of the schema of her fatal expectations, which had formed as early as during the first encounter with Vronsky at the railway station. The author indicates to us that the heroine is the draftsman and engineer of her fate insofar as one may conclude that the above-quoted scene is presented from Anna's point of view and embodies her fatal construction of her future life and death.

Cognitive narratology tends to neglect the artistic character of the structure of the literature from which it draws its examples. Of course, in theory, few cognitivists would not accept that fictional minds and social minds are elements that belong to the artistic design of a piece of literature. In practice, however, cognitivists tend to neglect the artistic nature of the fictional narrative and its fictional instances. They therefore do not take sufficient account of the fact that the content of a fictional mind can be motivated not so much by the nature of the character and the situation she or he is in as by the overall shape of the artistic design.

Victor Shklovsky pointed to the primacy of the *sujet*, i.e. the energetic artistic construction, over life-experience realities:

> The sujet constructions select fabula-situations that suit them and deform the material in the process. [...] Certain fabula situations can be selected according to sujet principles, i. e. there can be a certain sujet construction laid out in the situations themselves, a staircase-like construction, an inversion, a circular construction. In the same way, specific types of stone have a layered structure that makes them especially well-suited to certain arrangements. (1970 [1928], 220)

In a similar vein Shklovsky emphasized the primacy of the aesthetic construction with a wonderful *aperçu*: "In art, blood is not bloody. No, it just rhymes with 'flood' [Кровь в искусстве не кровава, она рифмуется с «любовь»]. It is material either for a construction of sounds or for a construction of images" (1990 [1921], 159). In well-made works the factors of the existential and the aesthetic tend to cohere with one another so closely that the seams between the characterological and artistic motivations are not visible. But cognitivists who approach a novel's characters and do not take into account the artistic fabric of the work's whole, should be advised to exercise a certain amount of caution in analyzing *Anna Karenina* and its heroine. They should understand certain mental developments that are seemingly motivated purely characterologically or socially to be justified no less (or even more) artistically, as superimposed by the overall aesthetic design.

The second shortcoming concerns cognitive narratology's focus on character. Contrary to empirical psychology, which says readers of the novel concentrate primarily on events (see Marisa Bortolussi's argument, mentioned above), cognitive narratology focuses on character, thereby subordinating events to character. However, Aristotle was early in pointing out the priority of action over character. In his *Poetics*, he defines a hierarchy of the parts of a narrative using the example of tragedy:

> The most important of these is the arrangement of the incidents [ἡ τῶν πραγμάτων σύστασις], for tragedy is not a representation of men but of actions [μίμησίς ἐστιν οὐκ ἀνθρώπων ἀλλὰ πράξεων] [...], and the end aimed at is the representation not of qualities of character but of some action. They do not therefore act to represent character, but character-study is included for the sake of the action. It follows that the incidents and the story [μῦθος] are the end at which tragedy aims, and in everything the end aimed at is of prime importance. (1940, 1450a, 15)[4]

The formula "arrangement of the incidents" implies a conscious constructive act, including even the admissibility of certain manipulations. The fact that a certain position was already taken by Aristotle is, needless to say, no absolute argument in favor of this view. Even so, we should give Aristotle some credit for being narratology's actual founder; what his short outline of the tragedy has to say about mimesis[5] and mythos has become a firm part of narratology's basic elements.

---

4 Original translation by W. Hamilton Fyfe revised by the author.
5 The term "mimesis" in the works of the mature Aristotle should not be translated as "imitation" but rather as "representation" or, better still, as the "presentation" of something that does not yet exist. The virtue of mimesis is not the resemblance to a certain given reality but such an "arrangement of incidents" that is capable of inducing the desired effect on the recipient.

One might argue that there are types of narrative that foreground character rather than action. But as far as these narratives are not descriptive, they cannot do without any action.[6]

In conclusion, this essay has argued that cognitive narratology should focus less on character and more on action. Also, character should be regarded as something that is implied in and through actions. This does not detract from the representation of mind, in which cognitive narratology is primarily interested. Much of what the representation of mind depicts are actions – mental actions. In literary narrative these mental actions often take the form of events. An event is a special occurrence, something that is not part of an everyday routine.[7] Thus, we would like to counter Palmer's formula that *Novel reading is mind reading*. We would argue instead that *Novel reading is event reading*, or, even better yet, *Novel reading is the mental event of reading mental events*.

References

Aristotle. 1940 [c. 335 BCE]. *Poetics*. Translated by W. Hamilton Fyfe. Oxford: Clarendon Press.
Bortolussi, Marisa. 2011. "Response to Alan Palmer's 'Social Minds.'" *Style* 45: 283–287.
Cohn, Dorrit. 1978. *Transparent Minds: Narrative Modes for Presenting Consciousness in Fiction*. Princeton: Princeton University Press.
Dinkler, Michal Beth. 2015. "'The Thoughts of Many Hearts Shall be Revealed': Listening in on Lukan Interior Monologues." *Journal of Biblical Literature* 134: 373–399.
Fernyhough, Charles. 2011. "Even 'Internalist' Minds are Social." *Style* 45: 271–275.
Fludernik, Monika. 1996. *Towards a 'Natural' Narratology*. London: Routledge.
---. 2011. "1050–1500. Through a Glass Darkly; or, the Emergence of Mind in Medieval Narrative." In *The Emergence of Mind: Representations of Consciousness in Narrative Discourse in English*, edited by David Herman, 69–109. Lincoln: University of Nebraska Press.
Forster, Edward Morgan. 1927. *Aspects of the Novel*. London: Arnold.
Genette, Gérard. 1990. "Fictional Narrative, Factual Narrative." Translated by Nitsa Ben-Ari, with Brian McHale. *Poetics Today* 11: 755–774.
---. 1993 [1990]. "Fictional Narrative, Factual Narrative." In *Fiction and Diction*, edited by Gérard Genette, translated by Catherine Porter, 54–84. Ithaca: Cornell University Press.
Hamburger, Käte. 1973 [1957]. *The Logic of Literature*. 2nd rev. ed., translated by Marilyn J. Rose. Bloomington: Indiana University Press.
Herman, David, ed. 2011. *The Emergence of Mind. Representations of Consciousness in Narrative Discourse in English*. Lincoln: University of Nebraska Press.

---

[6] On the delimitation of descriptive and narrative texts and the role of interpretation in this classification, see Schmid 2010, 5–6.
[7] On the narratological concepts of event and eventfulness, see Schmid 2003; 2010, 8–21; Hühn 2014 [2009].

---. 2011a. "Introduction." In *The Emergence of Mind: Representations of Consciousness in Narrative Discourse in English*, 1–40. Lincoln: University of Nebraska Press.
---. 2011b. "Post-Cartesian Approaches to Narrative and Mind: A Response to Alan Palmer's Target Essay on 'Social Minds.'" *Style* 45: 265–271.
---. 2014. "Cognitive Narratology." In *Handbook of Narratology*, 2nd fully revised and expanded ed., edited by Peter Hühn, Jan Christoph Meister, John Pier, and Wolf Schmid, 46–64. Berlin and Boston: De Gruyter.
Hogan, Patrick Colm. 2003. *Cognitive Science, Literature, and the Arts: A Guide for Humanists*. London: Routledge.
---. 2011. "Palmer's Anti-Cognitivist Challenge." *Style* 45: 244–248.
Hübner, Gert. 2003. *Erzählform im höfischen Roman. Studien zur Fokalisierung im „Eneas", im „Iwein" und im „Tristan"*. Tübingen and Basel: A. Francke.
Hühn, Peter. 2014 [2009]. "Event and Eventfulness." In *Handbook of Narratology*. 2nd fully revised and expanded ed., edited by Peter Hühn, Jan Christoph Meister, John Pier, and Wolf Schmid, 159–178. Berlin and Boston: De Gruyter.
Hutto, Daniel D. 2011. "Understanding Fictional Minds without Theory of Mind!" *Style* 45: 276–282.
Jahn, Manfred. 2011. "Mind = Mind + Social Mind?: A Response to Alan Palmer's Target Essay." *Style* 45: 249–253.
Kafalenos, Emma. 2011. "The Epistemology of Fiction: Knowing v. 'Knowing.'" *Style* 45: 254–258.
Lagoni, Frederike F. E. 2016. *Fiktionales versus faktuales Erzählen fremden Bewusstseins: Eine korpusbasierte Kritik der ‚Signposts of Fictionality'-These*. Berlin and Boston: De Gruyter.
Palmer, Alan. 2002. "The Construction of Fictional Minds." *Narrative* 10: 29–46.
---. 2004. *Fictional Minds*. Lincoln: University of Nebraska Press.
---. 2007. "Universal Minds." *Semiotica*: 165: 205–225.
---. 2010. *Social Minds in the Novel*. Columbus: Ohio State University Press.
---. 2011. "Social Minds in Fiction and Criticism." *Style* 45: 196–240.
Rimmon-Kenan, Shlomith. 2011. "Response to Alan Palmer." *Style* 45: 339–343.
Ryan, Marie-Laure. 2011. "Kinds of Minds: On Alan Palmer's 'Social Minds.'" *Style* 45: 654–659.
Schmid, Wolf. 2003. "Narrativity and Eventfulness." In *What is Narratology?: Questions and Answers Regarding the Status of a Theory*, edited by Tom Kindt and Hans-Harald Müller, 17–33. Berlin and New York: De Gruyter.
---. 2010. *Narratology: An Introduction*. Berlin and Boston: De Gruyter.
---. 2017. *Mentale Ereignisse. Bewusstseinsveränderungen in europäischen Erzählwerken vom Mittelalter bis zur Moderne*. Berlin and Boston: De Gruyter.
Shklovsky, Victor [Šklovskij, Viktor]. 1990 [1921]. "The Novel as Parody: Sterne's *Tristram Shandy*." In *Theory of Prose*, translated by B. Sher, 147–170. Normal: Dalkey Archive.
---. 1970 [1928]. *Material i stil' v romane L'va Tolstogo "Vojna i mir"*. Paris: The Hague.
Stanzel, Franz K. 1959. "Episches Präteritum, erlebte Rede, historisches Präsens." *Deutsche Vierteljahrsschrift für Literaturwissenschaft und Geistesgeschichte* 33: 1–12.
---. 1979. *Theorie des Erzählens*. Göttingen: Vandenhoeck & Ruprecht.
---, ed. 2002. "Der Durchbruch. Die Kontroverse mit Käte Hamburger." In *Unterwegs. Erzähltheorie für Leser*, 41–44. Göttingen: Vandenhoeck & Ruprecht.
Tolstoy, Leo. n. d. [ca. 1936]. *War and Peace*. Translated by Constance Garnett. New York: Random House.

---. 1965. *Anna Karenina*. Edited and introduced by Leonard J. Kent and Nina Berberova. The Constance Garnett Translation revised by the editors. New York: Random House.

Vygotsky, Leo S. [Vygotskij, Lev S.]. 1987 [1934]. "Thinking and Speech." In *The Collected Works of L. S. Vygotsky*, vol. 1, edited by Robert W. Rieber and Aaron S. Carton. New York: Plenum.

Wertsch, James V. 1991. *Voices of the Mind: A Sociocultural Approach to Mediated Action*. Cambridge: Harvard University Press.

Woledge, Brian. 1988. *Commentaire sur „Ivain (Le Chevalier au lion)" de Chrétien de Troyes*. Tome II, vv. 3412–6808. Genève: Droz.

Zunshine, Lisa. 2006. *Why We Read Fiction: Theory of Mind and the Novel*. Columbus: Ohio State University Press.

Eva von Contzen
Dido's Words: Representing Speech and Consciousness in Ancient and Medieval Narrative

In 2003, Monika Fludernik outlined the prospects and the urgent need for a diachronic narratology: "a reorientation of narratology in the direction of diachronic inquiry is now on the cards – no longer as a weird antiquarian interest but as a vital and exciting new area of research" (332). In the ensuing decade and particularly in recent years, both historical and diachronic narratology have indeed gained momentum. At the same time, a growing sensitivity to the temporal restriction of many key parameters of narrative theory has been discernible among narratologists. These developments suggest that the paradigm shift Fludernik envisioned is in full swing. The significance of this shift cannot be overestimated. Classical narratology, after all, had largely ignored the fact that narrative practices are historically dependent. The few cases in which scholars did turn to genres prior to the modern novel, such as Tzvetan Todorov in his 1969 study of the *Decameron* (mid-fourteenth century), offer structuralist readings that prefer the identification of abstract categories over the analysis of specific narrative practices in their historical circumstances. And even though postclassical narratology has admirably succeeded in taking contextual parameters into account, the objects of study have remained rather narrow in terms of their historical and diachronic scope (the modern novel, film, hypertext, graphic novels).

A tension that underlies the agenda of historicizing narratology is the need, on the one hand, for systematic approaches that rely on established parameters and theorems, and thus necessarily proceed deductively, and the necessity, on the other hand, to approach texts inductively so as not to impose categories that do not (yet) apply to the text in question. The latter case, however, does not, strictly speaking, require narratological approaches, as Hartmut Bleumer has pointed out (2015, 213–215). A second problem concerns the differentiation between a 'historical' and a 'diachronic' narratology: the former is synchronic in that it considers narrative practices at a specific point in time, usually in a premodern context, while the latter sets a historical narrative practice in relation to earlier and later developments. Even though the two obviously overlap, they correspond to different views on narrative: in their most vehement applications, historical narratology is interested in its objects of study as an end in themselves, while a diachronic narratology considers narrative texts as building bricks, or stepping stones, in a larger trajectory of narrative developments. Both approaches of course have their validity, and to my mind are best used in combination: starting from an informed historical narratological study, one can then proceed to comparative studies and focus on aspects of narrative developments and change.

Monika Fludernik's work on medieval and early modern English narratives is clearly diachronic. In both her monographs *The Fictions of Language and the Languages of Fiction* (1993) and *Towards a 'Natural' Narratology* (1996), as well as in several articles (1995, 2000, 2003, 2007) she is concerned with the question of change: when and why does a certain narrative feature (scene shifts, discourse markers, metanarrative comments) emerge and/or become replaced by another feature? A crucial issue in this context is the representation of speech and consciousness in premodern texts. Here Fludernik has conducted much important groundwork: for instance, she demonstrates that passages of free indirect speech exist in medieval narrative, if only sparingly (1993, 93–95; 98–99). Also, she has shown that the communicative situation required for narrating speech and consciousness is more flexible than traditional theories – which posit the existence of a narrator at all cost – would hold (1993, 442–443). In a recent article, she introduces six categories of thought representation that can be found in Middle English texts and makes a strong case for reconsidering the categories of speech and thought and their narrative representation when it comes to medieval literature (2011b).

In what follows, I revisit the question of how speech, thought, and consciousness are represented in selected premodern texts, and complicate the issue by adding a further parameter: the fact that characters are often taken from traditional material. Characters in medieval narrative generally tend to be less internally motivated; they are characterized by their actions; there are fewer, if any, passages that provide insight into their minds and their reasoning (von Contzen 2015b). That premodern characters, too, exhibit psychological dimensions goes without saying, even though these dimensions may be calibrated differently from those we find in modern texts.[1] There have been fruitful attempts to approach the category of 'character' in terms of James Phelan's triad of mimetic, synthetic, and thematic dimensions (1989). These three aspects, simultaneously present, refer to characters as individuals, that is, their life-like qualities, their constructedness, and the representation of superordinate qualities; characters as types.[2]

---

[1] On character in medieval narrative, see e.g. Haferland 2013 and Stock 2010; on character more generally, Jannidis 2004.
[2] See Meyer 1999 for applications of Phelan's theory to medieval German texts.

In medieval literature, thematic aspects can prevail when a character functions as a representative of a particular ethics or moral. But there is a further dimension, different from the thematic dimension and issues of typification: the frequent case that characters are implicated in dense intertextual contexts. Rather than being invented from scratch, many characters in premodern narratives are taken from previous literary and cultural traditions. Heroes such as Achilles, Alexander, or Arthur belong to the received tradition and already bring with them a set of relatively fixed attributes, character traits, and patterns of behavior. These details function as a necessary backdrop and prerequisite for new versions and stories in which they are featured. This aspect is not covered by Phelan's categories. The synthetic dimension with its focus on the 'makedness' and artificiality of character comes closest, but it does not account for intertextual references. Phelan defines the synthetic as "that component of character directed to its role as artificial construct in the larger construction of the text; more generally, the constructedness of a text as an object" (1996, 220). The practice that characters who exist beyond individual texts in a shared cultural context of narratives can be transferred from this shared material into new contexts, is not so much an issue of constructedness than of referentiality and intertextuality. A fourth dimension appears to be at stake here: for want of a term, I call it the *referential* dimension, which complements the three categories as suggested by Phelan. As part of the referential dimension, character transcends the boundaries of a particular text. Links are invited and established between the same character(s) in different transformations, across different narrative contexts. For each of these occurrences in a specific narrative text, one can, in a second step, differentiate again between the mimetic, synthetic, and thematic aspect.

How, then, do authors come to grips with representing well-known heroes and heroines and their consciousness when they take up traditional material? My test case will be the depiction of Dido, Queen of Carthage, in the *Aeneid* (first century BC), Geoffrey Chaucer's dream vision *The House of Fame* (late fourteenth century), and William Caxton's *Eneydos* (1490). I will also briefly refer to Chaucer's "Legend of Dido" in *The Legend of Good Women* (late fourteenth century). In all four cases, Dido is the same Dido: the point of reference is always the same (pseudo-historical) figure. From its Vergilian beginnings, Dido is trapped between clashing, eventually irreconcilable, demands. Vergil's Dido is subjected to the larger patterns of the epic framework; her love cannot compete with the divinely ordained mission of Aeneas. In the medieval tradition, the emphasis is shifted to Aeneas's role in the affair, reinterpreting Dido as a courtly lady betrayed by a weak knight. While the overall material (*materia*) is constant, the *modus tractandi*, that is, the presentation of the material, underlies the individual author's choices and decisions.³ In all versions, Dido's words and her mental states are key to her representation. Three aspects of the narrative depiction are of special importance: first, the representation of direct and indirect discourse; second, the description of consciousness, emotions, and patterns of behavior; and third, the degree to which the narrator controls and frames the characters' discourse.

1 The *Aeneid* and the *Eneydos*

In the *Aeneid*, direct discourse is paramount: the passages in which the characters interact verbally bring to the fore the action-focused nature of the epic and the speech-actions performed through their direct discourse.⁴ Dido provides a particularly striking example of the close interrelationship between action and direct speech. In the fourth book of the *Aeneid*, there are eight speeches of considerable length made by Dido: her words to Anna, in which she reveals her burning love and seeks her sister's advice (4.9–29); the first speech to Aeneas in which she confronts him about his plans of leaving Carthage (4.305–330); her increasingly enraged reply to Aeneas's evasive response (4.365–387); two further speeches to Anna, making explicit her wish to die (4.416–436) and feigning an alternative solution while in truth masking her preparations for her suicide (4.478–498); her soliloquy while the pyre is built (4.534–452); an apostrophe to Jupiter and the gods upon seeing the shore empty, in which she curses Aeneas and the Trojans (4.590–629); and a second, shorter soliloquy immediately before her suicide (4.651–662).⁵ With respect to Dido, the *Aeneid* uses two main strategies in representing her consciousness: direct speech and descriptions by the narrator about her mental state (psychonarration). The latter often coincides with

---

3 On medieval theories and practices of writing, see Minnis 1988. The reception history of Vergil, and the Dido tragedy in particular, is rich; see recently Manuwald 2014; Hamm 2008; and the impressive bibliography by Kailuweit 2005. For the first fifteen hundred years of reception, see Ziolkowski and Putnam 2008; for the Vergilian reception in the manuscript tradition in England in particular, Baswell 1995.
4 See e.g. Highet 1972, 1974 with respect to the importance of speech in the *Aeneid*.
5 I use the edition by Conte (2009). Highet counts thirteen speeches made by Dido in total in the *Aeneid*: "four in the first book and no less than nine in the fourth. Only three of these (a libation prayer, a request, and an order) are brief. The others are relatively long, carefully wrought, full of strong emotions. Her speeches amount to 231 lines" (1972, 26).

the description of emotional gestures.[6] At the same time, the epic narrator – 'Olympic' in his knowledge about the events, both among the gods and the mortals – accompanies the narrative with his comments. Dido's death is anticipated long before its actual conduction. She is referred to as *infelix* [unhappy; 4.68], *demens* [without sense; 4.78], *furentem* [raging; 4.465], and *moritura* [moribund; 4.519]. Upon the episode of the cave wedding, the narrator remarks: "this was the day which gave first cause to death and first cause to unhappiness" [*Ille dies primus leti primusque malorum / causa fuit*; 4.169–170]. When the Trojans prepare their ships for their departure, the narrator inserts an apostrophe to Dido in which he laments how painful the events are for the queen (4.408–412).

Because of and despite her institutional power, Dido is unable to change the course of events and her own fate, and she has already failed to make Aeneas stay by means of her direct pleas. Dido's powerlessness is reflected in her speech, which no longer conveys the power of a sovereign. It does not matter that her diction is dominated by words from the semantic field of 'power' (Helzle 1996, 55). The only actions Dido is able to perform are her speech actions, which, however, remain without effect. Wishes, curses, hypothetical possibilities and her feelings take over her sense of reality. The discrepancy between the spoken, executed word and the passivity in view of her future fate, against which all words are ineffective, is shown in the queen's direct discourse. Dido's death is the ultimate subjection to her powerlessness, which goes hand in hand with her having to admit that the only deed she can still accomplish cannot change her fate but at least dissolve it. Ovid can thus end Dido's epistle in the *Heroides* with her wish to have inscribed on her tomb that Aeneas caused her death but she accomplished it.[7]

When, in 1490, William Caxton published an English translation of the Aeneas myth, the fine balancing between Dido's two roles and her downfall was lost. Instead, the spectacular takes precedence: Caxton's version is a voyeuristic exuberance of Dido's pain and madness. The *Eneydos* is the translation of a translation: Caxton used the prose French *Livre des Eneydes*, printed in 1483 in Lyons by Guillaume Le Roy, which in turn was a loose paraphrase of Vergil. The *Eneydos* consists of 65 chapters of varying length, which retell the *Aeneid* very freely. The work incorporates passages from other authors, most notably Boccaccio, and

---

[6] See e.g. 4.300–301, when she rages [*bacchatur*] through town, and 4.465–473, when she experiences visions and bad omens. As to examples of emotionally charged descriptions, Dido looks at Aeneas rolling her eyes (4.363–364) and beats her breast and tears her hair (4.589–590).
[7] The passage is the following: PRAEBVIT AENEAS ET CAVSAM MORTIS ET ENSEM / IPSA SVA DIDO CONCIDIT VSA MANV; 7.193–194. I use the edition by Knox (1995).

shifts the emphasis considerably in some respects.[8] The Dido story, which covers chapters 11 to 29, belongs to the latter group. Even though the overall plot remains the same, the narrative is much longer and more detailed. In the modern editors' words, the whole Dido episode is "long, verbose, and exaggerated" (Culley and Furnivall 1890, xi).[9] Dido's speeches, which in the *Aeneid* are carefully constructed and present her tragic story as a developing narrative arc, are expanded on to such a degree that the narrative progression is halted.

The effect is startling: neither do Dido's speeches add anything to the story, nor do they advance her character or present her in a different light. Rather, Caxton maximizes what is known about Dido (her despair and anger of Aeneas, putting her in a situation of inescapable doom), and thereby invites his audience to take delight in the known. When Dido shows Aeneas the city, her words lose her: "she yet spekynge, her speche deffaylleth alle sodeynly, and can not kepe purpos ne countenaunce, as a person transported from her vndrestandynge, and ouertake wyth oure grete loue inestymable" (Ch. 13, 48). In the *Aeneid*, the corresponding passage covers merely one line: *incipit effari mediaque in voce resistit* (4.76). A similar inflation occurs in chapter 14, which recounts how Carthage falls into decay and chaos because Dido, due to her fervent love, neglects her duties as queen: "Alle the werkes and doynges of Dydo are taryed, and lefte in the astate of Inperfection" (49). While the equivalent passage in the *Aeneid* is short (4.86–89), here a long list follows in which Dido's shortcomings are spelled out: bridges and streets crumble, the city is no longer defended, grass grows over the buildings, all construction sites are stopped (Ch. 14, 49).

As a general strategy, then, Caxton inflates Dido's story with details that add little to nothing to the plot. This pertains especially to the length of Dido's speeches.[10] Since full chapters are devoted to her words, the dialogic quality of the Vergilian account is lost. Dido seems to speak generally rather than to her interlocutors. The effect is one of a greater distance between the character of Dido and the development of the plot, and thus a greater distance between her and the audience. This holds even true for the one passage in which the events are focalized through Dido exclusively (Ch. 22, 79–81). When Dido's despair increases, she

---

[8] See in more detail on the *Livre des Eneydes* Singerman 1986, 211–216, and Leube 1969, 65–76. On Caxton's use of Vergil, see Hall 1960.

[9] All quotations from Caxton are taken from the edition by Culley and Furnivall (1890). I refer to the relevant chapter and page number(s).

[10] The speeches are the following: in chapters 11, 21, 23, 24 to her sister; in chapters 18 to 20, her lament and accusation of Aeneas; in chapters 25 and 26, two further extended laments; in chapter 27, her angry words when she sees the leaving ships and her final, excessive speech before her suicide.

retreats, first to her chamber, then wandering about town on her own. She experiences visions and omens, such as birds of doom and holy water blackening. Only the readers are witnessing her desolation: "a grete malencolie enuaded thenne her herte & her wittes, all ynoughe troubled of the thynges precedent / whiche things she kept clos & shette withynne the shryne of her sorowfull thoughtes, without to notyfye them to eny body lyuynge" (Ch. 22, 79). One should note that Dido's despair is described as "malencolie." Her state is medicalized. In the final scene, too, the narrator stresses that the sanguine humor has gained full control of Dido (Ch. 27, 103–104). Her madness is a case of her humors in imbalance.

In Caxton's account of Dido, there is only one instance in which the audience is granted access to Dido's mind. When she is on her own, she desires her beloved's presence: "by Imagynacyon impraynet wyth-in the fauntasme of her entendemente, Her semeth that she seeth hym there presente, heringe after his words playsaunte / And deuysynge wyth hym / and there she passeth ouer a parte of the nyghte in suche medytacyons and contynuell thoughtes" (Ch. 13, 48). This is a rare example of psychonarration, highlighting Dido's longing for Aeneas. Yet the depiction is detached and formal: the narrator uses technical terminology in order to describe how she recalls Aeneas's image in her mind (*Imagynacyon*; *fauntasme*), evoking Aristotelian models of mental recollections.[11]

These examples point to a strategy of rationalizing Dido's story, perhaps in order to increase her 'mimetic' dimension. That Dido should be imagined as a flesh and blood woman is also stressed in the description of her suicide, which is, indeed, bloody: "her handes, & her persone alle couered & defyled with blood without mesure, & the swerde that dropped yet of bloode, and alle blody, laye by her" (Ch. 28, 106). She sheds her own blood and frees herself from her ill humoral balance. The narrator remarks upon the scene of her dying that she was "without eny more langage" (Ch. 28, 106). Caxton's Dido hovers curiously between verbal excess, and thus extreme outspokenness, and stark narratorial control that seeks to rationalize her behavior. Even though Dido talks a lot she says little. She is so well-known that her story has become emblematic and does not require careful narrative development. Instead, the audience is invited to take delight in her suffering (the excessive laments and curses) and to find explanations for her behavior on a more 'human' scale.

---

[11] For instance in *De memoria et reminiscentia* and *De memoria*. See Carruthers 2008 in more detail on medieval theories of recollection.

2 Chaucerian Dido

Turning to the depiction of Dido in Chaucer, we see quite a different approach to the representation of her speech and thought. This is partly due to the influence of a different tradition to which Chaucer takes recourse: Dido's letter to Aeneas in Ovid's *Heroides*. The Ovidian rendering builds on and playfully engages with the depiction of Dido in the *Aeneid*. In her letter, Dido is less the furious and desperate partner left behind, but appears as a more sensible and thoughtful character. Heroism has been replaced by pathos. Dido thus becomes the epitome of the abandoned lover in the medieval tradition; she is the victim of a cruel Aeneas who decides against her. Chaucer's treatment of Dido is clearly shaped by this tradition.[12] In *The House of Fame*, the story of Dido is central to the description of the images in Venus's Temple of Glass. The dreamer in the temple recalls the passage from the beginning of the *Aeneid* in which Aeneas, standing in the temple of Venus in Carthage, is looking at the images of the Trojan War (1.446–493). Even though the introduction and the inscription on the "table of bras" (1.141) suggest that the *Aeneid* in its entirety will be depicted, the ekphrasis focuses on the Dido story in particular.[13] The dreamer's perception punctuates the account: the phrase "I sawgh/saugh" leads from one panel and scene/episode to the next. The Dido story, though, falls out of the description: here the dreamer turns away from, or rather, is drawn further into, the events. The description gives way to narrative: he mentions the descriptive "Ther sawgh I" in line 253 and picks it up again only in line 433. The Dido episode is thus a narrative digression from the ekphrasis, reversing the more usual digressive qualities of descriptive passages in narrative accounts.

Twice we hear Dido's own words in *The House of Fame*. The first instance is introduced by a description of her inner turmoil: "She gan to wringe hir hondes two" (1.299). Dido laments her faithfulness towards an unfaithful man who sought nothing but his own fame (1.300–310). What follows is an emotional soliloquy ("Quod she to hirselve thoo"; 1.319), apostrophizing Aeneas. Here Dido anticipates that she will become a model and exemplum for other women. From her particular situation, she generalizes, addressing men in general ("O, have ye men such godlyhede / In speche, and never a del of trouthe?", 1.330–331), and categorizes herself with all women in opposition to mean men: "Thus we be

---

12 See Desmond on the Ovidian changes (1994, 37–45). McTaggart (2012) argues that *The House of Fame* is characterized by a tension between the Vergilian and Ovidian tradition.
13 All quotations from Chaucer are taken from Benson (1987).

served euerychone.... Certaynly we ben deceyvyd" (1.337; 340). She laments the destructive power of Fama and the shame Aeneas brought on her (1.349–360). The ensuing conversation with Anna is provided in free indirect speech; Dido blames her for having counseled her in giving in to her love in the first place: "And seyde that she [= *Anna*] cause was / That she [= *Dido*] first loved him, allas" (1.369–370).

The two speeches constitute the heart of the passage. Dido not only voices her despair and disillusionment – which, in contrast to Vergil, does not develop or turn into madness –, she is also acutely aware of her exemplarity and her afterlife as an epitome of the abandoned woman. The dreamer does everything in order to silence Dido: he describes her from the very beginning as fully controlled by external forces; first through Venus, who makes Dido fall in love with Aeneas; then through Aeneas, whom she cannot get away from. Ultimately, she appears to be firmly in the narrator's hands, who comments on the events and frames them in his way, summarizing the love story rather shrewdly: "she / Becam hys love and lete hym doo / Al that weddynge longeth too" (1.242–244). The dreamer foregrounds Aeneas's faultiness, who is good only in appearance: "Allas, what harm doth apparence, / Whan hit is fals in existence!" (1.265–266). But he also criticizes Dido who "loved al to sone a gest" (1.288).

Yet despite the narrator's seeming dominance over the material, it is Dido and her narrative which cannot be silenced or glossed over. Interpreting the hasty account and the dreamer's comments as a parody or trivialization of the heroic love affair (both of which can be substantiated) misses the point (Clemen 2001). The episode shows the dreamer's succumbing to the overbearing power of tradition, as epitomized by Dido's narrative. After Dido's first speech, the dreamer comments:

> In suche wordes gan to pleyne
> Dydo of hir grete peyne,
> As me mette redely –
> Non other auctour alegge I. (1.311–314)

He claims to have dreamed ("as me mette") Dido's words as he represents them, and not have drawn on any other "auctour." The passage makes a strong claim of authorial independence.[14] Why, though, does such a statement occur at exactly this point rather than at any other passage in the poem? Clearly the dreamer felt the need to justify himself: in disclaiming any other source, he strengthens his

---

14 See in more detail Miller 1986.

own position as teller of the tale. At the same time, he actually represents someone else's story and speech in spite of the disclaimer. The material has reached a status of independence so that no other authority is necessary. This argument is carried further when the dreamer breaks off his account of Dido by referring his readers to Vergil and Ovid:

> And al the maner how she deyde
> And alle the words that she seyde,
> Whoso to knowe hit hath purpos,
> Rede Virgile in Eneydos
> Or the Epistle of Ovyde,
> What that she wrot er that she dyde. (1.375–380)

Dido functions as an index on several levels: she has become an exemplary case, and is implicated in a web of intertextual references. The dreamer-narrator in a poem about fame, the poet's fame in particular, wrestles with a traditional story and its protagonist which cannot be channeled. The transgression from the ekphrasis, a digression in reverse, demonstrates the power of such traditional material. *The House of Fame* draws attention to the constructedness of Dido (her synthetic dimension), but even more so to her referential dimension. Any Dido must be measured against other Didos, and thereby retains a status of independence – the idea or essence of Dido – that remains constant. The fact that her death, in *The House of Fame*, covers merely two lines (1.373–374), cannot be attributed only to a narrator who loses interest in her story. Her death is a known fact, it sets an example that no longer requires detailed speeches or descriptions. The narrative can be condensed and suppressed in any way imaginable. Ultimately, the name Dido already evokes and encapsulates the story.

Chaucer's second rendering of the Dido story, in *The Legend of Good Women*, at first sight appears to be a victory of narrative again. After all, "The Legend of Dido" covers more than 1,360 lines and delves into many details of the story.[15] It begins with a praise of Vergil and acknowledges Ovid as a source (924–929). There are six instances of direct discourse in total, plus an account of her letter in direct speech.[16] Yet there are many striking similarities: the narrator is overt and

---

15 I can only refer to the wide range of interpretations of "The Legend of Dido" here, from it being a parody to a serious proto-feminist account. See Delaney 1972; Desmond 1994; Sanderlin 1986; Percival 1998; Phillips and Havely 1997.
16 These are: her two turns in the conversation with Aeneas at their initial meeting (978–982 and 989–993); her promise to help the Trojans (1086–1089); the talk to her sister in which she reveals her burning love (1170–1181); another two addresses to Aeneas after it is clear that he will leave her (1303–1308; 1316–1324); and the letter (1355–1365).

frequently comments on his arrangement and selection of the material (953–957; 1002–1003; 1160–1161; 1210). He establishes himself as the authority of his material. Conspicuously, Dido is referred to as "sely," i.e. 'innocent,' three times (1157; 1237; 1336). This innocence is Dido's attribute: it recalls the reference 'holy' of saints in hagiographic texts. Just as the ensuing narrative is 'proof' of a saint's sanctity, so does Dido's adjective anticipate the outcome and final evaluation.[17] The ending of Chaucer's "Legend of Dido" is once more the beginning of another tale: he directs the reader's attention to the *Heroides*: "Rede Ovyde, and in hym he shal it fynde" (1367). Again Dido's textual and narrative fixedness comes to the fore. Her story has become a point of reference – yet the referent, she herself, remains the focal point in all these accounts.

3 Tradition and Premodern Characters

In order to elicit the narrative strategies that underlie the depiction of Dido in these different contexts, the analysis of direct discourse and the representation of her mental states, which often occur closely together, proves to be a useful method. In particular, the distribution of speech and thought representation in its various forms is an effective means of measuring the degree of the narrator's control over a character and her story. My approach may not come across as particularly 'narratological' in that I have refrained from using any elaborate terminological framework, or imposing preconceived categories. This is not necessary: in a first step, the focus on the narrative forms themselves can direct our attention to identifying strategies and structures, which in a second step can be rendered fruitful for interpretation. Here narrative theory offers useful tools and cues. Forms and structures are not ends in themselves, but employed as means to an end. In order to tease out these purposes in a historical trajectory, historical narratology has to rely on both these sides of the narratological coin.

In every new rendering of the story, Dido remains the same character, even though Caxton's Dido and Chaucer's Dido differ considerably in their depiction. In the *Eneydos*, Dido has become almost a parody of herself: with many words, she says little. The dialogic quality of the *Aeneid* is replaced with long speeches that overstress Dido's fears and madness. As if to counterbalance Dido's verbosity

---

[17] John Lydgate's legends are a good example of this practice, which effectively shuns down narrative development (von Contzen 2015a). But see Frank for the opposite view: he ascribes the legend's power to its high degree of narrativity (1972, 59–78).

that suppresses the development of character as much as of the plot, Caxton attempts at rationalizing her behavior. Dido is physically ill; her phantasies are a case of memory recollection. Yet these references are too scarce to heighten Dido's mimetic dimension. In Chaucer, the narrator struggles to contain Dido within his narrative. The dreamer in *The House of Fame* is challenged by the weight of tradition and the constant referential quality of his heroine to which he eventually gives in. Chaucer's Dido is far less outspoken and verbose than Caxton's (and also than Vergil's). Her direct discourse cannot be controlled, though, because her story itself speaks louder than the narrator's voice. Here we can witness the full impact of a character's referential dimension, which runs crosswise the mimetic, thematic, and synthetic dimension.

Against the backdrop of a four-fold dimension of character depiction (mimetic, synthetic, thematic, and referential), it becomes difficult to maintain that Dido is 'psychologized' in any way comparable to heroines in the modern novel. Raymond Tripp has suggested that "Chaucer's transformation of Vergil's Dido anticipates his development away from medieval conventions toward modern, psychological people" (1970, 52). In Chaucer, Tripp maintains, Dido has acquired psychological depth and become "highly self-conscious" (55). In her lament, "she speaks about herself, almost as if she were another person" (56). While Tripp's findings are true, the conclusions he draws miss the point: Dido's self-consciousness results from her awareness as an exemplum, embedded in a traditional framework of intertextual references that competes with authorial and narratorial control and inhibits closure. Much work lies ahead for narratologists in order to further our understanding of how character depiction operates in premodern narratives, and how and why it changes. Dido, as an exemplum of a great love failed, is but one example of a character entangled in her own intertextuality.

References

Baswell, Christopher. 1995. *Virgil in Medieval England: Figuring the Aeneid from the Twelfth Century to Chaucer*. Cambridge: Cambridge University Press.
Benson, Larry D., ed. 1987. *The Riverside Chaucer*. 3rd ed. Oxford: Oxford University Press.
Bleumer, Hartmut. 2015. "Historische Narratologie." In *Literatur- und Kulturtheorien in der Germanistischen Mediävistik*, edited by Christiane Ackermann and Michael Egerding, 213–274. Berlin and Boston: De Gruyter.
Carruthers, Mary. 2008. *The Book of Memory: A Study of Memory in Medieval Culture*. 2nd ed. Cambridge: Cambridge University Press.
Clemen, Wolfgang. 2001. "The Dido Episode in *The House of Fame*." In *Chaucer*, edited by Corinne Saunders, 76–83. Malden: Blackwell.

Conte, Gian Biagio, ed. 2009. *P. Vergilius Maro: Aeneis. Bibliotheca Scriptorum Graecorum et Romanorum Teubneriana*. Berlin: De Gruyter.
Contzen, Eva von. 2015a. "Narrating Vernacular Sanctity: The *Scottish Legendary* as a Challenge to the 'Literary Turn' in Fifteenth-Century Hagiography." In *Sanctity as Literature in Medieval Britain*, edited by Eva von Contzen und Anke Bernau, 172–190. Manchester: Manchester University Press.
---. 2015b. "Why Medieval Literature Does Not Need the Concept of Social Minds: Exemplarity and Collective Experience." *Narrative* 23.2: 140–153.
Culley, M. T., and F. J. Furnivall, eds. 1890. *Caxton's "Eneydos."* London: Kegan Paul, Trench, Trübner & Co., 1890. Repr. 1913.
Delaney, Sheila. 1972. *Chaucer's House of Fame: The Poetics of Skeptical Fideism*. Chicago: University of Chicago Press.
Desmond, Marilynn. 1994. *Reading Dido: Gender, Textuality, and the Medieval Aeneid*. Minneapolis: University of Minnesota Press.
Fludernik, Monika. 1993. *The Fictions of Language and the Languages of Fiction: The Linguistic Representation of Speech and Consciousness*. London and New York: Routledge.
---. 1995. "Middle English *po* and Other Narrative Discourse Markers." In *Historical Pragmatics: Pragmatic Developments in the History of English*, edited by Andreas Jucker, 359–392. Amsterdam: Benjamins.
---. 1996. *Towards a 'Natural' Narratology*. London and New York: Routledge.
---. 2000. "Narrative Discourse Markers in Malory's *Morte D'Arthur*." *Journal of Historical Pragmatics* 1.2: 231–262.
---. 2003. "The Diachronization of Narratology." *Narrative* 11.3: 331–348.
---. 2007. "Letters as Narrative: Narrative Patterns and Episode Structure in Early Letters, 1400 to 1650." In *Methods in Historical Pragmatics*, edited by Susan M. Fitzmaurice and Irma Taavitsainen, 241–266. Berlin: De Gruyter.
---. 2011a. "The Representation of Mind from Chaucer to Aphra Behn." In *Narrative Developments from Chaucer to Defoe*, edited by Gerd Bayer and Ebbe Klitgård, 40–59. New York: Routledge.
---. 2011b. "1050–1500: Through a Glass Darkly; or, the Emergence of Mind in Medieval Narrative." In *The Emergence of Mind: Representations of Consciousness in Narrative Discourse in English*, edited by David Herman, 69–100. Lincoln: University of Nebraska Press.
Frank, R. W., Jr. 1972. *Chaucer and The Legend of Good Women*. Cambridge: Harvard University Press.
Haferland, Harald. 2013. "Psychologie und Psychologisierung: Thesen zur Konstitution und Rezeption von Figuren. Mit einem Blick auf ihre historische Differenz." In *Erzähllogiken in der Literatur des Mittelalters und der Frühen Neuzeit: Akten der Heidelberger Tagung vom 17. bis 19. Februar 2011*, edited by Florian Kragl and Christian Schneider, 91–117. Heidelberg: Winter.
Hall, Louis. 1960. "Caxton's *Eneydos* and the Redactions of Vergil." *Mediaeval Studies* 22: 126–147.
Hamm, Joachim. 2008. "*Infelix Dido*: Metamorphosen einer Liebestragödie." In *Das diskursive Erbe Europas: Antike und Antikerezeption*, edited by Dorothea Klein and Lutz Käppel, 1–24. Frankfurt am Main: Peter Lang.
Helzle, Martin. 1996. *Der Stil ist der Mensch: Redner und Reden im römischen Epos*. Stuttgart: Teubner.
Highet, Gilbert. 1972. *The Speeches in Vergil's "Aeneid."* Princeton: Princeton University Press.

---. 1974. "Speech and Narrative in the *Aeneid*." *Harvard Studies in Classical Philology* 78: 189–229.
Jannidis, Fotis. 2004. *Figur und Person: Beitrag zu einer historischen Narratologie*. Berlin: De Gruyter.
Kailuweit, Thomas. 2005. *Dido – Didon – Didone. Eine kommentierte Bibliographie des Dido-Mythos in Literatur und Musik*. Frankfurt am Main: Peter Lang.
Knox, Peter E. 1995. *Ovid's "Heroides": Selected Epistles*. Cambridge: Cambridge University Press.
Leube, Eberhard. 1969. *Fortuna in Karthago: Die Aeneas-Dido-Mythe Vergils in den romanischen Literaturen vom 14. bis zum 16. Jahrhundert*. Heidelberg: Winter.
Manuwald, Gesine. 2014. "Dido: Concepts of a Literary Figure from Virgil to Purcell." *Proceedings of the Virgil Society* 28: 19–40.
McTaggart, Anne. 2012. "Shamed Guiltless: Criseyde, Dido, and Chaucerian Ethics." *The Chaucer Review* 46.4: 371–402.
Meyer, Matthias. 1999. "Struktur und Person im Artusroman." In *Erzählstrukturen der Artusliteratur. Forschungsgeschichte und neue Ansätze*, edited by Friedrick Wolfzettel, 145–163. Tübingen: Niemeyer.
Miller, J. T. 1986. *Poetic License: Authority and Authorship in Medieval and Renaissance Contexts*. Oxford: Oxford University Press.
Minnis, Alastair. 1988. *Medieval Theory of Authorship. Scholastic Literary Attitudes in the Later Middle Ages*. 2nd ed. Philadelphia: University of Pennsylvania Press.
Percival, Florence. 1998. *Chaucer's Legendary Good Women*. Cambridge: Cambridge University Press.
Phelan, James. 1989. *Reading People, Reading Plots: Character, Progression, and the Interpretation of Narrative*. Chicago: University of Chicago Press.
---. 1996. *Narrative as Rhetoric: Technique, Audiences, Ethics, Ideology*. Columbus: Ohio State University Press.
Phillips, Helen, and Nick Havely, eds. 1997. *Chaucer's Dream Poetry*. London and New York: Longman.
Sanderlin, George. 1986. "Chaucer's 'Legend of Dido': A Feminist Exemplum." *The Chaucer Review* 20.4: 331–340.
Singerman, Jerome. 1986. *Under Clouds of Poesy: Poetry and Truth in French and English Reworkings of the Aeneid, 1160–1513*. New York: Garland.
Stock, Markus. 2010. "Figur: Zu einem Kernproblem historischer Narratologie." In *Historische Narratologie – Mediävistische Perspektiven*, edited by Harald Haferland and Matthias Meyer, 187–203. Berlin: De Gruyter.
Todorov, Tzvetan. 1969. *Grammaire du Décaméron*. Paris: Mouton.
Tripp, Raymond P., Jr. 1970. "Chaucer's Psychologizing of Virgil's Dido." *The Bulletin of the Rocky Mountain Modern Language Association* 24.2: 51–59.
Ziolkowski, Jan M., and Michael C. J. Putnam, eds. 2008. *The Virgilian Tradition: The First Fifteen Hundred Years*. New Haven: Yale University Press.

Miriam Nandi
Narrative Identity and the Early Modern Diary

1 Introduction

Diaries are narrative prose forms located in the interstitial space between life and narrative. As Phillippe Lejeune suggests in his seminal *On Diary*, "[t]he private diary is a practice. The text itself is a mere by-product, a residue" (2009, 31). It may be for this reason that diaries are hardly ever put on a par with literary genres (see, however, Bunkers and Huff 1996; Dusini 2005), while autobiographies and letters are typically read as properly narrativized and stylized texts. Typically, the diary is deemed a "primitive form of a practice which would, by the nineteenth century, produce the narrativized autobiography and the concept of the individualist self" (Mascuch 1997, 71).

In her ground breaking study *Towards a 'Natural' Narratology*, Monika Fludernik scrutinizes the difference between narratives in everyday life and in literary narrative forms, arguing that both are characterized by "the quasi-mimetic evocation of real-life experience" (1996, 12). Here, she does not take a revisionist stance on verisimilitude but builds largely on Ricœur's threefold model of mimesis (1984, 1985) to assess the various ways in which "narrative draws on the dynamic patterning of human temporality" (Caracciolo 2014 [2013], 150).

In this article, I will not be able to restore the bad reputation of the diary as genre. Instead, I take my cue from Fludernik's model and address the way in which life and narrative interact in the diary as a genre. Specifically, I investigate the way in which diaries construct what Paul Ricœur calls "narrative identity" (1991b).[1] I suggest that diaries are a practice of articulating, formulating, and reformulating narrative identity along sequential, serial lines. I take the diary of Lady Anne Clifford, one of the first extant diaries by a woman[2] as a test case for my claim. Taking my cue from the feminist critic Megan Matchinske (2009), I argue that the cumulative, serial form of the diary is crucial for Clifford's decade-long struggle to develop a narrative voice, identity, and sense of ownership. It is

---

[1] On Ricœur's legacy in narratology, see Nünning 2013.
[2] The first diary by an Englishwoman is Margaret Hoby's diary, which was composed between 1599 and 1605, see Hoby 2001.

my contention that Matchinske's feminist reading can be fruitfully amended when combined and specified with Ricœur's notion of narrative identity.

This essay falls into three parts. I will start by offering a formal definition of the diary, and then move on to a brief summary of Ricœur's model of narrative identity. In the final and longest section, I shall investigate how Clifford constructs a particular kind of gendered narrative identity in her diary.

2 What Is a Diary?

The diary can be defined as a "log or record" of activities, events, experiences, feelings, and thoughts that is kept on a regular basis (Abbott 2008, 106). The lexeme *diary* derives from etymological roots meaning "day,"[3] to denote its mode of composition. The "genetic," i.e. the mode of composition of the diary, is different from other autobiographical genres.[4] The diary, unlike the memoir or the autobiography, is not written from a vantage point of looking back but from a position of being "immersed in the present," as Rachel Cottam points out in *The Encyclopedia of Life Writing* (2001, 268). One would have to specify and amend this statement since many diaries do in fact contain retroactive passages. Yet the stretch of time upon which the narrator looks back is considerably smaller than in an autobiography.

As H. Porter Abbott has pointed out, one of the key characteristics of the diary is its "intercalated mode of production" (2008, 106), which means that the writing process is occurs *between* the narrated events.[5] In contrast to the autobiography, in which the narrated events are molded to fit into a linear pattern, the diary is written in a spontaneous and unplanned manner (Abbott 2008, 106).

---

[3] The words *diary* and *journal* are usually used synonymously, though the lexeme *journa'* tends to be used to denote a diary that covers a specific period in the life of the writer such as a travel journal, for instance see Cottam (2001, 240). Some critics associate the diary with a more intimate form of writing, arguing that the journal focuses on public events (Smith and Watson 2001, 196). Since Anne Clifford's diary was composed at a time when the division between public and private was not yet stable, and her text clearly links public and private occurrences, I use the terms *journal* and *diary* interchangeably.

[4] On genetic criticism, see Deppman et al. 2004.

[5] Phillippe Lejeune has objected to the term *intercalated*, arguing that the diarist does not write from a position of being in-between or "intercalated" between "two equivalent things" (2009, 208). Instead, he suggests that writing a diary is "progressive": "it advances with the moving front of life, digesting the near past and filling the near future with plans" (2009, 208). Since

The practice of dating the text can be traced back to the practices of letter writing and/or keeping an account book (Lejeune 2009, 81–82). The date of the diary entries creates an aura of trustworthiness and authenticity, like the stamp on an official document. It is probably due to this aura of authenticity that the diary has such an appeal in historiography.[6]

The shortness of the narrative form and the inclusion of dates link the diary with the letter generically, although there are important differences between the two: The letter always has an explicit addressee, while the diary only *implies* the potential of its being read in the future (see also Lejeune 2009, 84). Another crucial disparity between the diary and the letter is that the diary usually consists of one medium form containing many dated entries. I would suggest dividing the diary into two levels: The level of the diary in its entirety, which I will call "D" and usually is contained in one form, and the level of the respective entries "E." The following chart helps to illustrate the typical formal make-up of the diary:

```
D_____
E1____ E2_____ E3____ E4 ...
```

Sometimes, the diary consists of several volumes: in this case, its formal structure needs to be described as follows:

```
D1_____
E1____ E2_____ E3____ E4 ...
D2_____
E1____ E2_____ E3____ E4 ...
```

On level D, the diary is perfectly chronological: Each dated entry follows after the last one. There are no prolepses or analepses on this level, since this would entail a later date preceding an earlier one. As the chronological structure of level D is connected with the "intercalated" mode of composition of the diary, anachrony does not take place. On level E, however, there can be "achronic" instances of storytelling – such as plans for the future (Genette 1993, 62). Another typical characteristic of the diary on level D is that it hardly ever uses "iterative narration" (Genette 1993, 64), i.e. "acceleration by means of an identifying sillepsis of events posited as relatively similar ('Every Sunday...')." Instead, diaries are replete with repetitions. Diarists quite literally write about going to church

---

"progressive" connotes a teleological development within diaries, an assessment with which I disagree, I prefer the term *intercalated*.

6 On the use of diaries in historiography see, for instance, Dekker 2002.

every Sunday, rather than mentioning their general habit at some point, as an autobiographer would do. In terms of pace or tempo, the diary is paradoxically decelerated with respect to level D, and accelerated with respect to level E. On level D, diaries are often much lengthier than autobiographies, novels or even epics. The most famous example is *The Diary* (1971–1983) of Samuel Pepys, which fills ten volumes. As the diary is kept on a regular, if not a daily basis, the storytelling that occurs on level D is automatically slowed down. An autobiography, by contrast, can describe the events of several years within a few sentences. Such summaries only rarely occur in diaries.

Diaries, like most other forms of life writing, are always single-authored texts (Abbott 2008, 106);[7] they are also typically homodiegetic (Genette 1993) or first-person narratives (Stanzel 1986). Unlike fictional first-person narratives, such as the classical *Bildungsroman* for instance, the diary is not structured around a crucial divide between the narrating and the experiencing self (Stanzel 1986, 201). Due to its intercalated mode of composition, the diary hardly ever contains moments in which an older and 'mature' narrating self looks back on the experiences of a younger, 'naive' self to note reflexively how she has grown or matured over the course of time. Instead, diaries are more adequately analyzed as texts that construct, articulate, and maybe also document what Paul Ricœur (1991b) calls "narrative identity" along serial and sequential lines.

3 Diaries and Narrative Identity

Paul Ricœur's work has been very influential in literary criticism (see Fludernik 1996), and psychology (see Lucius-Höhne 2004), but he has also come under some scrutiny because he is "an overtly Christian philosopher" (Simms 2003, 7). Yet, dismissing Ricœur as revisionist would be a bit rushed. Ricœur's philosophy may be problematic in our contemporary post-secular context, which has witnessed a traumatic return of religious fundamentalism. Nonetheless, this philosophy can be particularly resonantly applied to autobiographical texts of the early modern era given the overt religiosity of the period. For an early modern diarist, selfhood always already implies spiritual duty; it is not constructed in opposition

---

[7] The notion of authorship may have to be complicated with respect to diaries, which have a long and fraught editorial history. See Dusini 2005 for an excellent discussion of how diaries are edited.

to religious norms. In Ricœur's words, early modern narrative identity is "prefigured" in terms of Christian ideas of a good life (1984, 54; see also Nandi 2012).

What makes Ricœur particularly interesting for this essay is his concern with temporality, which overlaps with the way diaries are constructed. Diaries are narrative genres which tell about a life *as it passes*, creating situative "concordance" (1991a, 22) out of the heterogeneity of everyday experience. As Ricœur points out convincingly, it is "narrative [which] constructs the durable properties of a character, what one could call his narrative identity, by constructing the kind of dynamic identity found in the plot which creates the character's identity" (1991b, 195). Narrative identity is the work of creating "discordant concordance" (1991b, 195), of grasping together disjointed elements in our life (see also Simms 2003, 85). It is a temporary attempt to establish a "synthesis of the heterogeneous" or the "integration" and "culmination" (1991a, 22) of disparate elements into an intelligible plot. For Ricœur, introspection, self-awareness, and self-interpretation rely heavily on narrative mediation (1991b, 198). The self can only be pictured as persisting and unique because it constantly re-figures itself through self-narratives. To oversimplify Ricœur's notion, we become what we are through the stories we tell about ourselves, and these stories are not always coherent or teleological. Crucially for Ricœur, life narratives always also imply the existence and centrality of other people, as he suggests in his later work on alterity (1992). Thus selfhood is qualitative, it implies otherness (the actual other person as much as the sense of being a stranger to oneself) to such an extent that the two cannot be separated.

It is important to note that Ricœur's model of narrative identity does not envision the self along essentialist lines. On the contrary, Ricœur constantly draws attention to the volatile, fluid, and contradictory nature of identity as in the following passage from the third volume of *Time and Narrative*:

> In the first place, narrative identity is not a stable and seamless identity. Just as it is possible to compose several plots on the subject of the same incidents (which, thus, should not really be called the same events), so it is always possible to weave different, even opposed, plots about our lives. [...] Narrative identity thus becomes the name of a problem at least as much as it is that of a solution. (1985, 248–249)

This quotation illustrates that Ricœur's model is not essentialist, but actually quite attuned to the situative and fragmented character of diary-narratives. Therefore, his concept of narrative identity offers an interesting model for analyzing narrative identity in the early modern diary, precisely because of the genre's characteristic emphasis on fluidity and change on the one hand and synthesis and concordance on the other.⁸ The following reading of the diary of Lady Anne Clifford is a first "test-drill" for reading the early modern diary along the lines of Ricœur's phenomenology.

4 Lady Anne Clifford's "Activist Diary"

Lady Anne Clifford was born on 30 January 1590 at Skipton Castle in Craven, Yorkshire as the only surviving child of George Clifford, third earl of Cumberland (1558–1608), one of Elizabeth's "most flamboyant courtiers" (Seelig 2006, 24) and Lady Margaret (1560–1616), née Russel. The death of Queen Elizabeth and the accession of James I meant that Anne, who had spent a considerable time of her childhood at court, became gradually less favored as she grew up (Acheson 1995, 78). Lady Anne was married twice, first to Richard Sackville, the third earl of Dorset in 1609; and after being widowed for six years, to Phillip Herbert, earl of Pembroke in 1630 (see Acheson 1995, 78; Suzuki 2009, xxix). Both her family lineage and her marriages placed her among the elite in seventeenth-century England. Neither of the two marriages were happy (see Seelig 2006, 24), but the relationship with Sackville was particularly fraught. One of the issues that gave rise to marital conflict was Anne Clifford's struggle to re-gain her patrimony. Her father George had willed his title and estates away from Anne to his brother and Anne's paternal uncle Francis Clifford (1559–1641). This was not unusual at the time (see Matchinske 2009, 204); but according to a deed dating from the reign of Edward II these were entailed upon "the heir of the body [...] regardless of sex" (Acheson 1995, 78; see also Lewalski 1990, 90; Lamb 1998, 12). Therefore, the Northern estates and titles were legally Anne's (Matchinske 2009, 204–205). Supported by her mother Margaret, Anne Clifford refused to acquiesce to the settlement that worked to her disadvantage (Acheson 1995, 78; see also Suzuki 2009, xii). The ensuing lawsuit was one of "the most publicized and celebrated marital property dispute[s] of the seventeenth century" (Suzuki 2009, xii; see also Erikson 1993, 111). Her husband Richard Sackville exercised tremendous pressure

---

8 On Ricœur's legacy, see Straub 2013; Taylor 1991. In his polemic "Against Narrativity," Galen Strawson levies a sharp attack against Ricœur's legacy in the humanities. Strawson not just rejects the view that narrative underlies human experience, but he also critiques what he calls the "ethical Narrativity thesis" (2004, 428), i.e. the claim that experiencing life along narrative lines is essential to a well-lived life or full personhood. See Schechtmann 2007 for a discussion of Strawson's claims.

to force her to agree to a cash settlement[9]: He threatened her with social shaming and withdrawal of the servants (Acheson 1995, 78) and eventually took custody of their daughter Margaret, the only surviving child. The entries in the diary from May 1616 relate Anne's passionate (and failed) attempts to get Margaret back.

Despite considerable pressure from her husband and although the Archbishop of Canterbury and even king James himself were set against her aims, Anne refused to sign her rights away. This refusal to sign the cash settlement enabled her to inherit the property after her uncle died without male issue in 1643 (Acheson 1995, 79; Klein 2001, 18). Only posthumously in 1691, was she assigned the title of Baroness (Acheson 1995, 79).

Anne Clifford not just survived all her male ancestors and relatives, but also the Civil War. Her Northern castles had been a stronghold on the royalist side during the War and were left intact. From the 1650s onwards, the diarist established herself in her castles of Brougham, Brough, Appleby, and Skipton. There, she financed and curated the restoration of churches and commissioned the fine arts and a family history. Until her death in 1676, Clifford kept a record of her life.

Anne Clifford's diaries were introduced to the greater reading public by Vita Sackville-West, who traced her own heritage to Clifford's first husband Richard Sackville. In her 1923 edition of the diary, Sackville-West announces her solidarity with the early woman writer and thus sets a landmark for later generations of feminist critics.[10] Most notably in the early 1990s, second-wave feminists read Clifford's writings as testimonials to the power of matrilineal kinship relations, see Acheson (1995); Lewalski (1991). Arguably, the importance of the struggle for her patrimony in her diary can hardly be overstated. What is interesting, and less often discussed, are Anne Clifford's later diaries, which she composed when the Northern castles were safely in her hands.[11]

Indeed, Anne Clifford represents her life in a variety of cultural texts: The first and most famous text is the so-called *Knole Diary*, which covers the years between 1616 and 1619. The second text dates from the 1650s onwards and could also be defined as a yearly chronicle, although it is usually called *The Kendal Diary*. With respect to the definition I have suggested in section one, both of Anne Clifford's narratives can be adequately defined as diaries. They both have a serial, cumulative form, and they both lack an overarching organizing principle or *telos* (see

---

9 King James I offered the following award: Anne and Dorset were to receive 17,000 pounds in compensation for the titles and estates. The latter were supposed to go to Francis Clifford, see Suzuki 2009, xxix; Acheson 1995, 79.
10 For a discussion of Clifford's impact on Sackville-West and Virginia Woolf, see Hallett 2009.
11 See, however, Matchinske 2009 for an intriguing discussion of Clifford's later diaries.

also Seelig 2006, 36). They hardly ever employ "iterative narration" (Genette 1993, 64). Instead, Clifford writes about every single move from one Northern castle to the other, rather than reporting a summary or mentioning her general habit of travelling the North of England. Therefore, also the *Kendal* does not connote the "already over" (Matchinske 2009, 203) so characteristic of the memoir or autobiography. As Megan Matchinske states, Clifford's diaries "offer constant and repetitive pronouncements that operate directionally, spatially, and metaphorically in opposition to patrilineal networks" (2009, 207). I would like to specify and amend Matchinske's thesis in reading Clifford's journal in terms of Ricœur's notion of narrative identity. It is my contention that Clifford's diary is not just "serial" and "sequential" (2009, 210), as Matchinske correctly assumes. Rather, it is also characteristically "synthetic" and relational in Ricœur's sense.

One of the first things that strikes the reader are Anne Clifford's frequent references to her female kin. Already at an early age, Anne Clifford frequently writes about the "greatness" between her and other female relatives she cares for. The following passage dating from the summer of 1603, when Anne was only thirteen, is a telltale example:

> [1603] About this time my Aunt of Bath and her Lord came to London and brought them my Lord Fitz-Warren & my Cousin Frances Bourchier, whom I met at Bagshot where I lay all night with my Cousin, & Mrs Mary Carey, which was the beginning of the greatness between us. About 5 miles from London there met my Mother, my Lord of Bedford and his Lady, my Uncle Russel & much other Company so that we were in number about 300 which did all accompany them to Bath House, where they continued most of that summer. Whither I went daily & visited them & grew daily more inward with my Cozen Frances & Mrs Carey. (Clifford 2009, 23)

Anne names all her relatives and the places they visited, also invoking female relations to whom she is particularly attached: her cousin Frances Bourchier and Mary Carey. In a gesture of hospitality, Frances and Mary Carey offer to share the bed with Anne for the night, which Anne accepts with gratitude: "I lay all night with my Cousin & Mary Carey."[12] Anne Clifford constructs herself as part of such a gendered network of hospitality, emphasizing the affection that grows out of Frances and Mary's generosity: "[It] was the beginning of the greatness between us. [...] Whither I went daily & visited them & grew daily more inward with my Cozen Frances & Mrs Carey." Viewed through the lens of Ricœur's theory of narrative identity, Clifford constructs a "synthetic" or "concordant" image of herself

---

12 As historian Gabriele Jancke (2005) has shown, offering a guest to share the bed for the night was very common in the early modern era, since it was part of its culture of hospitality.

– she is not an isolated persona in a group of disparate people but is safely immersed in a network of kinship relations. The material objects, the servants, whom she often refers to as "family" (see also Wilcox 2009, 151), and the houses in particular, echo, mirror, and demonstrate Anne Clifford's entitlement to her patrimony. Knowing that her rank is at risk under the new king, Anne constructs a safety net of influential men and women, and eventually creates a powerful entourage of 300 people. Characteristically, she mentions the places owned by her family. Moreover, she tells us here that she is intimately connected to these women of rank and that she has been granted their generous hospitality, which she will return, of course, once she has won her land and her titles back.

Clifford's emphasis on community and affectivity ties in with Ricœur's notion that selfhood always implies alterity (see Ricœur 1992). Such relational identities were particularly prominent in the early modern era, a time that considerably predated our contemporary system of "democratic individualism" (Seelig 2006, 4; see also Bedford, Davis, and Kelly 2007). Early modern writers had to rely on what Verena Lobsien has called the "heterological" (1996) mode of writing the self, i.e. of portraying the subject in relation to one or more other persona (usually, a patron or a near kin). This heterological, synthetic way of writing the self was probably the only possible way for the woman writer to construct a self-narrative.

Another characteristic that the above passage shares with Ricœur's theory of narrative identity is that – even at the age of thirteen – Anne Clifford presents her consciousness along very "concordant" lines, creating an identity that is both spatially responsible and temporally accurate. The young Anne makes sure she narrates exactly where she spent her summer, with whom she spent it, and how long her stay at Bagshot lasted. Instead of presenting spontaneous outbursts of emotions without much narrative control (as one might expect from a teenager today), Anne chooses her subjects very attentively, thus creating a "concordant" image of the time she spent with her family.

Intriguingly, the temporality of Clifford's visits to Bath House – she visits them daily – is echoed in the attachment which forms between the women: she grows "daily more inward" with them; and in the narrative form of the diary itself. She writes daily about her visits and relationships. This sequential and repetitive structure is crucial to Clifford's construction of narrative identity. On the one hand, it serves a strategic function in the struggle for her patrimony, and thus for her (contested) identity as female landowner: Anne stresses *repeatedly* that she has influential relations, who trust and love her and that she has the moral support of women of power and standing. On the other hand, writing her diary may also serve the purpose of a preparation for the legal and interpersonal struggle that stood before her, as Sharon Seelig suggests: "Anne Clifford writes [...] in the deepest possible sense for herself. She writes to construct her life, to understand it, to place herself in relation to her husband, [...] and she writes to justify her actions to herself" (2006, 39). The diary thus is a means to construct a concordant narrative identity – it establishes a "face" (Seelig 2006, 39) to *face* with the men that pressure her to give up her titles and lands. At the same time, the diary is also a means of documenting her struggle. Her diary thus constructs, mirrors, and reflects on Clifford's narrative identity, pointing this identity in several different temporal directions. It reflects on her bravery in the struggle for her property, thus pointing to the *past*. It reflects on the ups and downs of her struggle as it occurs, thus establishing a *simultaneity*. It also reflects the image Anne has of herself and the one which she wants to be remembered by, thus pointing to the *future*.

From the year of 1616 onwards, the diary also recounts moments of crisis and despair. The following passage, in which Clifford relates the death of her mother, is characteristic of the way the diary narrativizes identity in moments of crisis:

> Upon the 24th, being Friday, between the hours of 6 and 9 at night died my dear Mother at Brougham, in the same Chamber where my father was born, 13 years and 2 months after the death of Queen Elizabeth and ten years and 7 months after the death of my Father. I being 26 years and five months, and the Child 2 years wanting a month. (2009, 37 FN 17)

Clifford hints at her affective connection to her mother whom she calls "my dear mother." Moreover, she draws some very striking spatial and temporal connections that suggest that she has some private magical numerology and spatial arrangement patterns. Margaret dies in the "same Chamber" in which her father was born and is therefore connected and united with him even after death. The juxtaposition of birth and death connotes the cycle of life and thus a way of coming to terms and making sense of an otherwise painful event. Anne Clifford is at pains to commemorate the exact time of her mother's passing ("between 6 and 9 in the evening"), her own age ("26 years and five months"), and that of her daughter Margaret ("2 years wanting a month"). Clifford here attempts to "grasp together" (as Ricœur would put it) disconcordant occurrences and facts – i.e. the sudden death of her mother, the death of the late Queen, her own age – into a concordant or synthetic whole. Clearly she seems to be looking for some kind of numerical pattern, but she does not actually discover one in the juxtaposition of events. Furthermore, here as in the opening passage of the *Knole Diary*, she positions herself, her mother, and her daughter in a close relationship with the late Queen Elizabeth I: Margaret dies "13 years and 2 months after the death of Queen

Elizabeth," and intriguingly "7 months after the death of my Father," who stands for a very different legacy.

In this painful scene of loss, Anne Clifford tries to establish connections; one might even say that she writes in order to connect with her father, her mother, with places (the chamber in which her father was born), and with the dead queen. The whole passage reads like a chant or a litany, invoking a greater pattern and a deeper meaning, hence, also a form of synthesis.

This curios synthetic, chant-like tone sets the atmosphere for Clifford's later writings, now known as the *Kendal Diary*. The Kendal Diary is marked by an intriguing sense of spatial awareness: Anne Clifford documents every place she visits, and every visitor she entertains in her Northern castle, drawing connections between the places and the people she sees in an "epic sweep" of temporal register (Matchinske 2009, 203). The affective intensity of the *Knole Diary*'s records of her mother's death and her daughter's custody has faded, but the repetitive, synthetic patterning is even more pronounced:

> [1667] And the 18th October in this yeare after I had layed in Appleby Castle in Westmerland in the chamber wherein I used to lye ever since the 8th day of August last, being two months and some 10 diaes over, did I remove from thence in my Horslitter with my family, going along the usual high Road, and not through Whinfeild Parke, into Brougham Castle in the same Countie, in which Castle of Brougham I had not bin since the 1st day of August in 1665 till now, and where I now continued to lye as I used to do in the Chamber wherein my Noble Father was borne, and my Blessed Mother dyed, till the 26th day of June next following, that I removed from thence back againe to Appleby Casle aforesaid, to lye there in it for a time. (Clifford 2009, 192)

Here, as in almost every other entry of the *Kendal* diary, Clifford marks each destination, the exact route she took and the time-span of her journey and visits in a cumulative order. The various places are associated with domestic intimacy, which is conveyed in the repeated use of the verb "lye." What is more, she again draws connections between places and kin: She stays in the same room in which her mother died and her father was born. She describes her parents with two striking adjectives, which she both capitalizes: Her father is "Noble" – thus denoting his aristocratic lineage, and her mother is "Blessed" and therefore protected and sanctified by God. Thus Anne Clifford presents herself as the heir of a religious and a secular power. The *Kendal Diary* mirrors her "noble" and "blessed" lineage. Therefore, we are tempted to conclude that Anne Clifford's accounts "serve an evidentiary role in the process of self-justification" (Matchinske 2009, 205).

Intriguingly, however, Clifford's sequential musings continue when the Northern castles and estates were "securely in her hands" (2009, 206), as the above extract illustrates. As Megan Matchinske points out convincingly, Clifford continued to inhabit a precarious position as female landowner and therefore had to defend "again and again *and again*" (2009, 206) what she considered her right: "In a culture so inherently antagonistic to land claims like Clifford's, her discursive status as a female property owner had to be vigilantly and recursively maintained. Seriality offered an effective albeit anxious solution to that problem" (Matchinske 2009, 211).

If the *Kendal Diary* serves as an "anxious" vindication of Anne Clifford's rights, then the cumulative pattern indeed represents a very important part of this vindication. In a very important way, the struggle for her patrimony was never actually over since Clifford's identity as female landowner was a contested one. Concomitantly, the *Kendal Chronicle* also needed to have a serial and iterative structure rather than a retrospective and teleological one. Clifford creates synthesis or concordance not by means of causality or teleology, but by means of repetition and spatial and temporal connection.

5 Conclusion

Diaries are not coherent, teleological narratives, but typically construct serial, sequential "mini-narratives" that are open-ended and lack closure. However, they can still serve as a means to construct what Ricœur calls "narrative identity." Diaries are then a medium for creating concordance and durability, for bringing the disparate elements of life together in a "synthetic" whole. This is also the case in the diary of Lady Anne Clifford, one of the first extant women diaries in English. Lady Anne Clifford uses her diary to prepare herself for the tremendous hostility in her struggle for her patrimony. Before becoming a woman landowner – an anomaly and a scandalous position in her time – Anne Clifford creates the narrative image of herself as a woman of rank who is morally and spatially entitled to the estates of her ancestors, and through the legitimating ties of powerful kinship.

Characteristically, she continues to vindicate her position as woman landowner even when the castles are securely in her hands because her situation did not cease to be precarious. I would therefore conclude that Ricœur's model of narrative identity needs to be amended or fine-tuned, as it were to gendered identities. As constructed by early modern women diarists, narrative identity creates a concordance by means of repetition, by means of spatial and temporal responsibility, and through connection with other powerful female rulers.

The (male-)gendered self-assurance of the teleological autobiography so prominent in the eighteenth century was not a model for early modern women diarists such as Clifford. Rather, early modern women's diaries such as Lady Anne's present chant-like repetitive patterns drawing synthetic connections in time and space. They articulate an experience of a subjectivity *in process*, which gains coherence by dint of succession and accumulation of detail. Clifford is not (yet) an "autobiographical subject" (Nussbaum 1989), i.e. a writer who appears to be the owner of her own self, an autonomous agent or even a person endowed with a plethora of legal rights. Nonetheless, she *claims* legal personhood, voice, and agency, over and over again, through writing her diary. In this vein, her diary is indeed more of a practice in Lejeune's sense. Characteristically, however, it is a practice endowed with cultural and historical meaning.

References

Abbott, Porter H. 2008. "Diary." In *Routledge Encyclopedia of Narrative Theory*, edited by David Herman, Manfred Jahn, and Marie-Laure Ryan, 106–107. London: Routledge.
Acheson, Katherine. 1995. "Lady Anne Clifford." In *British Prose Writers of the Early Seventeenth Century*, edited by Clayton D. Lein, 77–81. Detroit: Gale.
Bedford, Ronald, Lloyd Davis, and Philippa Kelly. 2007. *Early Modern English Lives: Autobiography and Self-Representation 1500–1660*. Aldershot: Ashgate.
Bunkers, Suzanne L., and Cynthia A. Huff. 1996. Eds. *Inscribing the Daily: Critical Essays on Women's Diaries*. Amherst: University of Massachusetts Press.
Caracciolo, Marco. 2014 [2013]. "Experientiality." In *the living handbook of narratology*, edited by Peter Hühn et al. Hamburg: Hamburg University. Accessed 28 May 2017. Web.
Clifford, Lady Anne. 2009 [1616–1619]. *The Diaries of Lady Anne Clifford*. Edited by D. J. H. Clifford. Gloucestershire: History.
Cottam, Rachel. 2001. "The Diary." In *Encyclopedia of Life Writing: Autobiographical and Biographical Forms*, edited by Margaretta Jolly, 267–269. London: Fitzroy Dearborn.
Dekker, Rudolf, ed. 2002. "Introduction." In *Egodocuments and History: Autobiographical Writing in Its Social Context Since the Middle Ages*, 7–20. Hilversum: Verloren Publishers.
Dusini, Arno. 2005. *Das Tagebuch*. München: Fink.
Erikson, Amy Louise. 1993. *Women and Property in Early Modern England*. London: Routledge.
Fludernik, Monika. 1996. *Towards a 'Natural' Narratology*. London: Routledge.
Genette, Gérard. 1993. "Fictional Narrative, Factual Narrative." In *Fiction and Diction*, 54–85. Translated by Catherine Porter. Ithaca: Cornell University Press.
Hallett, Nicky. 2009. "Anne Clifford as Orlando: Virginia Woolf's Feminist Historiology and Women's Biography." In *Anne Clifford and Lucy Hutchinson*, edited by Mihoko Suzuki, 3–22. Surrey: Ashgate.
Hoby, Margaret. 2001. *The Private Life of an Elizabethan Lady: The Diary of Lady Margaret Hoby, 1599–1605*. Edited by Joanna Moody. Stroud: Sutton.
Jancke, Gabriele. 2005. "Bettgeschichten. Gastfreundschaft in der Frühen Neuzeit." *querelles-net* 6.17. Accessed 3 June 2016. Web.
Klein, Lisa M. 2001. "Lady Anne Clifford as Mother and Matriarch: Domestic and Dynastic Issues in Her Life and Writings." *Journal of Family History* 26: 18–38.

Lamb, Mary Ellen. 1998. "Tracing a Heterosexual Erotics of Service in Twelfth Night and the Autobiographical Writings of Thomas Whythorne and Anne Clifford." *Criticism: A Quarterly for Literature and the Arts* 40.1: 1–25.

Lejeune, Philippe. 2009. *On Diary*. Edited by Jeremy E. Pomkin and Julie Rak. Honolulu: University of Hawai'i Press.

Lewalski, Barbara K. 1991. "Re-Writing Patriarchy and Patronage: Margaret Clifford, Anne Clifford, and Aemilia Lanyer." *Yearbook of English Studies* 21: 87–106.

Lobsien [Olejniczak], Verena. 1996. "Heterologie. Konturen früneuzeitlichen Selbstseins jenseits von Autonomie und Heteronomie." *Zeitschrift für Literaturwissenschaft und Linguistik* 101: 6–36.

Lucius-Höhne, Gabriele. 2004. "Narrative Identität und Positionierung." *Gesprächsforschung* 5: 166–83.

Matchinske, Megan. 2009. "Serial Identity: History, Gender and Form in the Diary Writing of Lady Anne Clifford." In *Anne Clifford and Lucy Hutchinson*, edited by Mihoko Suzuki, 203–218. Surrey: Ashgate.

Mascuch, Michael. 1997. *Origins of the Individualist Self*. Cambridge: Polity.

Nandi, Miriam. 2012. "Narrating Emotions – Narrating the Self? Representation and Regulation of Emotions in Early Modern Diaries." In *Proceedings of the Anglistentag 2011*, edited by Monika Fludernik and Benjamin Kohlmann, 135–146. Trier: WVT.

Nünning, Vera. 2013. "Erzählen und Identität: Die Bedeutung des Erzählens im Schnittfeld zwischen kulturwissenschaftlicher Narratologie und Psychologie." In *Kultur – Wissen – Narration*, edited by Alexandra Strohmeier, 145–170. Bielefeld: transcript.

Nussbaum, Felicity. 1989. *The Autobiographical Subject: Gender and Ideology in Eighteenth-Century England*. Baltimore: Johns Hopkins University Press.

Pepys, Samuel. 1971–1983. *The Diary of Samuel Pepys*. 11 vols. Edited by Robert Latham and William Matthews. Berkeley: University of California Press.

Ricœur, Paul. 1984. *Time and Narrative*. Vol. 1. Translated by Kathleen Blamey and David Pellauer. Chicago: University of Chicago Press.

---. 1985. *Time and Narrative*. Vol. 3. Translated by Kathleen Blamey and David Pellauer. Chicago: University of Chicago Press.

---. 1991a. "Life in Quest of Narrative." In *On Paul Ricœur: Narrative and Interpretation*, edited by David Wood, 20–33. London: Routledge.

---. 1991b. "Narrative Identity." In *On Paul Ricœur: Narrative and Interpretation*, edited by David Wood, 188–199. London: Routledge.

---. 1992. *Oneself as Another*. Chicago: University of Chicago Press.

Schechtmann, Maria. 2007. "Stories, Lives, and Basic Survival: A Refinement and Defense of the Narrative Life View." In *Narrative and Understanding Persons*, edited by Daniel Hutto, 155–178. Cambridge: Cambridge University Press.

Seelig, Sharon Cadman. 2006. *Autobiography and Gender in Early Modern Literature: Reading Women's Lives, 1600–1680*. Cambridge: Cambridge University Press.

Simms, Karl. 2003. *Paul Ricœur*. Routledge Critical Thinkers. London and New York: Routledge.

Smith, Sidonie, and Julia Watson. 2001. *Reading Autobiography: A Guide for Interpreting Life Narratives*. Minneapolis: University of Minnesota Press.

Sperl, Irmela. 2010. *Geschriebene Identität: Lebenslinien in Tagebüchern*. München: Utz.

Stanzel, Franz K. 1986. *A Theory of Narrative*. Translated by Charlotte Goeschde. Cambridge: Cambridge University Press.

Strawson, Galen. 2004. "Against Narrativity." *Ratio* 4 December: 428–452.

Straub, Jürgen. 2013. "Kann ich mich selbst erzählen – und dabei erkennen? Prinzipien und Perspektiven einer Psychologie des Homo narrator." In *Kultur - Wissen - Narration: Perspektiven transdisziplinärer Erzählforschung für die Kulturwissenschaften*, edited by Alexandra Strohmeier, 75–144. Bielefeld: Transcript.

Suzuki, Mihoko. 2003. *Subordinate Subjects: Gender, the Political Nation, and Literary Form in England, 1588–1688*. Aldershot: Ashgate.

---, ed. 2009. "Introduction." In *Ashgate Critical Essays on Women Writers*, xii–xxiv. Farnham: Ashgate.

Taylor, Charles. 1991. "Ricœur on Narrative." In *On Paul Ricœur: Narrative and Interpretation*, edited by David Wood, 174–179. London: Routledge.

Wilcox, Helen. 2009. "Anne Clifford and Samuel Pepys: Diaries and Homes." *Home Cultures* 6.2: 149–161.

Susan Lanser
The Diachronization of *Jane Eyre*

"Reader, I married him": so begins the final chapter of *Jane Eyre: An Autobiography*, edited by Currer Bell and published in 1847. No sentence in this novel, and few sentences in any novel, have been more resonant. At least seven books, from scholarly studies of Victorian marriage plots to a collection of short stories, take their titles from the phrase.[1] A *Huffington Post* article notes the "lavish overuse" of the sentence in Facebook posts, Instagram announcements, and wedding blogs (Fallon 2016). Predictably, occasional blogs and stories reverse the idyll to "Reader, I left him." But 170 years after its first inscription, the original sentence still holds sway.

Jane Eyre's famous declaration is more than a cultural touchstone; its four simple words bear multiple points of emphasis, each with a specific narratological import. The most obvious of these, "Reader, I *married* him," rounds out a plot that has taken Jane Eyre far from Thornfield, almost indeed to India. In returning Jane to Rochester, the sentence recalls the marriage that did not take place at the novel's midpoint, which would have been, in any case, an unlikely structural position for a heroine's marriage were it not for Richardson's *Pamela* (1740). Jane's initial refusal thus also resists aligning Brontë's impoverished governess with Richardson's impoverished servant in a plot that could well liken Rochester to the would-be seducer Mr. B–, all the more as Jane alludes to reading *Pamela* in *Jane Eyre*'s opening chapter. The emphasis on Jane as the subject of the marital enunciation – "Reader, *I* married him" – marks an innovation in cultural expression, creating the distinctive agency we do not hear, for example, in the voice of Defoe's Moll Flanders, who merely and more typically reports that "behold, we were Married" (1989 [1722], 101), or even in Anne Brontë's Agnes Grey, who "became the wife of Edward Weston; and never found cause to repent it" (1988 [1847], 250). That Jane Eyre "married *him*," the high-handed patriarch, the deceiver, the would-be bigamist who is later blind and disabled, reminds us that Rochester has never been a storybook husband and that Jane may be following passion rather than prudence in choosing him over St. John Rivers. That Jane marries at all (*"I married"*) is equally significant, marking a consent very different from the one she made earlier, as an impoverished dependent. When Rochester

---

[1] The titles listed in WorldCat for *Reader, I Married Him* include novels by Michèle Roberts (2006) and Anne Green (1931), a collection of short fiction (edited by Chevalier, 2016), a volume of poetry by Dorothea Smartt (2014), and two scholarly works, respectively by Patricia Beer (1974) and Isabel Clark (1998).

proposes what would have been an illicit marriage, Jane insists that "I am a free human being with an independent will, which I now exert to leave you" (Ch. XXIII, 293)², but the destitution that ensues, so "absolute" that Jane "wandered about like a lost and starving dog" (Ch. XXVIII, 377), dramatizes the consequence of that principled choice.

The final "I married" thus provides contrast for the economic liberty that undergirds Jane's second decision to accept Rochester, and thus the novel's penultimate chapter, in which Jane returns to Ferndean, uses the word "independent" four times to insist that she is "independent, sir, as well as rich: I am my own mistress" (Ch. XXXVII, 501). Marriage is rewritten here, as the briefest memory of Jane Austen's novels should remind us, as grounded fully in desire: Whatever Elizabeth Bennet feels for Darcy, Fanny Price for Edmund Bertram, and Anne Elliot for Frederick Wentworth, all of them need to marry for economic and social security; even Emma Woodhouse, while not financially needy, could not sustain her position in Highbury as an "old maid" (2005 [1816], Ch. X, 91)

Jane Eyre's – and Charlotte Brontë's – simple sentence thus arguably carries within itself the very history of the English domestic novel, modifying traditional investments in female agency, in romantic masculinity, and in the rationale for marriage. What may be less apparent is the contribution *Jane Eyre* makes to the history of narrative voice and the powerful innovation evoked in that famous and simple sentence through its direct address to a public, extradiegetic narratee: "*Reader,* I married him." For if Rochester is the object of Jane-the-character's desire, the equally potential object of Jane-the-narrator's desire is that reader, who is directly invoked no less than thirty-five times over the course of her narrative and repeatedly interpellated as a sounding-board and confidant/e. Just as Jane's assertive, aggressive, defensive, and/or apologetic "Reader, I married him" marks a watershed moment in the history of marriage plots, so too does that sentence, and this novel, offer a watershed in the history of narration.

For narration does, of course, have a history. Like other elements of narrative, the behaviors of narrators, their relationship to authors, characters, and narratees, their governing conventions and their modes of interaction, have rich and varied lives in time and space. The analytical and theoretical study of the "nature, form, and functioning of narrative" (Prince 2003 [1987], 65) should thus logically encompass understanding narrative elements in terms of their historical context, with attention to the shape, implications, and resonances of both change and

---

2 Because there are so many editions of *Jane Eyre*, I have chosen to use chapter numbers in addition to page numbers for references; this will make easier the search for a quotation in any given edition of the novel.

continuity in narrative practices across time and place. Nearly any narratologist would acknowledge, for example, that the novel, whether seen as a genre that dates back to antiquity or considered as a modern phenomenon, has changed its formal contours over time. Nearly any narratologist would also agree that free indirect discourse, now ubiquitous in fiction, attained what Brian McHale calls a "threshold of visibility" (2011, 10) in the later nineteenth century. Yet from the outset, narratology has been, and remains, one of literary study's most synchronic fields. Even as classical, postclassical, postcolonial, feminist, natural, unnatural, and cognitive approaches have proclaimed themselves, diachronic investigation, by contrast, or even sustained attention to pre-modern texts, has barely appeared on the narratological map.

It is only a slight exaggeration to say that we can thank Monika Fludernik for its being there at all. Fludernik's "The Diachronization of Narratology," published in *Narrative* in 2003, notes with surprise the field's "comparatively little interest on a theoretical level in the history of narrative forms and functions," and rightly observes that much of that interest occurs only "on the margins of mainstream narratological theorizing" (331–332). Pointing to recent work in both historiography and the origins of the novel, Fludernik celebrates the "sheer number of relevant topics and their significance" and predicts that a "major breakthrough" in diachronizing narratology is "imminent." Her essay proposes its own "programme for diachronic narratological study" and seeks "to provide some guidelines for the prospectors keen to participate in this paradigm shift" (2003, 332). By way of advancing the project herself, Fludernik goes on to analyze changes in narrative beginnings from medieval through early modern to modern texts and to explore ways in which metafictional commentary and attendant scene shifts operate in works "from Malory to modernism" (2003, 334). In the process, and with her characteristic precision in drawing on specific and detailed literary examples, Fludernik not only offers important insights into the history of narrative but raises provocative methodological questions for further research.

Fludernik's brief essay augurs a paradigm shift in the practice of narratology. By way of corrective, she shows how phenomena attributed by Genette and other narratologists to the nineteenth or twentieth century were already in practice four or five hundred years earlier. To take one prominent example, Fludernik is able to provide a surprising back history to what Genette in *Narrative Discourse* called "narrative metalepsis" (1980, 235) by demonstrating that "the metanarrative strategies of the Malory type survive well into the nineteenth-century novel" (Fludernik 2003a, 338) and come to carry an increasingly heavy "metafictional load" (2003, 344). The result in this instance is that "what initially appeared to be a very minor example of historical change" becomes much more significant "in relation to the more general development of narrative structure between the late Middle Ages and the nineteenth century" (2003, 344). The scene shifts that Fludernik studies also show that "the novel, despite its diegetic surface structure, comes to obey the deep-structural patterns of drama, in which scene changes occur either when a new setting is introduced or when a new set of protagonists appear on stage. The introduction of lengthy dialogue scenes and, later, of consciousness scenes in the novel underlines this development" (2003, 343). The rich insights that "The Diachronization of Narratology" is able to draw even from these modest examples of textual practice seen over time is indeed inspiring. As Fludernik concludes,

> If even such basic features of narrative have so far remained unanalyzed from a diachronic perspective, it becomes self-evident how many questions there still are to be answered, how much there is still to be done in narrative studies, particularly from a diachronic perspective. If such historical analysis is taken into account, the field of narratology could be on the brink of a major revolution. (2003, 344)

But the revolution is yet to arrive, and the most accomplished practitioner of diachronic narratology on a historically broad scale is still Monika Fludernik herself. The book that is often considered her magnum opus among magna opera, *Towards a 'Natural' Narratology*, argues that "only by means of [a] diachronic journey through English literature" can "the conceptual tools" of a "'natural' narratology" be developed (1996, ix); and she sees diachrony as enabling a natural narratology to "lay claim to wider historical relevance" (1996, 250). *The Fictions of Language and the Languages of Fiction* (1993) uses historical evidence to argue for instances of free indirect discourse not only in medieval texts but (against Ann Banfield) in oral narrative, while a more recent essay (Fludernik 2011) charts representations of mind and especially of emotion in works from Chaucer to Behn, showing Chaucer's innovative role in the development of psychonarration. Fludernik's *Erzähltheorie* (2006, published in English in 2009) is unique among introductions to narratology in devoting a full chapter to the "Geschichte der Erzählformen [the history of narrative forms]" that, though brief, lays out promising paths for future inquiry and calls especially for "an extension of narratological research to the periods before the eighteenth century and a focus on questions of diachronic development and change" (Fludernik 2009, 118). Fludernik frequently credits her mentor Franz Stanzel for a "historical slant that allows the theory [of natural narratology] to be applied on a diachronic scale" (1996, 248), and she follows his lead in drawing her examples, and thus her postulates about narrative, from a wide historical range.

In part because of the combined influence of Stanzel and Fludernik, and probably (as Fludernik notes in her *Introduction to Narratology*) because of the demands of the German *Habilitation*, scholars with German ties have been well ahead of other narratologists in engaging diachrony. Ansgar Nünning is one of the earliest scholars to call for a stronger historical turn (2000). Jan Alber has considered historical change in his discussion of unnatural narrative (2011). The *Living Handbook of Narratology*, based in Hamburg, added in 2013 an entry on "Diachronic Narratology. (The Example of Ancient Greek Narrative)" contributed by Dutch scholar Irene J. F. De Jong. The journal *Diegesis*, sponsored by the University of Wuppertal, focused a full issue on "Historische Narratologie" in 2014, with six articles on the subject that together hark back to early texts as well as delineating long trajectories. In this journal issue, Eva von Contzen calls for a medieval narratology; Caroline Frank explores the historical contours of space in *Simplicissimus* (1668), *Werther* (1774), and *Malte Laurids Brigge* (1910); Harald Haferland examines changing "forms of finality" from oral folktales to modern fiction; and Silvia Reuvekamp explores characterization in medieval and early modern narratives; while essays by Matthias Grüne and Martin Klepper take on, respectively, the past and future of historical narratology itself. Of course, some of the theorizing that underwrote narratology *avant la lettre* – one thinks of Northrop Frye's *Anatomy of Criticism* (1957) and Erich Auerbach's *Mimesis* (1953) – do span centuries, and a few pioneering narratologists have certainly studied such early works as the Hebrew Bible (Meir Sternberg) and *The Decameron* (Tzvetan Todorov).

Notwithstanding such signal contributions, how often, Reader, have you found substantial engagements with diachrony in the anthologies, encyclopedias, monographs, and journal articles where narrative theory has been articulated and advanced? How often has a non-European narratologist insisted on diachrony? How often, indeed, do major works of narrative theory draw their sources of insight from narratives published before 1740, or before 1848, or even, for that matter, before 1920? To offer a bit of data in evidence: At the 2014 conference of the International Society for the Study of Narrative, of 114 organized panels, all but ten focused on twentieth- and twenty-first-century narratives, and among some 300 papers in mixed panels, just twenty concerned texts produced before 1900, with almost none of those twenty focusing on works written before the nineteenth century. A search of the *MLA Bibliography* for the historical distribution of texts discussed in the journal *Narrative* confirms my point: of the 272 entries for essays in *Narrative* that the bibliography has coded for one or more historical periods[3], fully 65% focus on literature after 1900 and another 27% on nineteenth-century works, leaving a meager 7% for all other periods. Lest I seem to be singling out these instances, let me hasten to assert that I fault myself here as well, for my book *The Narrative Act* (1982) barely extends beyond Austen; and although *Fictions of Authority: Women Writers and Narrative Voice* (1992) attends to changes in formal practices in texts by women from the eighteenth through the twentieth centuries, it does not consider a broader historical spectrum or look outside of the global North. In focusing on *Jane Eyre*, this very essay arguably perpetuates the degree zero presentism of the field. I must thus count myself among the vast majority of narratologists who Monika Fludernik is calling to account.

Fludernik herself has already amply demonstrated the value of diachrony for narratology 'proper,' showing the ways in which it renders our understanding of form more precise, stitches questions of form more fully to questions of function, corrects presentist assumptions about narrative innovations, and expands the narratological canon from its predominantly nineteenth- and twentieth-century repertoire. Diachrony also expands the reach of narratology to scholars working in arenas other than the modern novel and thus both invites those scholars to consider the benefits of narratology and expands the sphere of historical expertise within the field. A diachronic dimension to narratological practice challenges us to scrutinize concepts and distinctions in order to see whether they do in fact describe all narratives, or have mistaken narratives of a specific time and place for the whole. At least as importantly, a diachronic approach promotes the study of narrative form as cultural knowledge. It recognizes that a narrative practice is neither a fixed nor an arbitrary phenomenon, but a lens into aspects of a society that may be less apparent than we can glean through more obviously manifest content. I think, for example, of the illuminating way in which Celtic scholar Joan Newlon Radner asks what scholars can learn about medieval Ireland by looking at the complementary narrative strategies specific to Irish annals, legends, and chronicles, and the differing account of historical causation that each of these genres implies. Radner persuasively demonstrates that the formal conventions of Celtic narratives "begin to suggest answers to major questions about the people who generate them: What is their image of the past? How do they believe that the past is related to the present? What do they believe is the place of human kind in the world?" (1999, 312). These are not questions that the texts articulate overtly; they are questions inscribed in rhetorical practices, in structures of events, and

---

[3] Of course, many of the essays published in a theoretically oriented journal like *Narrative* cannot be coded according to historical period.

in the behavior of narrators toward their implicit narratees, and from them Radner gleans a rich sense of a complex society. Reading – and reading about – earlier narratives also shifts our understanding of later works, for it provides the comparative perspective that, as the historian Christopher Hill (1965, 3) has put it, often comes as close as textual scholars can get to the methodology of the laboratory experiment.

A diachronic narratology enables us to consider the long history of narrative elements, to see how, where, and (speculatively) why specific practices accrue and sometimes also disappear. A diachrony that is also global – rather than, as is more usual in today's narratologies, European and Anglo-American – would also show us the time-travels of narrative elements, revealing whether a particular formal practice located in the past of one culture might be currently at work in another, and whether similar material, social, or cultural conditions might prevail in those contexts where a form recurs. We could then chart more and less conventional practices along a temporal axis and consider what contextual factors might account for innovations. The ebbs and flows of epistolary narrative offer a promising case in point. While scholars have recognized the rise of epistolary fiction across the long eighteenth century, sometimes also looking back to Ovid or forward to *Frankenstein* (1818), we have still not fully accounted for the dramatic waning of epistolarity in early nineteenth-century Europe or for epistolarity's global travels, spotty recurrences, and fascinating resurgences.

Historical knowledge might be particularly enhanced by distinguishing between the quite different epistolary projects represented, respectively, by the monovocal *Lettres portugaises* of disputed authorship (1669) and by Aphra Behn's polyphonic *Love Letters Between a Late Nobleman and His Sister* (1684–1687). Like the *Lettres portugaises* and Françoise de Graffigny's *Lettres d'une péruvienne* (1747), the Senegalese writer Mariama Bâ's *Une si longue lettre* (1980) and the African-American Alice Walker's *The Color Purple* (1982) give primacy to the single, female voice to articulate a sexual subjectivity against patriarchal abuses or constraints. The polyphonic *Love Letters*, on the other hand, evokes as much through its form as through its content a political culture in which secrecy, spying, intrigue, and caballing were the fabric of government in the wake of the Exclusion Crisis in England; similarly Laclos's 1782 *Les liaisons dangereuses* uses the polyphony of secrets and lies to characterize *ancien-régime* France.[4] Mapping

---

[4] I would make the same political argument for the polyphony of Samuel Richardson's *Clarissa* (1747–1748), and I would compare the monologic epistolary novels to his *Pamela*, since although Pamela's is not the exclusive voice, it is by far the dominant one. I also see resonances between "Mr. B–" and Walker's "Mr. –."

these early European novels with later incarnations may reveal similar cultural imaginaries beneath obvious situational differences. For example, Amos Oz's multi-voice novel in letters, *Black Box* (*Kufsah shechorah*, 1987), explicitly adopts eighteenth-century practices not only, in the words of Joshua Getz and Thomas Beebee, "to give long-suppressed discourses a voice in the Israeli public sphere" but also to explore "the terms under which political discussion and mutual understanding may take place" (1998, 63; 46). And one might also think about the epistolary forms that have recently emerged with email and text message structures, interrogating their particular popularity in, say, Japan, and asking whether the new technologies refashion epistolarity around both emergent and recurrent cultural concerns.

As my initial focus in this essay on *Jane Eyre* means to emphasize, however, a diachronic narratology can be, and arguably should be, pursued even at the level of the single text. For the text is the point where diachrony and synchrony meet; it is not the choice of text but the questions we ask of it that will determine our approach. I would argue, and I suspect Monika Fludernik would agree, that a full narratological understanding of any individual work requires not only reading the text 'in itself,' or exploring its relationship to its contemporaries, but understanding its place in the history of narrative. We can ask whether a text changes the narrative landscape by influencing other texts or affirming new formal possibilities. We can consider how the text's narrative practices embed new social concerns. We can locate a work's formal dimensions in relation to its precursors, its local and global contemporaries, and its imitators and descendants as a way to map narrative practices in time and space and, if we wish to probe further, along such axes as gender, genre, and race. In short, we can put into narratological practice the truism that no text, however recent, lives outside history. I am not, of course, suggesting that every text will yield a story of narrative innovation of the kind that I have been proposing for *Jane Eyre*. But mapping noncanonical as well as canonical texts for their formal dimensions, as proponents of Franco Moretti's 'quantitative formalism' have proposed, may end up showing us unexpected departures, anomalies, and repetitions in the history of narrative.

As I have suggested in my toyings with "Reader, I married him," I see *Jane Eyre* as sitting at a diachronic turning point: the articulations of subjectivity, desire, marriage, masculinity, and narration that converge not only in the novel as a whole but even in the key sentence "Reader, I married him" are all distinctive and in some ways innovative in Brontë's text. For the purposes of this brief inquiry, I will focus on narration, asking how Brontë's construction of the relationship between narrator and narratee is positioned in narrative history; what that positioning might tell us about the social imaginary of England in the 1840s; and whether we can speak of a legacy of narrative practice in the wake of Brontë's still-popular novel.

Jane Eyre certainly fits Robyn Warhol's concept of the "engaging narrator," the one who "uses narrative interventions" earnestly to address "a 'you' that is intended to evoke recognition and identification in the person who holds the book and reads, even if the 'you' in the text resembles that person only slightly or not at all" (1986, 811). Like the heterodiegetic narrators of Gaskell, Stowe, and Eliot that form the focus of Warhol's book *Gendered Interventions: Narrative Discourse in the Victorian Novel* (1989), Brontë's narrator sets up the narratee as a textual presence with whom the narrator establishes a bond. When she stops at the Millcote inn on the way to take up her new position at Thornfield, for example, Jane invites her reader into both her physical surroundings and her mental unrest:

> When I draw up the curtain this time, reader, you must fancy you see a room in the George Inn at Millcote, with such large figured papering on the walls as inn rooms have; such a carpet, such furniture, such ornaments on the mantelpiece, such prints, including a portrait of George the Third, and another of the Prince of Wales, and a representation of the death of Wolfe. All this is visible to you by the light of an oil lamp hanging from the ceiling, and by that of an excellent fire, near which I sit in my cloak and bonnet; my muff and umbrella lie on the table, and I am warming away the numbness and chill contracted by sixteen hours' exposure to the rawness of an October day: I left Lowton at four o'clock a.m., and the Millcote town clock is now just striking eight. (Ch. XI, 111)

The wealth of detail to describe a temporary stopping-place makes sense when we imagine that it is created not so much for the benefit of the story as for drawing in the narratee as a substitute intimate. For she follows this description by acknowledging,

> Reader, though I look comfortably accommodated, I am not very tranquil in my mind.... It is a very strange sensation to inexperienced youth to feel itself quite alone in the world, cut adrift from every connection, uncertain whether the port to which it is bound can be reached, and prevented by many impediments from returning to that it has quitted. (Ch. XI, 111)

Here narration becomes the antidote to experience: even as the narrator recreates the character's isolation, she alters it by invoking the narratee not only as the witness to her loneliness but as the presence who changes the scene and enables a gap between the scene as remembered and the scene as retold.

Once Jane leaves Millcote behind for the greater isolation of Thornfield, the narratee, consistently named as "reader," is evoked directly and as an intimate, and an intimate who is expected to respond in certain ways more appropriate to an individual friend than to an anonymous and collective public. After she arrives at Thornfield, for example, Jane asks the reader's forgiveness for "telling the plain truth" (Ch. XII, 130); later, after Rochester acknowledges his marriage to Bertha Mason, she asks the reader's forgiveness for forgiving him "at the moment and on the spot" (Ch. XXVII, 344). On at least one metaleptic occasion, she asks the reader to "stay till [Rochester] comes, reader; and, when I disclose my secret to him, you shall share the confidence" (Ch. XXV, 318). When she leaves Thornfield, she hopes that the "gentle reader" may "never feel what I then felt!" (Ch. XXVII, 370); and when she is unhappy with St. John Rivers's coldness, the reader is again called into her confidence. It is thus not surprising that the reader is also evoked in the famous marital declaration, which not only announces Jane's decision to marry Rochester, but introduces the wedding scene recounted in the very next sentence: although Jane Eyre tells us that she and Rochester had a "quiet wedding" with the parson and the clerk "alone present," she also implicitly places the reader at the nuptial event, creating in effect a marital closure on the level of narration as well as story and affirming the importance of the reader as the site of the narrator's desire.

From our twenty-first-century vantage point, it may be hard to imagine the innovative nature of this extradiegetic reader figure interpellated so directly and so often in the text, but a diachronic narratology can perhaps illuminate what a synchronic approach might well obscure. In my book *Fictions of Authority: Women Writers and Narrative Voice*, I argued for the novelty of Jane's narrative practices within the history of female personal voice. Here, I want to take a longer view but also a narrower focus, to suggest that the kind of intimacy the eponymous narrator creates with a public reader-figure is exceptional for its time among both male and female narrators and may have helped to shape not only the tradition of "engaging narrators" but the afterlife of private disclosure as public narrative act.

I cannot, of course, claim to have accomplished a large-scale Morettian survey of all previous narratives or even of all previous English novels, but it is possible to speak of trends. My evidence suggests the value of distinguishing three somewhat historically sequential – though also accruing – patterns of relationship between extradiegetic narrators and their public-reader narratees, which I will call, respectively, *impersonal, ironic,* and *intimate*. Irene J. F. De Jong's extensive work on classical narratives shows us the paucity in ancient Greek and Roman texts of any direct address to a public reader or listener beyond the invocation of the Muses; the most common form of address, where it exists at all, appears in the generalizing form that M. P. Cuypers calls the "indefinite second person" and which she illustrates with this example from the *Argonautica* of

Appolonius of Rhodes: "'You would say that there was no escape from fate'" (2004, 53–54). De Jong identifies only rare exceptions to this already rare form, the most overt of which seems to be a single direct reader-address in Apuleius that veers slightly from the impersonal form: "But perhaps as a careful reader you will find fault with what I tell and reason as follows…" (qtd. in de Jong 2014, 29). Medieval and early modern fictions seem likewise reticent to address an extradiegetic readerly 'you,' though Rabelais's prefaces are an exception; and Monika Fludernik offers the example of Chaucer's "Knight's Tale" for its rarity as a moment when the narrator "tries to elicit sympathy from the audience" (2011, 45), and as the audience in this case are the pilgrims, they remain in attenuated relationship to a reader-figure.

It is in the late seventeenth and eighteenth centuries that we begin to see the emergence of more fleshed-out extradiegetic reader-narratees. Most frequently, a reader figure or figures are invoked by a heterodiegetic narrator in a relationship that I would designate as ironic. Henry Fielding's narrator of *Tom Jones* (1749) is of course the most famous prototype, invoking variously characterized male and female narratees in witty ways that also sometimes mime a struggle for authority between authorial narrator and implied audience; Susanna Rowson's *Charlotte Temple: A Tale of Truth* likewise engages a range of narratees from critics who "cavil" to "my dear sober matron" or "the young and thoughtless of the fair sex" (1791, 147; 59; 35). Defoe's extradiegetic narrators also address a reader on a few occasions, though most references to the reader come by way of the indefinite and impersonal mode of the third person in histories that the Defoe editor-figure claims must be "altered" so that the narrator can "tell her own tale in modester words than she told it at first" (*Moll Flanders* 1964 [1722], v). The famous *auto*-diegetic exceptions are of course Sterne's *Tristram Shandy* (1759) and Diderot's *Jacques le fataliste* (1796), but both of these novels, while technically closer in form to *Jane Eyre* than to *Tom Jones,* stage witty power struggles between narrator and reader-narratee with Fieldingesque irony. In all of these instances, moreover, the text creates a multiplicity of overt narratees rather than a singular or cohesive reader-figure.

To be sure, the form of relationship between narrator and narratee that I am calling *intimate* and attributing to *Jane Eyre* is already widespread in eighteenth-century fiction; it is perhaps even the hallmark of that period. But it is almost never *extradiegetic,* and thus never evokes a *reader* as the intimate recipient of a personal history. As is commonly acknowledged, nearly all homodiegetic narration in eighteenth-century Europe is also intradiegetic, "sealed off" in a "diegetic balloon," as Gerard Genette puts it (1988, 138), through structures of memoir and epistolarity that confine the narratee to the status of private respondent and render the public reader either an indirect eavesdropper or a later-stage audience for the editor-figure who claims to be publishing private materials. The reasons for this monopoly of the "diegetic balloon" are complex and certainly include the hegemony of authentication, the lure of privacy, the new culture and technology of letters, and the emerging fashion for interiority. What is often considered the first modern novel, the anonymous *Lazarillo de Tormes* (1554), models the monologic version by addressing its story from the eponymous hero to an unnamed and silent "Vuestra Merced." Novels with more complex epistolary structures enable not only confidences but the movements of plot, but they also highlight intimacies among characters, sometimes reciprocally when characters confide in one another, and sometimes unidirectionally from protagonist to confidant(e). Most often, narrators and their confidantes are of the same sex and, *pace* Lovelace and his ultimately unfaithful Belford, they are most often female.[5]

What eighteenth-century novels generally *do not* do, at least as far as my informal survey goes, is to create narrator-protagonists who address narratees that stand in for the reading public. One of the earliest to do so, Mary Brunton's *Discipline* (1815), serves England's Evangelical moment well by using abject language that we might see as the antithesis of the ironic address of a Tristram Shandy: "Detest me, reader. I was worthy of your detestation! Throw aside, if you will, my story in disgust" (1986, 50).

What a dramatic leap, then, when we get to the engaging extradiegetic narrator of *Jane Eyre*, and to some extent also of Charlotte Brontë's sister Anne's *Agnes Grey*, published in the same year. In innovative ways, both these novels invest deeply – and *Jane Eyre* much more deeply – in creating narrators whose autobiographical disclosures resemble those of epistolary or memoir confidence but who explicitly evoke the public reader as their recipient. Moreover, while *Agnes Grey* bills itself "a novel" (in its initial publication as the third-volume appendage to Emily Brontë's *Wuthering Heights* [1847]), *Jane Eyre* is one of the first works of any genre ever to proclaim itself "An Autobiography," foregrounding its status as a private individual's public account. In what strikes me as a post-Romantic move – and indeed it is in the period of high Romanticism that the word "autobiography" is first used in English[6] – we find a narrator daring to believe

---

5 Pamela's letters to her parents and Evelina's to her guardian remind us, however, that there are certainly exceptions to these generalizing remarks.
6 The *OED* shows sparse uses of the term, and none before 1796, but Robert Folkenflik's *The Culture of Autobiography* (1993) provides several examples dating from 1786 and intensifying in

that her story is worth telling, to the stranger who stands in for the reading public, as it might more traditionally have been told to an intimate friend. We might further speculate that this intimate relationship between narrator-protagonist and reader-narratee is a substitute for that earlier form of intimacy. Certainly *Agnes Grey* gives us a clue to such a purpose when the narrator promises to "candidly lay before the public what I would not disclose to the most intimate friend," and Jane's repeated claims of isolation make an implicit similar claim. This sense that the reader is the appropriate recipient of intimate confidence is echoed in Dickens's *David Copperfield* (1850), which opens with the authorial confession that "I am in danger of wearying the reader whom I love, with personal confidences, and private emotions." Whether substitute for or extension of intimate friendship, this "reader whom I love" is a relatively new entity as a narratee. Moreover, the intimate engagement with the narratee as reader that we find in *Jane Eyre* and to a lesser extent in *Agnes Grey* sets the transformative trend at this moment for the English novel as a whole: both the heterodiegetic engaging narrators of *Mary Barton* (1848) and *Adam Bede* (1859) and *Uncle Tom's Cabin* (1852) that Warhol describes in *Gendered Interventions* and the autodiegetic narrators of Dickens's *David Copperfield* and *Great Expectations* (1861) all postdate *Jane Eyre*.

What is also striking about *Jane Eyre*'s construction of the intimate reader figure is the gender-neutrality – and thus gender-inclusiveness – of its narratee. In her *Introduction to Narratology*, Monika Fludernik comments that in most novels the narratee is "usually implicitly or explicitly identified as male or female" (2009, 23), and she offers the examples of Sterne and Eliot in evidence. I agree with Fludernik, and I think *Jane Eyre* stands as an exception – and perhaps a deliberate exception – to this trend. The reader is rarely even characterized except *as* reader (only once "romantic," only once "gentle") as the person who *knows* the narrator, who must sometimes be reminded not to misjudge or misunderstand, but who is never marked by social attributes that would exclude any implied member of the public by virtue of age, gender, or class. We might recall Jane the character's chastising of Rochester:

> Do you think I am an automaton? – a machine without feelings? and can bear to have my morsel of bread snatched from my lips, and my drop of living water dashed from my cup? Do you think, because I am poor, obscure, plain, and little, I am soulless and heartless? You think wrong! (Ch. XXIII, 292)

---

the 1830s. Folkenflik agrees, though, that *Jane Eyre* may mark the first use of the term for a book by a woman (1993, 6).

Such a figure perhaps needs that external reader, the reader whose personal identity will not align that reader with anyone other than Jane. Where in *Fictions of Authority* I emphasized the Brontës's new confidence in the reading public, I see here as well a new distrust of intimates, of private relations and charitable safety nets, a new awareness of the dehumanizing of automation, a new imperative to create public affiliations between those poor, obscure, plain, and little folks and a large public at a moment when class revolution on a major scale was taking hold.[7]

"Reader, I married him" thus stands as a double signpost, not only for its dynamics of story but for its explicit, extradiegetic, and autodiegetic engaging narrator intimately connecting herself to a narratee who could potentially encompass all willing and sympathetic readers. I would go so far as to suggest that what *Jane Eyre* helps to inaugurate is a new culture in which telling one's story to strangers becomes the vehicle not only for the novel as an instrument of social change, as Warhol elucidates so well in *Gendered Interventions,* but also for the emergence of fictional autobiography and the confessional culture that arose in its wake, a culture in which it is deemed safer and more productive to tell one's story to strangers than to friends or, put differently, to turn strangers into friends not only despite but because of the anonymity of the exchange. The transgressive nature of this divulging mode is niftily visible in J. D. Salinger's *Catcher in the Rye* (1951), in which the rebellious Holden Caulfield opens his narrative with an aggression that might help remind us how strong was Jane Eyre's voice in 1847, and with an explicit address to a blatant stranger of a reader-narratee, with disclosures that as explicitly violate parental dicta:

> If you really want to hear about it, the first thing you'll probably want to know is where I was born, and what my lousy childhood was like, and how my parents were occupied and all before they had me, and all that David Copperfield kind of crap, but I don't feel like going into it, if you want to know the truth. In the first place, that stuff bores me, and in the second place, my parents would have about two hemorrhages apiece if I told anything pretty personal about them. (2006, 3)

The enduring popularity of *Jane Eyre,* not only in English classrooms but with common readers, may likewise suggest that confiding in a reader still carries its weight.

---

[7] In *Fictions of Authority*, I discuss the negative implications of Jane's reach for hegemony as narrator and character, and in particular the implications for the racially othered Bertha Mason and perhaps also for subsequent narratives by women of color. Although I am not discussing this aspect of Jane's practice here, I have not altered my viewpoint. See Lanser 1992, 190–193.

Although I have just scratched the surface here even vis-à-vis the singular instance of *Jane Eyre*, I hope that this essay helps to advance Monika Fludernik's eloquent call for a diachronic narratology. This is new ground for most of us who have not been as assiduous as Fludernik in attending to change and continuity across time. But we might take comfort in a closing passage from *Jane Eyre*. In the final chapter, Rochester gains back some sight: "He cannot now see very distinctly [...] but he can find his way [...] the sky is no longer a blank to him – the earth no longer a void" (Ch. XXXVIII, 520). I hope that new if still vague vision is also true for the challenge – indeed the revolution – of a historicized narratology. Thanks to Monika Fludernik, that horizon is no longer blank.

References

Alber, Jan. 2011. "The Diachronic Development of Unnaturalness: A New View on Genre." In *Unnatural Narratives, Unnatural Narratology*, edited by Jan Alber and Rüdiger Heinze, 41–67. Berlin: De Gruyter.
Austen, Jane. 2005 [1816]. *Emma*. Edited by Richard Cronin and Dorothy McMillan. Cambridge: Cambridge University Press.
Brontë, Anne. 1988 [1847]. *Agnes Grey: A Novel, by Acton Bell*. London: Thomas Cautley Newby. Rpt. London: Penguin.
Brontë, Charlotte. 2006 [1847]. *Jane Eyre: An Autobiography. Edited by Currer Bell*. London: Smith, Elder, & Co. Rpt. London: Penguin.
Brunton, Mary. 1986 [1815]. *Discipline*. London: Pandora Press.
Cuypers, M. P. 2004. "Appolonius of Rhodes." In *Narrators, Narratees, and Narratives in Ancient Greek Literature*, edited by Irene J. F. De Jong, René Nünlist, and Angus Bowie, 43–62. Leiden and Boston: Brill.
Defoe, Daniel. 1989 [1722]. *Moll Flanders*. London: Penguin Books.
de Jong, Irene J. F. 2013. "Diachronic Narratology. (The Example of Ancient Greek Narrative)." In *the living handbook of narratology*, edited by Peter Hühn et al. Hamburg: Hamburg University. Accessed 5 September 2017. Web.
---. 2014. *Narratology and Classics: A Practical Guide*. Oxford: Oxford University Press.
Diegesis: Interdisciplinary E-Journal for Narrative Research (2014). "Historische Narratologie." 3.2. Accessed 29 May 2017. Web.
Fallon, Claire. 2016 "'Reader, I Married Him': The Unfeminist Reason We Love Charlotte Brontë." *Huffington Post*, 21 April. Accessed 28 August 2017.
Fludernik, Monika. 1993. *The Fiction of Languages and the Languages of Fiction: The Linguistic Representation of Speech and Consciousness*. London: Routledge.
---. 1996. *Toward a 'Natural' Narratology*. London and New York: Routledge.
---. 2003. "The Diachronization of Narratology." *Narrative* 11: 331–348.
---. 2006. *Einführung in die Erzähltheorie*. Darmstadt: Wissenschaftliche Buchgesellschaft.
---. 2009. *An Introduction to Narratology*. Translated by Patricia Häusler-Greenfield and Monika Fludernik. London and New York: Routledge.

---. 2011. "The Representation of Mind from Chaucer to Aphra Behn." In *Narrative Developments from Chaucer to Defoe*, edited by Gerd Bayer and Ebbe Klitgard. London: Routledge.

Folkenflik, Robert. 1993. "Introduction: The Institution of Autobiography." In *The Culture of Autobiography: Constructions of Self-Representation*, edited by Robert Folkenflik, 1–20. Stanford: Stanford University Press.

Genette, Gérard. 1980. *Narrative Discourse: An Essay on Method*. Translated by Jane E. Lewin. Ithaca: Cornell University Press.

---. *Narrative Discourse Revisited*. Translated by Jane E. Lewin. Ithaca: Cornell University Press.

Getz, Joshua M., and Thomas O. Beebee. 1998. "The Epistolary Politics of Amos Oz's *Black Box*." *Prooftexts* 18: 45–65.

Hill, Christopher. 1965. "Introduction." In *Crisis in Europe, 1560-1660: Essays from "Past and Present,"* edited by Trevor Astton, 1–4. London: Routledge.

Lanser, Susan. 1982. *The Narrative Act: Point of View in Prose Fiction*. Princeton: Princeton University Press.

---. 1992. *Fictions of Authority: Women Writers and Narrative Voice*. Ithaca: Cornell.

McHale, Brian. 2011. "Speech Representation." In *the living handbook of narratology*, edited by Peter Hühn et al. Hamburg: Hamburg University. Accessed 29 May 2017. Web.

Nünning, Ansgar. 2000. "Towards a Cultural and Historical Narratology: Concepts, Diachronic Approaches and Projects." In *Anglistentag 1999 Mainz: Proceedings*, edited by Bernhard Reitz and Sigrid Rieuwerts, 345–373. Trier: WVT.

Prince, Gerald. 2003 [1987]. *A Dictionary of Narratology*. Lincoln: University of Nebraska Press.

Radner, Joan N. 1999. "Writing History: Early Irish Historiography and the Significance of Form." *Celtica* 23: 312–325.

Rowson, Susanna. 1964. *Charlotte Temple: A Tale of Truth*. New Haven: College and University Publishers.

Salinger, J. D. 2006 [1951]. *The Catcher in the Rye*. Boston: Little, Brown.

Warhol, Robyn. 1986. "Toward a Theory of the Engaging Narrator: Earnest Interventions in Gaskell, Stowe, and Eliot." *PMLA* 101.5: 811–818.

---. 1989. *Gendered Interventions: Narrative Discourse in the Victorian Novel*. New Brunswick: Rutgers University Press.

Philippe Carrard
Historiographic Discourse and Narratology: A Footnote to Fludernik's Work on Factual Narrative

Over the past years, Monika Fludernik has published several essays on the relations between factual and fictional narratives. She has, among other things, revisited her concept of 'experientiality' as applied to historical discourse (2010), asked whether a different kind of narratology was needed to account for the features of factual narrative (2013), and examined how collective minds were represented in fictional and non-fictional texts in the early modern period (2014). She co-edited the volume *Faktuales und Fiktionales Erzählen*, in which her own contribution surveys narratological problems related to factual narrative, especially to 'descriptions' in both novels and texts that aim at representing real events (2015).

My purpose is to continue Fludernik's analyses by looking at a specific type of factual narrative, namely, current scholarly historiography. Let me stress *current* and *scholarly*. Conventions of researching and representing the past are neither eternal nor universal, and history, in its current state, is far from monolithic. Its productions run the whole gamut from popular biographies to learned studies grounded in quantitative methods, through a wide range of texts targeted to various audiences. I will restrict my inquiry to the scholarly kind for the sake of homogeneity, and I will take most of my examples from contemporary French historiography due to my familiarity with it. I will focus on the four questions that Fludernik asks at the end of her essay on factual narrative as a "missing narratological paradigm" in order to determine which features of classical narratology can be "preserved" and which ones can be "discarded" or "marginalized" (2013, 130).

1 Narration

The first such question is narration, that is the problem of determining who is speaking/writing and to/for whom. In historiography, as Dorrit Cohn (1999, 123–131) and Gérard Genette (1991, 78–88) have argued in their contrasting descriptions of factual and fictional discourses, the initial contract between text and reader implies that author and narrator refer to the same person. To put it otherwise, historians as authors are responsible for what their narrators are asserting, whether it is factual statements or comments bearing on the meaning of the events that they are reporting. When Henry Rousso (1992, 13), at the beginning of one of his studies of the Occupation, writes for example, "on 16 June 1940 a new government was formed in Bordeaux by Marshall Pétain," he as author supports what his narrator is stating. In so doing, he also implicitly performs what might be viewed as the historian's basic speech act, which could be formulated as: "I have done research, believe me, and if you do not believe me, go check my sources."[1]

Though merged in the speech act that opens every historiographic study, the functions 'author' and 'narrator' may at times be dissociated in the course of the text. That is, historians do not always mean what they say; they may also quote discourses that they do not endorse, and do so without necessarily marking off the quotes by way of punctuation. When the film historian Geneviève Sellier, for instance, writes that in French movies of the 1950s "active women are dangerous" and form "a pack of hussies desperately attempting to destroy men," she as author does not stand behind what her narrator is stating (1999, 285). Here, Sellier introduces the conception of women that prevailed in many postwar films, but that conception obviously is not hers. Similarly, the medievalist Georges Duby does not 'mean it' when he asks in his examination of the Church's thirst for material riches in the early 1000s: "Doesn't he [God] deserve to possess a treasure more radiant than that of all the powerful of the earth?" (1976, 60). The question here has the value of an assertion, but an assertion that the historian does not underwrite. Duby, as author, makes his narrator express beliefs that clearly are not his, and beliefs that temporal distance makes even more foreign and objectionable.

These occasional disjunctions between author and narrator make it necessary to modify some received ideas about historiographic discourse. In the first place, quotations from another discourse ("pack of hussies") show that historiography is not necessarily – to use Bakhtin's terms – "monologic" and "authoritative" (1981, 342). Specifically, historiographic studies may include quotations that evolve from Bakhtin's "characters' zone," in this case, from a zone of culture that encroaches on the historian's zone without being explicitly separated from it (1981, 316). The presence of expressions for which the historian cannot be held

---

[1] I am paraphrasing Paul Ricœur, for whom a witness makes the basic statement: I was there, believe me, and if you do not believe me, ask someone else (2000, 206). The historian, of course, in most cases 'was not there' and thus must rely on sources.

responsible also challenges the view of historiography as an entirely "serious" discourse, in John Searle's sense (1979, 60). Paul Hernadi, in an essay on historians' language, has argued that a sentence such as that which opens Jane Austen's *Pride and Prejudice* ("It is a truth, universally acknowledged, that a single man in possession of a good fortune, must be in want of a wife" [1813]) is incompatible with historical discourse (1975, 252). For it is not a 'true statement,' and historians have pledged to make true statements exclusively. Descriptions of active women as "dangerous" and affirmations that God deserves a treasure "more radiant than that of all powerful of the earth," however, show that Hernadi has a restricted view of how tropes in general – and irony in particular – may be used in historiographic texts. In this instance, it shows that irony does indeed occur in those texts, provided that it not be reduced to antiphrasis but defined, with Dan Sperber and Deirdre Wilson (1978), as 'quotation' of another discourse: a discourse that ironists do not 'use,' but 'mention' as they signal that they disapprove of it. While turning to irony, historians thus remain reliable. They play with language and do so against the instructions of their style manuals and the expectations of literary theorists, but these games – if properly understood – are not incompatible with the 'reliability contract' that binds historiographic texts and their readers.

The second question on Fludernik's list also concerns narration. It bears on *we*-narratives, that is, on stories in which "the protagonists are more than one person and the autodiegetic narrator *persona* is either part of that protagonist group or additionally coparticipates in the narration with one or more of the relevant protagonists" (Fludernik 2013, 130). This type, Fludernik notes, is rare in fictional narratives, while it is frequent in memoirs and oral stories in which the author-narrator speaks 'for' a group whose activities he/she has shared to various extents. Yet contemporary historians do not recount events in which they themselves have participated as part of a collective, and 'we' (or at least 'nous' in French scholarship) has a different reference in their texts. The first-person plural may designate the author-narrator and the reader ("we must now stop to consider…"), the author-narrator and his/her research community ("we do not have the necessary documents to…"), and even the author-narrator him/herself, when discursive conventions prescribe not to use the first-person singular ("as we have tried to show…"). Commenting on this 'we,' Michel de Certeau has stressed that it has an important ideological function: it enables historians to eliminate "the alternative that would consist of ascribing history *either* to an individual (the author, his/her personal philosophy, etc.) *or* to a global subject (time, society, etc.)" (1975, 72). According to Certeau, resorting to 'we' allows history to be located in an institutional place from which the historian's discourse can be articulated without being reduced to it. Because historical studies are rarely collective endeavors, 'we' referring to actual colleagues seems to be reserved for the two or more scholars who introduce the anthology they have edited; it seldom includes a research team that is responsible for the whole work, as is frequently the case in papers in the 'hard' sciences.

We-narratives, of course, can also be inserted into traditional heterodiegetic historical texts in the form of quotations. Stephan Jaeger, in his examination of historiography as a mode of *Wirklichkeitserzählung* [factual narrative], devotes a whole section of his essay to an analysis of insertions of this type in Jörg Friedrich's *Der Brand: Deutschland im Bombenkrieg 1940–1945* [*The Fire: The Bombing of Germany, 1940-1945*] (2002). Focusing on the chapter programmatically titled "*Wir* [We]" he shows how Friedrich constructs a "collective perspective" that includes "public opinion and mood, propaganda, and rumors" (Jaeger 2013, 130). The whole civil population, as a result, becomes the implicit subject of a *we*-narrative that Friedrich may or may not reference in his footnotes. That narrative may communicate shared feelings of hate ("Die Rache kann für England nicht hart genug ausfallen [Revenge against England cannot be strong enough]"), quote the Bible ("Die ganze Brut gehört mit Stumpf und Stiel ausgerottet [The brood must be eradicated root and branch]") or cite Göring, who regrets not to be able to respond to the *Fliegerterror* with gas ("Wenn wir zurückschlagen könnten, hätten wir das schon lange getan, ehe der Kölner Dom kaputt ging, aber wir können nicht [If we could strike back, we would have done it long ago, before the Cologne Cathedral was destroyed, but we can't]") (2013, 131).[2] Friedrich's study, Jaeger concludes, does not join the category 'fiction' because of its reliance on different perspectives. At the least, this structural feature points to the book's nature as a "construct," as a "restaging" and "rewriting" of the events that it recounts (2013, 131). One might add that Friedrich is careful to separate his own text from the quoted text(s) with the help of punctuation. Whereas Sellier – to return to an earlier example – is confident that her readers will understand that "active women" for her are not "hussies," Friedrich puts statements coming from 'others' in quotation marks, making clear that England, for example, is not in his value system a "brood" on which "revenge" should at some point be taken.[3]

---

[2] The translations are taken from Allison Brown's English version of *Der Brand* (Friedrich 2006, 427). All other translations are mine.

[3] Concerned, like Jaeger, with Friedrich's strategies of enunciation, I will not dwell on the properly historical issues raised by *Der Brand* here. For a survey of the controversies brought

2 Context of Utterance

The third question that Fludernik asks of factual narratives concerns their "context of utterance" (2013, 131). Whether they are memoirists reflecting on their lives, witnesses in a courtroom, or economists describing a trend, authors of factual narratives all operate in an "institutional setting" (Fludernik 2013, 131). In historiography, this 'place' (Certeau) is usually established through the paratext, more precisely, through what Genette calls the "editorial peritext" (1987, 20): the information that figures on the exterior cover and the first pages of a book, such as the name of the publisher, the name of the series in which that book is appearing, and relevant facts about the author. The front cover of Duby's *Le Temps des cathédrals* [*The Age of Cathedrals*] (1976), for example, tells prospective readers that the book was brought out by Gallimard, a well-established French publisher, in one of that publisher's most prestigious series, the "Bibliothèque des histoires" ["The History Library"]. The peritex of Duby's other books (e.g., *L'An Mil* [*The Year One Thousand*, 1980]) also specifies that the historian belongs to the French Academy and that he teaches at one of the most distinguished French sites of higher education, the Collège de France. These references to an institutional setting play an important role in the initial negotiations between text and reader. By specifying from where the historian is speaking, they insure his/her legitimacy, granting him/her the authority that he/she needs with readers who may not be familiar with his/her work. Series names such as "Bibliothèque des histoires" also tell readers how to "take" the text, how to correctly decode its "intentions" (Fludernik 2013, 133). In this instance, "Bibliothèque des histoires" indicates that the text is not just referential in a general way (it is about the actual past), but also scholarly. That is, the series name here offers both a promise and a set of instructions: a promise that the text has been written according to the rules in force in the historians' community, and directions about the way it should be properly apprehended. To be sure, I can always 'read' *Le Temps des cathédrales* (or any book published in "Bibliothèque des histoires") as a novel; but I cannot 'take' it as a novel, that is, assign it to the category 'novel,' because the information displayed in paratext points to the membership of the text in the category 'historical discourse.'

While historical narratives originate in a certain place, their context of utterance also includes time. In other words, it is relevant to ask not only from where

---

about by Friedrich's study, including the historian's use of not always adequately identified quotations and inappropriate metaphors, see Arnold 2005.

historians are speaking, but also from when, from what point in time. Addressing this question, Arthur Danto has argued that historiographic texts are always written in light of the "now" of the researcher, that is, in light of "further information" (1985, xii). Sentences such as "The Thirty Year War began in 1618," he explains, are typical of historiography, as they "give descriptions of events under which the events could not have been witnessed, since they make essential reference to events later in time than the events they are about, and hence cognitively inaccessible to observers" (Danto 1985, xii). To put it otherwise, historians for Danto know more than 'the whole story' (i.e., the story they are recounting); they also know the whole history (i.e., the history of what happened before and especially after the stretch of the past that they are investigating). This unavoidable "presentism" (Hull 1979) has important consequences for the writing of history. For one thing, it accounts for the fact that historiographic studies can be continued, or even entirely rewritten, not solely because new documents have been uncovered, but also (and more fundamentally) because the temporal distance between the end of the story and the moment of writing has grown. This increasing span between 'now' and 'then' obliges historians to extend – to take obvious examples – national narratives such as those of Germany and Yugoslavia. Likewise, it offers the possibility to redo, from a different perspective or in light of new questions, the analysis of complex periods such as the French Revolution and World War II. At the level of individual descriptions, their presentism also allows historians to compare the aspect of the past they are exploring (e.g., religious fanaticism) with its current manifestations, to show the common points as well as the differences between 'then' and 'today.' Such comparisons of course risk committing what manuals deem to be one of the historian's worst sins: anachronism. The specialist of the Old Regime Roland Mousnier has thus attacked Marxist historians for describing that Regime's social structures in terms of class, instead of adopting the category in use during the period, that of estate (1964). Conversely, in an article programmatically titled "Eloge de l'anachronisme en histoire [In Praise of Anachronism in History]," the hellenist Nicole Loraux has pleaded for employing the modern concept of "public opinion" in the examination of Athenian democracy (1993). Following in her footsteps, Patrick Boucheron and Nicolas Offenstadt have proposed to apply to the Middle Ages Habermas's notion of the public sphere (*Öffentlichkeit*). This "intentional and controlled" use of anachronism, Boucheron and Offenstadt have argued, should provide the opportunity for reexamining some all-too common views of the Middle Ages, such as the belief in the period's "brutality of social domination" (2011, 14; my translation).

As historians occupy a certain place and cannot escape their own time, the context of utterance in which they write also includes addressees, in this instance, both actual and inscribed readers. The profile of the former is difficult to work out, because sales figures do not tell whether the book that was bought was really read, and how. Partial descriptions can be provided by examining reviews, which inform about a book's reception, or by conducting field studies, on the model of Janice Radway's (1984) analysis of the ways a group of women in the Midwest 'read the romance.' The attributes of inscribed readers are easier to identify. First, they are conspicuous in the paratext. To return once again to Duby's *Le Temps des cathédrales*, its membership in Gallimard's "Bibliothèque des histoires" shows that this work is targeted to what French publishers call "le grand public cultivé," that is, an audience made up of university graduates, or at least of people who are familiar with the conventions of scholarly discourse. Publishers' names such as "Publications de la Sorbonne" or "Presses universitaires de Rennes," on the other hand, denote a study aimed at a more restricted, more specialized audience. As for series titles such as Gallimard's "Les Journées qui ont fait la France" [The Days That Made France] and Hachette's "La Vie quotidienne" [Everyday Life], they point to a wider, more general audience, made up of the many readers interested in the detailed account of well-known events, as well as in the description of 'how ordinary people lived' at a certain time and place. In the text itself, inscribed readers can be characterized by looking at what Umberto Eco calls their "encyclopedia" (1979, 19): the knowledge that the historian ascribes to them, especially in the domain that the study covers. In *1515 et les grandes dates dans l'histoire de France* [*1515 and the Most Important Dates in French History*], for example, established scholars writing for a general audience posit a reader's encyclopedia whose range greatly varies. Commenting on the battle of Bouvines, Jean-Claude Schmitt thus feels the need to explain that the ritual meaning of the fight was that of an "ordeal," that is, in the first meaning of the term, of a "judgment coming from God" (2005, 89). Conversely, recounting in the same anthology how Napoléon III seized power, Michel Winock takes for granted that readers know that Morny, the coup's engineer, was also the Emperor's half-brother (2005, 395); he thus does not bother to provide this information, which would have been useful to readers who were not aware of the family relations between Louis-Napoléon and his main co-conspirator. As these few examples show, the figure of the inscribed reader in historiographic texts designed for a general audience is far from coherent. Writing for that audience is difficult, since scholars, depending on what they think is widely known and what deserves an explanation, can be charged with lending too much competence to their readers, or on the contrary with patronizing them. Yet a similar remark can be made about studies aimed at specialists. In the reviews they write in professional journals, historians frequently complain – among other things – that their colleagues resort to a jargon that is incomprehensible to ordinary scholars. Historians who have turned to 'theory' have often been taken to task for this misdeed, though they are not the only ones in whose works the figures of the inscribed and actual readers do not consistently fit together.[4]

3 Report vs. Experiential Narrative

The fourth and last question that Fludernik asks of factual narratives concerns their respective membership in the categories of the "report" and the "experiential narrative." Except for "oral storytelling and popular journalism," she points out, "report dominates over experiential telling" in factual narrative (2013, 133). This remark is certainly true of historiography, at least of the scholarly type. Just like popular journalism, popular historical studies and especially popular biographies frequently account for experience, as they have no qualms about reconstructing dialogs and telling how characters 'felt' about what they were doing.

The reluctance of professional historians to describe experience calls for two observations. First, it must be noted that if those historians, as Cohn has pointed out, hesitate to enter characters' minds, conventions of scholarly writing allow them to 'quote' those minds, provided that documents are available (1999, 117–118). Friedrich's *Der Brand* is a case in point, as the instances of *we*-narrative Jaeger mentions in his analysis of this text are all grounded in archival research, whether Friedrich footnotes his sources or not. To put it otherwise, Friedrich does not tell indiscriminately how the actors 'felt' about their ordeals; this would disqualify him as a serious historian in the eyes of his colleagues. He only provides access to those actors' thoughts when he has been able to reconstruct them on the basis of letters, memoirs, newspaper articles, and other personal or archival documents. Similar strategies are found in French history of 'mentalities,' a field that has now been incorporated into the capacious domain of 'cultural history.' The specialist of World War I Stéphane Audoin-Rouzeau has thus studied specific aspects of what he labels "war culture," seeking for example to describe the rapes committed by German soldiers in occupied territories by relying as far as possible on testimonies provided by "the victims themselves and eyewitnesses" (1995, 43).

---

[4] On this subject, see for instance Allan Megill's 1987 article on the reception of Foucault by the American historical community.

Turning in similar manner to records that communicate 'what things were like' or 'how people felt' at certain times and places, historians have sought to trace the evolution of attitudes toward such things as death (Ariès), smells (Corbin), corporeality (Vigarello), fear (Delumeau), sexuality (Flandrin), deliveries (Laget), and even skirts (Bard) and tanning (Ory). There is no end to what 'culture' might encompass, provided of course that the term not be reserved for 'high' forms of art, literature, and music.

The paradox of these studies – and this is my second observation – resides in the fact that while they deal with experience, they do not constitute "experiential narratives" in Fludernik's sense.[5] To begin with, several of them are not narratives properly speaking. They do not move from point A to point Z along temporal lines, "someone telling somebody else on some occasion and on some purpose that something happened" (Phelan 2007, 203), or representing in a logically consistent way "at least two asynchronous events, or one state and one event, that do not presuppose or imply each other" (Prince 2012, 25). Friedrich's and Audoin-Rouzeau's works on war, for instance, are organized thematically; they do include brief stories, usually employed as examples, but their overall structure is that of the analysis of a topic within a specific period, not that of a narrative. Insofar as they trace changes in attitudes, other studies take the form of what might be called 'stage narratives': they do not proceed from event to event (as traditional political and military histories do), but from situation to situation, slicing time into periods that correspond to successive 'attitudes towards.' The best-known instance of this type of textual arrangement is probably Philippe Ariès's *L'Homme devant la mort* [*The Hour of Our Death*] (1977), which divides outlooks on death into five time-spans extending from Antiquity to the twentieth century. Most of the studies I mentioned earlier (Corbin's on smells, Vigarello's on corporeality, Bard's on skirts, etc.) are organized like Ariès's, the historian seeking to distinguish among phases in the development of the domain that he/she has chosen to investigate, as well as to explain the shift from one phase to the next.[6]

Stage narratives of course pose a problem for literary theorists, that of knowing whether they possess enough narrativity to be included at all in the category

---

5 Fludernik has this type of inquiry in mind when she writes: "Cultural history, merging with the history of ideas and mentalities, is often concerned with the development of collective understandings and concepts, looking at the shaping and persistence of communal experience through the centuries" (2010, 41). She, however, does not ask what kind of textual structure studies like Ariès's on death may assume, and she moves on to examining a few "experiments" in historical writing (2010, 42).
6 For a more detailed analysis of the different types of structure used in current historical studies, see my *History as a Type of Writing*.

'narrative.' Fludernik, to my knowledge, has not commented on stage narratives specifically, but she has denied in earlier essays that historiography may have a place at all in the category 'narrative' because of its lack of experientiality. This criterion, as Daniel Fulda points out in his essay on historiographic narration, is a "minority view within narratology," and Fludernik has since then "softened her position" (2014, 4). She now stresses that "experientiality (and hence narrativity) occurs on a scale, and that the more academic a historical text is, the less experientiality there will be" (2010, 50). One could distinguish on this subject, as Prince (2008) does, between "narrativehood" and "narrativeness," that is, between the entities that constitute narrative and the qualities or traits of narrative.[7] Stage narratives would thus have narrativehood, because their structure fits Phelan's and Prince's definitions of narrative. Admittedly, such narratives proceed from state to state and only involve events as part of the situation that they describe. But these states are asynchronous, they follow each other on a temporal line, which makes their succession into a narrative. Whether texts of this type include elements of narrativeness (or narrativity) is open for debate. I would argue with Prince (and Fludernik) that narrativeness is a matter of scale, but I would add that experiencing such things as curiosity, suspense, and/or surprise – to use Meir Steinberg's (1978) well-known categories – depends on one's expectations while taking up and then reading a certain type of text. Medievalists, for instance, may not immerse themselves in *Le Temps des cathédrales* as they would in a detective novel; however, they may be eager to learn how Duby will shift from one stage to the next, and be surprised by the way the historian deals with, say, the transition from the stage of the 'monastery' to that of the 'cathedral.' Obviously, issues of narrativeness are not reserved for stage narratives; they may be raised about any historiographic text that has a narrative structure. But stage narratives, insofar as they may be at the lower end of narrativeness, allow to pose with much clarity the question of the relations between narrative and historiography – a question that I now will seek to reframe.

4 From Narratology to Poetics

Returning in her conclusion to the problem of determining "which aspects of the standard narratological models are useful in the analysis of factual storytelling,"

---

[7] For a survey of the definitions of 'narrativity' and the issues related to this concept, see Abbott 2014.

Fludernik states that such concepts as voice, narratee, and focalization as well as the story-discourse distinction might be useful, whereas categories related to time such as anachrony, frequency, and duration do not appear "absolutely necessary to the analysis of factual narrative" (2013, 134). One could of course quarrel with some of these affirmations, as time is doubtless a key aspect of historiographic narratives. While analyzing such narratives, it is indeed relevant to ask how strictly they follow chronological order (as manuals instruct apprentice historians to do); to what extent they rely on singular or iterative narration, as historiography often accounts for "what things were like" and then concerns itself chiefly with repeated actions; and at what speed the text proceeds, as historians can devote several hundred pages to a few hours and a short paragraph to a whole century. More basically, as Cohn has demonstrated, the story-discourse dichotomy must be supplemented to correctly account for the specificity of historiography (1999, 110–117). We need a third level, 'reference,' by which Cohn means the traces that the past has left – traces in which historians ground their inquiries.

The addition of 'reference' to the story-discourse dichotomy has important textual implications. First, it entails that only historiographic texts are properly speaking "emplotted," that is, based on "preexisting material" that they "transform" and "endow with meaning" (Cohn 1999, 114). Fiction, on the other hand, is "plotted," as its "serial moments do not refer to, and can therefore not be selected from, an ontologically independent and temporally prior data base of disordered, meaningless happenings that it restructures into order and meaning" (1999, 114). To be sure, fiction may be grounded in archival sources and play with well-known, frequently used topoi. But it does not, as historiography does, *have* to originate in prior materials to which it then *must* refer in the text itself. This latter requirement has significant implications for the layout of historiographic studies. Indeed, it accounts for what Michel de Certeau calls the "split structure" of historiographic texts (1975, 111): the fact that those texts include two categories of statements, namely (1) utterances that originate with the author-narrator, and (2) testimonials – citations and references whose function is to warrant the veracity of statements of the first category. Historiographies thus offer prime examples of the split page, that is, of the division of the page between a primary text and footnotes usually set in smaller print. But they also supply choice examples of the split chapter and the split study, that is, of works where notes are grouped not at the bottom of a page, but at the end of a larger textual unit. Such layouts (and especially the split page) give to historiographies a certain 'look,' and this look is not a phenomenon that could be dismissed as superficial. Indeed, it is among the immediately visible signs that provide readers with instructions, telling them how to 'take' the text that they are reading or merely leafing through. The split structure, in this instance, alerts them to the fact that the historian has followed the conventions of scholarly research and writing. He/she can thus be trusted, which does not mean that his/her inquiry should remain unexamined: Foot- and endnotes are also invitations to 'go see,' in this instance, to go consult the sources used in that inquiry and check whether they have been properly selected, quoted, and interpreted.

Adding emplotment and reference to the categories of classical narratology, however, does not account for a major aspect of current historiography: the fact that a large part of its production does not fall under narrative, at least not as defined by literary theorists like Prince and Phelan. In short, historiographic texts do not necessarily tell stories. While historians always situate their investigations in time, they do not organize their material along a time sequence in every case. The relevant question to ask about a piece of historiography, therefore, is not "What type of narrative does it belong to?" or "Does it have enough narrativeness to count as narrative?" but, more basically, "Does it have a narrative structure?" We saw earlier how texts such as Friedrich's *Der Brand* and Audoin-Rouzeau's *L'Enfant de l'ennemi* [The Enemy's Child] reside in the category 'analysis,' as they proceed from topic to topic and not from event to event, or from period to period. Organized after the rhetorical scheme of going from 'wrong' to 'right,' other analyses revisit well-known issues to dispel mistaken interpretations. Pierre Laborie's *Le Chagrin et le venin* [The Sorrow and the Venom] (2011), for example, moves from a survey of the 'wrong' views of the German occupation of France to what the historian holds to be the 'correct' ones.[8]

A different non-narrative model frequently employed in historiography is description. Fludernik, in a further essay on factual narrative, devotes several pages to the structure and role of description in this type of text, taking her examples in *Gebrauchsliteratur* – tour books and oral depictions of apartments (2015, 130–131). Focusing on description as a stop in the flow of a narrative, however, she does not consider cases when whole texts are shaped as descriptions, which can be of different types. One such type derives from anthropology. The historian describes a certain place at a certain time, in accordance with a grid that, as dissected by the anthropologist Mondher Kilani, has become standardized: they go "from the periphery to the center, from the visual to the less visual, from the objective to the subjective, from the material condition of a culture to its expression

---

[8] Laborie's title *Le Chagrin et le venin* obviously plays on the title of Marcel Ophüls and André Harris's much talked-about documentary film *Le Chagrin et la pitié* [The Sorrow and the Pity] (1969). Laborie takes on this film, as well as on well-known studies such as Robert Paxton's *Vichy France* (1972), as a *doxa* on the Occupation that must now be questioned.

of meaning" (1988, 11). Emmanuel Le Roy Ladurie's celebrated *Montaillou* (1975) unfolds by and large according to this pattern. Studying everyday life in a village in Southern France at the beginning of the fourteenth century, the historian examines successively the environment, housing, work, gestures, sex life, marriage, and beliefs.

Another non-narrative model frequently used in current historiography is the tableau. Whereas anthropological descriptions move from the outside to the inside, tableaus chart out different aspects of a certain society without privileging a specific order. Often employed in France in the 1950s and 1960s as a way of charting large regional studies, the tableau has now been adopted in global and connected histories, that is, in histories that aim at questioning the chronologies and political mappings in use in Western scholarship. *L'Histoire du monde au XVe siècle* [*History of the World in the Fifteenth Century*], for example, an anthology edited by Patrick Boucheron, covers the "territories of the world," the "time of the worlds," and the "writings of the world" (2009, 200). Boucheron and his collaborators offer an overview of the "world" in the fifteenth century, a term that they at times use in the plural to show that there was not one world, but several when we abandon the Eurocentric perspective that for a long time has dominated western historical research.

What analyses, anthropological descriptions, and tableaus have in common is to constitute synchronic cross-sections: they do not trace changes (as even stage narratives do), but provide flat accounts of the 'state of things' at a specific time and place. To be sure, synchronic cross-sections may include narratives. Germans, as we have seen, recount their experiences of the Allied bombing, and villagers in Montaillou tell anecdotes that Le Roy Ladurie can retell because they figure in the documents on which he is basing his inquiry.[9] *Der Brand* and *Montaillou*, moreover, could be understood as part of a larger story – of bombing during World War II and village life in the Middle Ages respectively. It remains that these two texts, considering their overall structure, are not narratives, as they do not report that 'something happened' (Phelan), are not made up of the succession of 'asynchronous events' (Prince), and more generally are not organized along a time sequence. Narratology, whether classical or postclassical, thus cannot describe them adequately, and must give way to a different, larger framework. I propose 'poetics,' by which I mean the study of the codes, rules, and conventions that shape any discourse, whether narrative or not. Poetics obviously

---

[9] It is possibly the number of these embedded stories that has led such a respected scholar as Lawrence Stone to regard *Montaillou* as a prime example of what he has labeled the "revival of narrative" (1979).

borrows the tools of narratology when dealing with narrative. But it also, more widely, borrows from literary theory and rhetoric, on which it draws to characterize – in the texts I have considered at least – figures of speech, models of description, and strategies of argument. Thus, there is no incompatibility between narratology and poetics in the analysis of historiography. Poetics, in this instance, takes over when narratology leaves off, that is, when the latter's toolbox is no longer appropriate because the texts to be accounted for follow models that do not have a narrative structure.

References

Abbott, Porter. 2014. "Narrativity." In *the living handbook of narratology*, edited by Peter Hühn et al. Hamburg: Hamburg University. Accessed 22 February 2016. Web.
Ariès, Philippe. 1977. *L'Homme devant la mort*. Paris: Seuil. L'Univers historique.
Arnold, Jörg. 2005. "A Narrative of Loss." Review of Jörg Friedrich, *Der Brand: Deutschland im Bombenkrieg, 1940–1945*. Accessed 22 February 2016. Web.
Audoin-Rouzeau, Stéphane. 1995. *L'Enfant de l'ennemi, 1914–1918*. Paris: Aubier. Collection historique.
Bakhtin, Mikhail. 1981. *The Dialogic Imagination: Four Essays*. Translated by Michael Holquist and Caryl Emerson. Austin: University of Texas Press.
Bard, Christine. 2010. *Ce que soulève la jupe: Identités, transgressions, résistances*. Paris: Autrement.
Boucheron, Patrick, ed. 2009. *L'Histoire du monde au 15e siècle*. Paris: Fayard.
Boucheron, Patrick, and Nicolas Offenstadt, eds. 2011. *L'Espace public au Moyen Age: Débats autour de Jürgen Habermas*. Paris: Presses Universitaires de France.
Carrard, Philippe. 2017. *History as a Type of Writing: Textual Strategies in Contemporary French Historiography*. Chicago: Chicago University Press.
Certeau, Michel de. 1975. *L'Ecriture de l'histoire*. Paris: Gallimard. Bibliothèque des histoires.
Cohn, Dorrit. 1999. *The Distinction of Fiction*. Baltimore and London: Johns Hopkins University Press.
Corbin, Alain. 1986. *Le Miasme et la jonquille: L'odorat et l'imaginaire social, 18e–19e siècles*. Paris: Flammarion. Champs.
---, ed. 2005. *1515 et les grandes dates dans l'histoire de France*. Paris: Seuil.
Danto, Arthur. 1985. *Narration and Knowledge*. New York: Columbia University Press.
Delumeau, Jean. 1978. *La Peur en Occident, 14e–18e siècles*. Paris: Fayard.
Duby, Georges. 1976. *Le temps des cathédrales: L'Art et la société, 980–1420*. Paris: Gallimard.
---. 1980. *L'An Mil*. Paris: Gallimard/Julliard. Archives.
Eco, Umberto. 1979. *The Role of the Reader: Explorations in the Semiotics of Texts*. Bloomington: Indiana University Press.
Flandrin, Jean-Louis. 2006. *L'Eglise et la contraception*. Paris: Imago.
Fludernik, Monika. 2010. "Experience, Experientiality, and Historical Narrative: A View from Narratology." In *Erfahrung und Geschichte: Historische Sinnbildung im Pränarrativen*, edited by Thiemo Breyer and Daniel Creutz, 40–72. Berlin and New York: De Gruyter.

---. 2013. "Factual Narrative: A Missing Narratological Paradigm." *Germanisch-Romanische Monatsschrift* 63.1: 117–134.
---. 2014. "Collective Minds in Fact and Fiction: Intermental Thought and Group Consciousness in Early Modern Narrative." *Poetics Today* 35.4: 689–730.
---. 2015. "Narratologische Probleme des faktualen Erzählens." In *Faktuales und fiktionales Erzählen: Interdisziplinäre Perspektiven*, edited by Monika Fludernik et al., 115–137. Würzburg: Ergon.
Friedrich, Jörg. 2002. *Der Brand. Deutschland im Bombenkrieg, 1940-1945*. Berlin: Propyläen.
---. 2006. *The Fire: The Bombing of Germany, 1940-1945*. Translated by Allison Brown. New York: Columbia University Press.
Fulda, Daniel. 2014. "Historiographic Narration." In *the living handbook of narratology*, edited by Peter Hühn et al. Hamburg: Hamburg University. Accessed 10 February 2016. Web.
Genette, Gérard. 1987. *Seuils*. Paris: Seuil. Poétique.
---. 1991. *Fiction et diction*. Paris: Seuil. Poétique.
Hernadi, Paul. 1975. "Clio's Cousin: Historiography as Translation, Fiction, and Criticism." *New Literary History* 7: 247–257.
Hull, David. 1979. "In Defense of Presentism." *History and Theory* 18: 1–15.
Jaeger, Stephan. 2013. "Erzählen im historiographischen Diskurs." In *Wirklichkeitserzählungen: Felder, Formen und Funktionen nicht-literarischen Erzählens*, edited by Christian Klein and Matias Martinez, 110–135. Stuttgart and Weimar: Metzler.
Kilani, Mondher. 1995. "Les anthropologues et leur savoir: Du terrain au texte." In *Le Discours anthropologique: Description, narration, savoir*, edited by Marie-Jeanne Borel et al., 65–100. Lausanne: Payot.
Laborie, Pierre. 2011. *Le Chagrin et le venin: La France sous l'Occupation, mémoire et idées reçues*. Montrouge: Bayard.
Laget, Mireille. 1982. *Naissances: L'accouchement avant l'âge de la Clinique*. Paris: Seuil. L'Univers historique.
Le Roy Ladurie, Emmanuel. 1975. *Montaillou, village Occitan de 1294 à 1324*. Paris: Gallimard. Bibliothèque des histoires.
Loraux, Nicole. 1993. "Eloge de l'anachronisme en histoire." *Le Genre Humain* 27: 23–29.
Megill, Allan. 1987. "The Reception of Foucault by Historians." *Journal of the History of Ideas* 48.1: 117–141.
Mousnier, Roland. 1964. "Problèmes et méthodes dans l'étude des structures sociales des 16e, 17e et 18e siècles." In *Spiegel der Geschichte: Festgabe für Max Braubach*, edited by Konrad Repgen and Stefan Skalweit, 550–564. Münster: Aschendorff.
Ory, Pascal. 2008. *L'Invention du bronzage: Essai d'une histoire culturelle*. Paris: Complexe.
Phelan, James. 2007. *Experiencing Fiction: Judgments, Progressions, and the Rhetorical Theory of Narrative*. Columbus: Ohio State University Press.
Prince, Gerald. 2008. "Narrativehood, Narrativity, Narratability." In *Theorizing Narrativity*, edited by John Pier and J. A. Garcia Landa, 19–27. Berlin and New York: De Gruyter.
---. 2012. "Récit minimal et narrativité." In *Le Récit minimal*, edited by Sabrinelle Bedrane et al., 23–32. Paris: Presses de la Sorbonne Nouvelle.
Radway, Janice. 1984. *Reading the Romance: Women, Patriarchy, and Popular Literature*. Chapel Hill: University of North Carolina Press.
Ricœur, Paul. 2000. *La Mémoire, l'histoire, l'oubli*. Paris: Seuil. L'Ordre philosophique.
Rousso, Henry. 1992. *Le Syndrome de Vichy de 1944 à nos jours*. Paris: Seuil. Points Histoire.

Schmitt, Jean-Claude. 2005. "1214: Le Roi Philippe-Auguste gagne la bataille de Bouvines." In *1515 et les grandes dates dans l'histoire de France*, edited by Alain Corbin, 87–90. Paris: Seuil.

Searle, John. 1979. "The Logical Status of Fictional Discourse." In *Expression and Meaning: Studies in the Theory of Speech Acts*, 58–75. Cambridge: Cambridge University Press.

Sellier, Geneviève. 1999. "Les contradictions du cinéma des années 50." In *Un Siècle d'antiféminisme*, edited by Christine Bard, 285–297. Paris: Fayard.

Sperber, Dan, and Deirdre Wilson. 1978. "Les ironies comme mentions." *Poétique* 23: 389–415.

Sternberg, Meir. 1978. *Expositional Modes and Temporal Ordering in Fiction*. Baltimore and London: Johns Hopkins University Press.

Stone, Lawrence. 1979. "The Revival of Narrative: Reflections on an Old New History." *Past and Present* 85: 3–24.

Vigarello, Georges. 2010. *Les Métamorhoses du gras: Histoire de l'obésité*. Paris: Seuil. L'Univers historique.

Winock, Michel. 2005. "1852: Napoléon fonde le Second Empire." In *1515 et les grandes dates dans l'histoire de France*, edited by Alain Corbin, 393–397. Paris: Seuil.

Dorothee Birke and Robyn Warhol
Multimodal You: Playing with Direct Address in Contemporary Narrative Television

TV has always been talking to 'you.' From the 1950s onward, commercial messages, news programs, variety shows, and anthology dramas, among other genres, have established structures of address that project an audience sometimes inside and sometimes beyond the studio, a viewing stance that is conceived as being open to the attitudes, values, beliefs, and tastes of the speaking voice. Conventions for constructing a viewer, and for encouraging actual audience members to identify with that virtual figure, have been strongly established throughout the history of broadcast television.[1] In this sense, television uses direct address in a more theatrical way than cinema: staged drama and television genres like newscasting or commercial advertising present themselves as directed to an audience, while in cinema the direct address to the camera is avoided or experienced as transgressive. A notable exception are fictional TV shows, which more closely resemble cinema than do other TV genres in that they conventionally maintain a strict division between the storyworld inhabited by the characters and the actual world in which flesh-and-blood people are watching television screens.

However, in the twenty-first century, the 'new golden age' of television (marked by what Jason Mittell calls "complex TV" and others have referred to as 'quality TV'), some of the most successful fictional television series conspicuously experiment with modes of direct address. This has happened across the spectrum from popular sitcoms at one end to self-consciously artistic full-drop series at the other. For instance, *How I Met Your Mother* (2005–2014) is framed as a story told to a pluralized 'you,' the future children of the main character; *Modern Family* (2009–present) periodically places the different members of the Delgado/Dunphy/Pritchett/Tucker family individually in front of the camera to address an unspecified audience; *House of Cards* (2013–present) has its villainous protagonist talk directly into the camera as to a familiar confidant. The play

---

[1] See, for example, John Fiske's collation of various studies that show how explicit modes of address on TV serve "to construct a complicity between presenter and viewer that provides a televisual way of living the ideology of the family" (1987, 54).

with modes of audience address seems to have become a signature feature of successful twenty-first-century series produced by networks and premium channels alike.

We have long been interested in the structure of second-person address in narrative, a topic Monika Fludernik pioneered early in her career.[2] In this paper we offer an anatomy of ways that contemporary fictional narrative TV series address 'you.' We posit that there are two main traditions in which direct address in TV shows can as a rule easily be naturalized as a device that is directed to fictive recipients.[3] The first evokes the narratorial structure of fiction told in the first person: in ways that are reminiscent of the novel, some TV programs represent narrator figures who relate their own experiences to a more or less specified fictive audience. The second involves the appropriation of documentary techniques that are familiar from news and so-called reality TV, where both presenters and interviewees can appear to address an audience by looking directly into the camera. In the following sections, we will examine how these two traditions of direct address are taken up, experimented with, and occasionally exploded in contemporary TV series. In the third section, we will discuss two examples of series that incorporate a more blatant type of transgression: they 'break the fourth wall' by having characters talk directly to a 'you' that cannot easily be situated as a part of the storyworld. We will argue that these shows use tropes from a medial tradition whose historical imbrication with television is even more obvious than the novel's – that of dramatic performance.

Our interest in modes of address in narrative TV series stems from our commitment to what we might call loose taxonomies of narrative form. We value narratology for (among other things) its attempts to categorize narrative structures according to their management of voice and address, a project whose chief attraction for us is the insight it offers not only into typical kinds of storytelling but also into narrative forms that trouble or defy neat categorization. In our analyses, we will make use of the concept of the narratee, or, as Wolf Schmid has usefully labeled it, the 'fictive addressee,' to discuss how more or less concrete recipients

---

[2] See especially her article "Second-Person Fiction: Narrative You As Addressee and/or Protagonist" (1993) and the special issue of *Style* on second-person narration that she edited (1994).
[3] We are using the term 'naturalization' in the broad sense suggested by Jonathan Culler: referring to the recipient's activity of reducing the strangeness of a text by "ways of constructing communicative circuits into which [he/she] can fit it" (2002 [1975], 156).

of address are constructed within the televisual storyworld.[4] Narratologists distinguish between the 'fictive addressee' (which is a complement to the 'fictive narrator') and an 'implied audience' or 'authorial audience' (a personification of the kind of reception towards which a text is geared).[5] Our investigations into multimodal ways of addressing a 'you' in contemporary TV series are also indebted to Markus Kuhn, who in his development of a narratology for film has highlighted the interplay of different channels of mediation in the medium of the movie. Whereas in written narrative, address is constructed through purely verbal means, film (like drama) adds an auditory channel (in particular, all the information conveyed through the speaker's voice as being *heard*, not *read* – but potentially of course also other audible features such as soundtracks or sound effects) as well as a visual channel. In our analyses, we will consider the verbal, the auditory, and the visual dimensions to pinpoint how the impression of address is generated, and where its limits appear to be.

1 Direct Address in the Narratorial Mode

In series such as *Sex and the City* (1998–2004) and *The Wonder Years* (1988–1993) as well as in the more recent examples *How I Met Your Mother* and *Gossip Girl* (2007–2012), the disembodied voice of one of the characters assumes the functions of a narrator, frequently commenting on the action in the show. This type of direct address on TV evokes the narrative situation in novels with character-narrators, such as the first-person *Bildungsroman*: a character in the storyworld speaks to a fictive addressee. To a greater or lesser degree, these series introduce a scenario that further explains the circumstances of the address, (more or less) specifying a fictive addressee and thereby naturalizing this commentary as a framing device. For example, Carrie Bradshaw (Sarah Jessica Parker) in *Sex and the City* is a newspaper columnist, who is frequently seen typing her commentaries on New York social life – utterances that are then elaborated in voice-over

---

[4] We use Wolf Schmid's term rather than the more established 'narratee' because the situation of address in television does not always serve a storytelling function, see Schmid 2013 [2007], 175.
[5] In our own analysis, we are less interested in the personification of an abstract or ideal viewer as a product than in the process of how a series projects stances for its viewers, constructing certain attitudes as appropriate modes of reception, see Birke 2016, 33–40.

sequences. Carrie speaks of her experiences in the present or the very recent past, thereby evoking a fictive addressee who is interpellated into her storyworld, not to mention her worldview.

Because Carrie's column details her present life, the distinction between the 'experiencing I' and the 'narrating I' that characterizes homodiegetic narration functions subtly in a series like *Sex and the City:* as in epistolary fiction, the speaker is only a few hours older and wiser than she was at the moment she is telling us about. An example in which the address more closely resembles the pattern of autobiographical fictions such as Charles Dickens's *David Copperfield* (serialized monthly from 1849–1850) would be *The Wonder Years*: in the case of the protagonist, Kevin Arnold, there is a discernible age difference between the self that tells the story and the self that lives it. The voice of an adult actor (Daniel Stern) frames dramatizations of his childhood, in which he is portrayed by Fred Savage as a little boy. An episode of *The Wonder Years* invariably begins with the adult Kevin Arnold's recollection of a childhood event and ends with his retrospective reflection on what it meant or why it mattered to him in the long run. Despite this marked difference in the temporal distance between experiencing and narrating self in the two series, the instances of address fulfil similar functions: Carrie's newspaper anecdotes about the sexual adventures she and her women friends alternately enjoy and endure in New York City frame the dramatizations of those adventures in the same way as the narration in *The Wonder Years* does. Moreover, although the auditory quality of Carrie's voice is identical in narration and in dramatization, her narrating-self typically finds a way to make some kind of rueful sense of the stories she is telling, even though they baffle and frustrate the experiencing self Parker portrays in the dramatizations. Within the world of the story, Carrie is making meaning for her column's readers; in a similarly pseudo-autobiographical gesture, the adult Kevin interprets his experience for a less defined, but still fictive addressee.

Both *Sex and the City* and *The Wonder Years* present an autobiographical narrative, then, as a way of reconciling a character to his or her distant or recent past, the kind of recuperative act undertaken by the homodiegetic narrators of Victorian *Bildungsromane*. The fictive addressees of these shows share the positioning of their counterparts in the *Bildungsroman*, imagined as virtual beings who recognize the typicality and the authenticity of the experiences being told, and who are looking for the meaning-making that these narrators offer at the end of each episode. In *Sex and the City* the identity of the fictive addressees is specified by Carrie's being an author who publishes her stories first in the newspaper and later in books. Carrie's addressees are the urban sexual sophisticates to whom her publications are directed, the people in the storyworld who buy her newspaper and her books. The fictive addressee of *The Wonder Years* occupies a position more similar to the fictive addressee in novels like *David Copperfield* or *Great Expectations* (serialized weekly from 1860–1861). The fictive autobiographer addresses a virtual interlocutor who has the patience and desire to attend to hundreds of pages of personal recollections, just as the adult Kevin Arnold speaks to an imagined person who will bear with his stories through six seasons of episodes. The target viewer is someone who can occupy the fictive addressee's imaginary position in the flesh; the series' longevity suggests that advertisers believed for a long time that a substantial number of actual viewers were willing to do so.

In both cases, direct address functions as what Robyn Warhol has called an 'engaging' move, whereby actual readers are encouraged to identify with the 'you' addressed in the text (1989). Conversely, 'distancing' address employs an ironic mode that the audience should recognize as part of a fictive exchange. In *Sex and the City* and *The Wonder Years*, viewers are encouraged to picture themselves as close to the lives of the narrators – whether as a part of a cosmopolitan crowd that appreciates Carrie's witty explorations of the problems of being a modern woman in the city, or as the confidante of an average member of the baby boomer generation, someone who can be expected to be sympathetic to the nostalgic evocation of the joys and trials of teenage life in the late 1960s.

More recent television series have employed direct address in the narratorial mode in ways that disrupt the easy naturalization afforded by series like *Sex and the City* and *The Wonder Years*. Probably the most prominent example of this is *How I Met Your Mother*, a series that makes heavy use of voice-over narration. It is particularly notable for its inclusion of visual elements in the representation of direct address. In the autobiographical TV narrations described so far, verbal-auditive mediation by means of voice-over is the most prominent technique, adding possibilities of expression (compared to address in the novel) through quality and sound of voice to the language content. *Sex and the City* further adds the visual component of sentences being typed into a computer, which situates the fictive audience as a reading audience, thereby distinguishing them from the actual viewers of the TV series.

How I Met Your Mother takes the use of visuality much farther by combining the off-screen voice of Ted Mosby (spoken by Bob Saget) with a visual (as well as verbal and auditory) representation of his audience, namely his two teenaged children (played by Lyndsy Fonseca and David Henrie). The children are shown sitting on a sofa facing the camera, alternately squirming with boredom, rolling their eyes, and becoming mildly interested in the nine-season-long account of the many failed relationships their father claims to have experienced before meeting their mother, who is never named until the final season. Framed by 'Future Ted's' narration, the stories are dramatized in each episode, featuring Josh Radnor as the younger Ted. In contrast with *Sex and the City*, then, the fictive addressees are not a generalized reading audience, but are specific characters. This set-up raises many of the questions that similarly structured novels inspire. Consider, for example, a prototypically framed novel like Emily Brontë's *Wuthering Heights* (1847). How many hours is Nelly Dean supposed to have been talking to Mr. Lockwood in order to get through the entire history of the Linton and Earnshaw families, and how accurate can her recollections be? *How I Met Your Mother* raises similar questions about Ted's reliability (is he presenting an aggrandized version of himself as he attempts to impress his children? Is he exaggerating the attractiveness or even the number of the many women he says he has dated?).[6] There are also instances where Ted is clearly editing the narrative for the benefit of his children, for example in the episode "How Lily Stole Christmas," in which Lily, slightly puzzlingly, is outraged at 'Past Ted' for having called her a 'Grinch,' and 'Future Ted' in a voice-over explains that the word he actually used was much worse. Questions of reliability are reinforced by the series's conclusion, which shows Ted's long narrative to have been misleading the actual audience, if not his kids (who know, as the actual audience does not, who their mother is and what her fate has been).

Direct address in *How I Met Your Mother*, then, is used both for comic effects and to explore the norms and values represented by the narrator and his fictive audience. But it also serves to highlight specific medial and generic conventions. *How I Met Your Mother*'s narratorial structure emphasizes the artifice and conventionality of multi-camera situation comedies, as does the obtrusive and noisy 'canned' laugh track that hearkens back to an earlier, less 'realistic' period of television comedy. The actual audience members are pointedly *not* to identify with Ted's kids, but rather to be constantly reminded that they are watching a show. Homodiegetic character narration, then, can strain the boundaries of the credible in much the same way that 'unnatural' narrative effects do, drawing deliberate attention to the artifice of the televisual narrative form and placing the actual audience in a position of (presumably amused) skepticism. On the one hand, the nostalgic gesture could be understood to set up a contrast between a more old-fashioned type of television as family entertainment and the more edgy type of show *How I Met Your Mother* is aspiring to be. On the other hand, there is also a suggestion of continuity. Just as Ted is positioned as a likeable, if a bit uncool, old-fashioned character who keeps looking for true love in a world populated

---

6 We owe this insight to Robyn's student Rachel Wainz.

with metrosexual adventurers like his friend Barney, so does the series also present itself as an heir to earlier sitcoms.

The artifice of television is also highlighted in an otherwise contrasting show with a narratorial mode of address: *Gossip Girl*, a soapy serial about teenagers attending an Upper-East-side private high school. In *Gossip Girl* the source of the narrator's voice is as mysterious to the characters as it is to the actual viewer, placing the fictive addressees and the actual audience at the same level of having only limited knowledge. "Gossip Girl here," each episode begins, in a snide, youthful female voice which proceeds to expose the secrets and criticize the personalities of a core group of eight to ten teenagers along with their parents and romantic partners. "Gossip Girl" is supposed to be an anonymous female blogger, someone who has an eerily intimate knowledge of the main characters' lives. Inside the storyworld, Gossip Girl's audience includes the main characters as well as teens and tweens all over the more privileged neighborhoods of New York City. The boundaries of that fictive audience are blurred and seem to include the viewing audience itself. Gossip Girl's voice-over interpolates sarcastic comments after a scene has just ended or before one is about to begin, and is often addressed directly to characters, using special nicknames for them, as in "Poor B." or "Look out, Little J."

Each episode begins with Gossip Girl's greeting to her fictive addressees: "Hey, Upper East-siders! Gossip Girl here." This would seem to exclude actual viewers, but each episode ends with a mocking direct address to the blog's audience that can just as easily speak to the series' fans: "You know you love me. XOXO, Gossip Girl." The final episode reveals Gossip Girl's identity: she is, somewhat expectedly, a member of the core group, who turns out, rather unexpectedly, not to be one of the girls, but rather Dan Humphrey (Penn Badgely), a male classmate of theirs from a slightly lower socioeconomic background who resents their higher status. As with other homodiegetically narrated TV series, the narrative situation stretches plausibility to the point of absurdity, since there is no way Dan could know the intimate details of, for example, the story's many bedroom scenes that do not involve him.

The voice of "Gossip Girl" is a narrative conceit; again, it is a structural acknowledgement of TV's self-conscious fictitiousness, and it projects the viewing stance of an audience whose sophisticated awareness of TV's narrative structures will make both the mystery and the revelation ironically amusing.[7] Both

---

[7] Not all fans of a show like this one are willing to play the part of ironic super-sophisticate; some internet fan-bloggers expressed dismay at how 'unrealistic' Gossip Girl's identity turned out to be.

How I Met Your Mother and *Gossip Girl*, then, feature self-referential, framed narrative structures that call into question their narrators' reliability while employing a dual direct address that encourages the actual viewer to imitate the fictive listeners' activity. At the same time, the actual viewer is also allowed to take on an amused, distanced stance. In these series, the actual audience gets to have it both ways, reveling in the enjoyment of lightweight entertainment while simultaneously enjoying an ironic take on material and, by inference, a medial activity, that does not aspire to be taken too seriously.

2 Direct Address in the Documentary Mode

The second type of address we shall take up has arguably been the most prolific in contemporary TV series: the documentary mode, which evokes news and interview formats. In examples fitting into this group, a speaker addresses either an interlocutor who is present on the scene, whether on or off-camera (as in a talk show or some kinds of documentary) or the apparatus itself (as in news programs). While this mode is similar to the narratorial mode in that it also involves verbal address, the central means of evoking the directedness towards an addressee here are usually visual, involving the positioning of the speaker's body, the *mise en scène*, and the camera. Address in documentary or interview modes has become a very frequently used feature in contemporary fictional TV, whether as an add-on in otherwise more classically fictional formats (as in *The Good Wife* [2009–2016]) and *Parks and Recreation* [2009–2015]), a device used in standalone documentary-style episodes, e.g. "X-Cops" in *The X-Files* (1993–2002), "Access" in *The West Wing* (1999–2006), or "These Arms of Mine" in *Grey's Anatomy* (2005–present), or as a key stylistic element framing a whole series (as in *The Office* [2005–2013] or *Modern Family*).[8]

Many series incorporate the interview as a particular medial situation into the storyline of an episode, depicting a character in the story as a moderator or an interviewee for a TV program. The production, broadcasting, and reception of this program can then be inserted into the story, as in a frame narrative. In *How I Met Your Mother*, for example, Robin's appearances as a TV reporter and news anchor are represented both directly and through the eyes of her friends, who

---

[8] See Warhol's analysis of direct address in mockumentary and reality TV in *Narrative Theory Unbound: Queer and Feminist Interventions* (2015).

become the intradiegetic audience for her broadcasts. This layered address is frequently used to create comic effects, for example when the professional demeanor Robin seeks to adopt on-camera is contradicted by information her friends have about her. In some instances these scenes also add to the complexity of her character, allowing the series to explore the relations between her public and her private persona, while placing the actual audience in the position of learning to know her in tandem with the other characters' apprehension of who she is.

A series that makes especially sophisticated use of such insertions is CBS's *The Good Wife*, whose title character, Alicia Florrick (Julianna Margulies), is a politician's wife who in the course of the series develops her own political ambitions. In order to advance her husband's and then also her own career, Alicia is obliged to participate in various news interviews, which are represented not just as products, but also in process. There are multiple levels of address in these representations: in the studio, Alicia addresses the host, who, as she understands, is an adversary as much as an interlocutor. More often than not, the interviews are represented as resembling duels, with Alicia striving to present a particular kind of image, while the interviewer tries to catch her off balance. Both characters are also in turn involved in a performance for the benefit of the fictive TV audience within the storyworld. That the reaction of this larger audience can be manipulated, but never fully anticipated or controlled is highlighted in plot strands involving the PR manager Eli Gold (Alan Cummings), whose job it is to let his clients appear in the best light and to assess publicity ratings after the interviews. Besides implying the power of the public as an important, but anonymous addressee, *The Good Wife* also represents specific members of the audience of Alicia's and her husband's medial performances – in particular, the reactions of their children, Zach (Graham Phillips) and Grace (Makenzie Vega). The multilayered representation of different levels of address and reception reinforces the main themes of the series, which explores the struggles involved in self-fashioning and the advantages and disadvantages of being assigned certain images in a hypermediated society. The series represents Alicia's story as a process of learning how to control her self-image, thus negotiating problems of morality and authenticity that are not at all resolved by the series's finale.

Moreover, through the complex layering of levels of address, the process of the actual viewing of *The Good Wife* is projected as involving processes of ethical evaluation. The TV series presents itself as a medium which can reflect on the problem of medial self-fashioning and thus perform a critique of contemporary media (both the more traditional news media and the new social/digital media, which in *The Good Wife* more often than not are represented as menacing).[9] The series's continued emphasis on the imbrication of media and identity contributes to its construction of a knowing viewer who understands the complexities of the media environment, an addressee with whom the sophisticated consumer of TV is invited to identify.

A different way of employing a documentary mode of direct address as a framing device can be seen in the ABC family sitcom *Modern Family*.[10] The most noticeable mockumentary element in *Modern Family* is the frequent shift to interview sequences with the characters, often in pairs. The style of some of these interviews is reminiscent of the confessional mode in reality shows such as *Keeping Up with the Kardashians* (2007–present) rather than a classical documentary: characters offer reactions and commentary to emotional subjects. There are also other aspects suggesting a reality show format, for example the at times jerky single-camera movements and the inclusion of 'authentic' footage such as wedding celebration videos. However, the characters in *Modern Family* do not refer to the presence of a camera crew, and there is no explanation for the mockumentary frame. The series, then, evokes the format of the reality show without in fact presenting itself *as* a reality show. It thus does not have to deal with all the implications of the format, for example the question why this family would invite a camera team into its everyday life. At times, its mode of address is distancing – in particular when situational irony is used in order to undercut a character's commentary. This happens particularly often in the case of Phil Dunphy, who rarely acts in ways that justify his self-image as a 'cool dad.' Ultimately, however, the interview sequences serve as devices enlisting the viewer's sympathy for the characters, who despite their various foibles show themselves to be good-hearted and loyal to each other.

In this sense, the effect of 'documentary' direct address in *Modern Family* is not unlike the 'writing to the moment' technique in the epistolary novel, which promises the fictive addressee access to both spontaneous reactions and authentic feelings on the part of the character. While in *The Good Wife*, the complex layering of documentary framing serves to project a critical viewing stance, *Modern Family* has assimilated the format of the mockumentary into the fictional storyworld, where it becomes a mainly engaging means of characterization. In both

---

9 See, for example, the fifth-season episode of "Whack-a-Mole," which revolves around the sinister implications of a site closely modeled on Reddit.
10 See also Robyn's discussion of documentary address in *The Office*, which uses the framing device of a fictive TV crew filming and interviewing the employees in the office of the equally fictive Dunder Mifflin Paper Company (Warhol 2015).

series, the foregrounded use of documentary modes of self-representation can be read as a reflection of how integral medial self-fashioning has become to everyday life in the age of social media.

3 Direct Address in the Dramatic Mode

Arguably the most startling alignment of a narrative 'you' with the actual TV viewer occurs in our third category, a form that imitates a convention of stage performance: the monologue addressed directly to the theatrical audience. Familiar from plays like Shakespeare's *Richard III*, the dramatic monologue spoken to the viewers has long been a performative device for constructing the subjectivity of a duplicitous character. Richard's monologues construct an addressee who understands and accepts the necessity of his criminal actions, positioning viewers, in spite of ourselves, as accessories or even accomplices to the atrocities he commits. In that it calls attention to the stage by transgressing its boundaries, 'breaking the fourth wall' is always a moment of anti-mimetic metadrama, and its metafictional effects have become familiar in certain twenty-first-century TV dramas that assert their audiences's complicity with their protagonists' cynicism and criminal intent. The most prominent current example is *House of Cards*, in both its 1980s British version and its more recent Netflix adaptation. Indeed, the star of the American series, Kevin Spacey, has said that the protagonist of *House of Cards* would not exist without Richard III.[11]

Direct address to the camera is the chief stylistic quirk of *House of Cards*, whose Richard-like main character (Ian Richardson's Francis Urquhart in the BBC version and Kevin Spacey's Frank Underwood in the Netflix adaptation) poses as a respectable holder of political office while secretly carrying on extramarital affairs, manipulating legislative outcomes, and eventually committing and covering up more than one murder. Francis/Frank regularly turns to the camera to explain the sociopathic principles guiding his actions. The 'you' he addresses is both generic and personal. To be sure, the referent could sometimes be 'one' or 'I' ("When the money is coming your way, you don't ask any questions", season 2, episode 7). Yet Frank's philosophizing can also be directed to a personified

---

[11] In an interview on IndieWire, Spacey said "The truth is Frank wouldn't exist without Richard III. I mean that literally. Michael Dobbs wrote the book and the original [BBC] TV show in Britain based on Richard's direct address. I didn't invent that: Shakespeare invented that whole idea of making the audience a co-conspirator, bringing you in on his ideas and plans" (Thompson 2014).

'you,' framed as advice to someone who wants to emulate him ("The road to power is paved with hypocrisy – and casualties. Never regret.", season 2, episode 9).

Spacey's Frank treats the fictive audience as a trusted confidant who will appreciate his little jokes at the expense of other characters and who can be persuaded, cajoled, or even bullied into approving of his increasingly horrific actions. Frank sometimes conspiratorially turns his head and lowers his voice to speak to 'you,' while the other characters show no awareness of 'your' presence in the scene. As with the breaking of the fourth wall of the stage, the obvious artifice of this structure of address constructs a multi-layered viewing stance. Actual viewers are invited to reflect on their own reactions to Frank's schemes and crimes and are possibly startled by their potential for cynicism.

More generally, we would argue, direct address in the American *House of Cards* appears as a playful acknowledgement of a tendency in recent TV series to push their audiences's limits with regard to engaging with unethical protagonists, such as Tony Soprano (*The Sopranos* [1999–2007]), Walter White (*Breaking Bad* [2008–2013]), or Dexter Morgan (*Dexter* [2006–2013]).[12] The ending of the first episode of the second season highlights this point: after fifty minutes in which Frank has not once addressed the camera, but has committed a startling murder, he finally confronts 'us' while speaking to his own reflection in a mirror: "Did you think I had forgotten you? [Looks into the camera, or rather into the spot on the mirror where an interlocutor would be reflected, if someone were actually present with him on the scene.] Perhaps you hoped I had. Don't waste a breath mourning Miss Barnes. [...] There is only one rule: hunt or be hunted. Welcome back." In this metaleptic fusion of an addressee as a confidant and as a TV consumer returning for a new season (possibly harboring doubts about his or her appreciation of the series's main stylistic device), *House of Cards* slyly comments on its own premises.

House of Lies (2012–2016) takes the staginess of 'breaking the fourth wall' several steps further. A dramedy about a group of consultants who earn extravagant wages for giving corporate clients unscrupulous advice on how to increase profits, *House of Lies* draws attention to its structure of address in the same way that Adam McKay's 2015 film *The Big Short* does, through dramatic monologues framed by tableaux, another old stage tradition. The action will be proceeding, and a character will say something technical whose meaning may not be obvious to a general audience. Suddenly everyone else in the scene freezes, and the central character (Ryan Reynolds in *The Big Short* and Don Cheadle in *House of Lies*)

---

12 See Martin 2013, who charts the rise of the antihero in television series.

turns to the camera to explain what is going on, while the camera pans around the room to show the other characters' faces fixed in a moment of time.

In a tableau on stage all the actors are silent, but in the dramatic mode one voice persists, speaking explicitly to 'you,' the viewer. Usually the tableaux are created by freezing the camera image, although *House of Lies* sometimes emphasizes the artifice by having Cheadle walk among the other actors who are actually standing perfectly still in place, as he moves someone's hand here or someone else's elbow there to suggest that the other characters' immobilized bodies are present on the same diegetic plane with him while he is speaking to 'you,' as they would be if they were standing on a stage. His ability literally to manipulate his fellow characters like puppets mirrors what the consultants do with their clients. Like Richard III and Frank/Francis, he is also acting out drama's ability to engage 'you' directly, while at the same time drawing ironic attention to that act. The irony here is structured differently from the irony in the documentary mode. Whereas the mock-documentary mode on TV draws attention to the apparatus, the theatrical mode pretends the apparatus is not there. The actor's aside to 'you' seems to pierce the boundary of the television screen and enter the viewer's domestic space, an effect that could not be achieved in a cinema or even a live theatre performance. In an even more pronounced way than in the narratorial mode and in the documentary mode, direct address in the dramatic mode both adds to and implicitly comments on the artificiality and anti-mimetic status of television programs while insisting on TV's salience to everyday 'real' domestic life.

4 Conclusion

In contrast to many narratologists who are mainly concerned with the categorical differences between fictive addressee and real-life recipient, we were equally interested in how viewing stances are designed to appeal to an actual viewer in her or his role as a consumer of a particular medial product. Narratives have for a long time used direct address to reflect on the recipient in her or his role as a medial consumer (see, for instance, the portrayal of 'the reader' as a guest in a restaurant in Henry Fielding's novel *Tom Jones* [1749]). In the case of television series, it seems to us, that the continued appeal to the viewer as a consumer has a special urgency. The traditional dependence on advertisement as a source of money in the case of broadcast television, the 'televisual flow' (Raymond Williams) between advertisements and different program blocks, the insertion of television viewing into domestic routines (see Bryce 1987), the actual viewer's option of switching to a different channel: these factors all shape a medial environment geared towards retaining old and attracting new audience members.[13] A continued appeal to 'you,' then, is particularly important in the case of broadcast TV series, but it has also become important in the competition between broadcast and cable TV, which needs to attract paying audiences, and more recently in the still emerging market of streaming media. Against this background, it seems not surprising that *House of Cards*, as the first self-produced series produced by the streaming service Netflix, should focus so explicitly on the recipient as somebody who is to be confronted and enticed.

By playing with modes of audience address, TV series in the twenty-first century produce comic as well as creepy effects; they enhance the possibilities of complex characterization. Most notably, they self-consciously reflect on the present moment in the history of TV and its relationship to past forms, both in its own medium and in other modes of narrative. Our three modes are not meant to be mutually exclusive, as a given example could be analyzed as belonging to two or more of these categories. We have organized our examples to highlight differences in their use of direct address, but our taxonomy is, as we have said, only a loose one. What we call the narratorial mode of address is a verbal framing of what is shown audiovisually. The documentary mode is mainly visual and auditory, as the addressing gesture is constituted by the character's look into the camera, and it uses visual means to draw attention to the apparatus. Also mainly visual and auditory, the dramatic mode downplays the apparatus or ignores it altogether. In all three modes, TV series make use of well-established functions of direct address in the corresponding traditions – whether to enhance characterization, to evoke or reflect on normative ideologies, or to problematize the concept of authenticity. Most importantly, direct address is for us a gesture that invites investigation of the status of television itself not just as a narrative medium but as an active presence in the lives of flesh-and-blood audiences.

References

The Big Short. 2015. Directed by Adam McKay. Paramount Pictures.
Birke, Dorothee. 2016. *Writing the Reader: Configurations of a Cultural Practice in the English Novel*. Berlin and Boston: De Gruyter.

---

[13] This famously contrasts with the case of a book or a cinema film, where with the purchase of the medial object or the ticket the main commercial transaction is concluded.

Bryce, Jennifer. 1987. "Family Time and Television Use." In *Natural Audiences*, edited by Thomas Lindlof, 121–138. Norwood: Ablex.
Culler, Jonathan. 2002 [1975]. *Structuralist Poetics*. London: Routledge.
Fielding, Henry. 1974 [1749]. *The History of Tom Jones: A Foundling*. Vol. 1–2. Edited by Fredson Bowers. Oxford: Clarendon.
Fiske, John. 1987. *Television Culture*. London: Routledge.
Fludernik, Monika, ed. 1994. *Second-Person Narration*. Special issue. *Style* 28.3.
---. 1993. "Second Person Fiction: Narrative You as Addressee And/Or Protagonist." *Arbeiten aus Anglistik und Amerikanistik* 18: 217–247.
The Good Wife. 2009–2016. Created by Michelle and Robert King. CBS.
Gossip Girl. 2007–2012. Developed by Josh Schwartz and Stephanie Savage. The CW.
Grey's Anatomy. 2005–present. Created by Shonda Rhimes. ABC.
House of Cards. 2014–present. Created by Beau Willimon. Netflix.
House of Lies. 2012–2016. Created by Matthew Carnahan. Showtime.
How I Met Your Mother. 2005–2014. Created by Carter Bays and Craig Thomas. CBS.
Keeping up with the Kardashians. 2007–present. Produced by Ryan Seacrest, Jonathan Murray et al. E!
Kuhn, Markus. 2011. *Filmnarratologie: Ein erzähltheoretisches Analysemodell*. Berlin and Boston: De Gruyter.
Martin, Brett. 2013. *Difficult Men. Behind the Scenes of a Creative Revolution: From "The Sopranos" and "The Wire" to "Mad Men" and "Breaking Bad."* New York: Penguin.
Mittell, Jason. 2015. *Complex TV: The Poetics of Contemporary Television Storytelling*. New York: NYU Press.
Modern Family. 2009–present. Created by Christopher Lloyd and Stephan Levitan. ABC.
The Office. 2005–2013. Developed by Greg Daniels. NBC.
Parks and Recreation. 2009–2015. Created by Greg Daniels and Michael Schur. NBC.
Schmid, Wolf. 2013 [2007]. "Textadressat." In *Handbuch Literaturwissenschaft*, vol. 1., edited by Thomas Anz, 171–181. Stuttgart: Metzler.
Sex and the City. 1998–2004. Created by Darren Star. HBO.
Thompson, Anne. 2014. "Kevin Spacey Q & A: 'House of Cards' Wouldn't Exist Without Richard III, Focus of Self-Released Doc." *IndieWire*, 2 May. Accessed 2 May 2016. Web.
Warhol, Robyn. 1989. *Gendered Interventions: Narrative Discourse in the Victorian Novel*. New Brunswick: Rutgers University Press.
---. 2015. "Giving an Account of Themselves: Metanarration and the Structure of Address in *The Office* and *Real Housewives*." In *Narrative Theory Unbound: Queer and Feminist Interventions*, edited by Robin Warhol and Susan S. Lanser, 59–77. Columbus: Ohio State University Press.
The West Wing. 1999–2006. Created by Aaron Sorkin. NBC.
The Wonder Years. 1988–1993. Created by Neal Marlens and Carol Black. ABC.
The X-Files. 1993–2002. Created by Chris Carter. Fox.

Vera Nünning and Ansgar Nünning
How to Stay Healthy and Foster Well-Being with Narratives, or: Where Narratology and Salutogenesis Could Meet

1 Introduction: Salutogenesis as a Challenge and Chance for Narratology and an Interdisciplinary Narrative Theory

Although narratology and narrative theory in general have been, and continue to be, among the most burgeoning disciplines or fields in the humanities and social sciences, the question about the performative quality of narratives implied in the title of this volume, *How to Do Things with Narrative*, has not yet received as much attention as it deserves. It has been widely acknowledged that narratives are among the most important and powerful ways of self-, community-, identity-, sense-, and worldmaking, but narrative theory has only recently begun to be concerned with the cultural work that narratives do, the storyworlds projected by factual or real-world narratives, and the performative functions that storytelling in such domains as politics, law, economics, journalism, medicine, and other areas can fulfil. While there is general agreement, e.g. in autobiography studies, that narratives and storytelling are key to making selves, as the felicitous subtitle of Paul John Eakin's seminal monograph *How Our Lives Become Stories: Making Selves* (1999) has it, narrative theory has not explored in much detail how people actually do things with narrative in many domains over and beyond literature.

One of the most interesting fields in question is arguably health studies, in which narratologists have hitherto, to the best of our knowledge, largely feared to tread. Narrative theorists' lack of interest in health and medicine comes as a particular surprise in the context of the issue raised by the title of this volume, in that both doctors and patients do a lot of interesting and important things with narratives. In addition, there is also considerable conceptual overlap between narrative studies and what has come to be known as 'salutogenesis.' Although narratives figure prominently in many natural or real-life narratives within the health-care system, the question of storytelling's health benefits has as yet neither been properly gauged nor been conceptually explored by narrative theorists, or in interdisciplinary narrative studies at large, for that matter. Anyone who wants to read up on the subject in what is certainly the best, most comprehensive and most up-to-date reference work on narratology, i.e. the seminal *Routledge Encyclopedia of Narrative Theory* (Herman, Jahn, and Ryan 2005), will find out that even this excellent encyclopedia has neither an entry on the term 'health' or 'health studies' nor on related concepts like 'salutogenesis' or 'sense of coherence.' To give this indispensable reference work its due, it is only fair to add that the *Routledge Encyclopedia* does feature an excellent entry on "Medicine and Narrative," which presents a very informative overview of recent research on the forms and functions of narratives in relation to medicine and illness, including some references on health. However, the emphasis in this entry is on illness narratives, narratives about illness, and narratives as a clinical tool. The default of the field of narrative medicine is thus pathography and pathogenetic issues rather than salutogenesis. One also looks in vain for entries on the subject of both this volume and our essay in other recent reference works in narratology, including the extremely useful *Handbook of Narratology* (2014 [2009]) edited by Peter Hühn and others, but also in encyclopedias and handbooks that cover approaches and concepts of literary and cultural theory at large.

In this essay, we will make a modest attempt at bridging the gap between the importance of storytelling for health and well-being, including the field known as 'narrative medicine' (see Charon 2008), and the scant attention that this phenomenon has so far been given by narrative theorists, but also by narrative medicine itself, which has mainly focused on pathographies and practical issues. This essay addresses some of the terminological and narratological issues pertaining to key concepts of salutogenesis, providing an outline of a salutogenetic narrative theory and of the functions narratives can fulfil for fostering health and well-being. Focusing on the interfaces between what is called a sense of coherence (SoC) and the qualities of narratives, the overarching objective of this essay is to offer a set of conceptual principles that can account for the formal features and the functions that narratives play for staying healthy and well.

More specifically, this essay stakes out three main aims: taking into consideration those fields in which the significance of narratives for health has been recognized, the first aim is to take stock, and provide a rough map, of those approaches and research areas in which some of the issues surrounding the proposed salutogenetic narratology have already been discussed (section 2). After this bottom-up introduction to the topic at hand, we will secondly try to outline a trajectory from the well-established field of narrative medicine to a salutogenetic narratology by exploring the interfaces between several of the key concepts developed in narrative theory and salutogenesis, teasing out some of the main conceptual overlaps, commonalities, and parallels of concern. In section 3, we will conceptualize and outline our notion of a salutogenetic narratology by providing a brief overview of some of the narratological approaches and concepts that could fruitfully be deployed in salutogenesis. The main aim is thus to enrich the conceptual repertoire of salutogenesis by developing a set of categories for the narratological description and analysis of narratives in the context of salutogenesis, with an eye to developing some steps towards a poetics of narrative continuity, coherence, and healing ruptures (section 3). The third aim of this essay is to provide some hypotheses about the functions that narratives and storytelling can fulfil for staying healthy and fostering well-being, further enriching the framework of a narrative salutogenesis or a salutogenetic narrative theory (section 4). A short summary and a brief look at some of the points and questions that future research could profitably explore will complete this essay (section 5).

2 Where Narrative Theory and Salutogenesis (Have So Far Failed to) Meet: Narratology, Narrative Medicine and the Co-Emergence of Multidisciplinary Narrative Research

The question of whether narrative and other key concepts developed in and by narratology are indeed 'traveling concepts' that have crossed the disciplinary border between literary studies and health and medicine seems as good a place to begin as any for anyone interested in exploring the questions of where narrative theory and salutogenesis could, but have so far largely failed to, meet, and why narratives can play an important role for staying healthy and well. Anyone reading such excellent collections of essays as *Narratology beyond Literary Criticism: Mediality, Disciplinarity* (Meister 2005), *Narratology in the Age of Cross-Disciplinary Narrative Research* (Heinen and Sommer 2009), or *Current Trends in Narratology* (Olson 2011), will probably be inclined to deduce from the very titles that narratology has indeed traveled far beyond literary studies and that it has become a truly inter- or even transdisciplinary endeavor in this 'age of cross-disciplinary research.' One might even jump to the conclusion that such recently emerging or established fields like narrative medicine were largely inspired by, or even inconceivable without, narratology. Whether this is really so, however, is an open question.

On the one hand, there are several reasons why one could indeed argue that narratology and some of its key concepts have become, or are becoming, 'travelers,' in that they have enriched cross-disciplinary narrative research or inspired work on narrative in disciplines outside the humanities. Three of these reasons deserve to be singled out. First of all, there has been a "Narrativist Turn in the Human Sciences" (Kreiswirth 1995) and a "Narrative Turn in the Humanities" (Kreiswirth 2005), as testified to by such volumes as *Narrative in Culture: The Uses of Storytelling in the Sciences, Philosophy, and Literature* (Nash 1990), the seminal and truly interdisciplinary *Routledge Encyclopedia of Narrative Theory* (Herman, Jahn, and Ryan 2005), and recent trends in narratology. Second, as Heinen, Meister, Olson, and other narratologists have shown, narratology has assumed an ever more important role in narrative research across the disciplines. What Heinen observes about narrative research has also become, at least partly, true of narratology:

> Narrative research is no longer confined to literary studies but has gained great currency in many other disciplines within the humanities and social sciences, ranging from cultural and media studies to linguistics, to historical theory and historiography, to anthropology, philosophy, theology, psychology, pedagogy, political science, medicine, law and economics. (Heinen 2009, 193)

Third, what Werner Wolf has called "The Transmedial Expansion of a Literary Discipline" (2011) is especially obvious and pertinent in transgeneric, intermedial, and interdisciplinary applications of narratology (see Nünning and Nünning 2002; Heinen 2009, 196). Narratology is indeed no longer merely a theory of verbal narrative (see Wolf 2011, 146), but has become equally interested in both issues of media and mediality, and in the forms and functions of narratives in other media (see Ryan 2004), and discourses (see Klein and Martínez 2009).

On the other hand, there are also a number of good reasons why one might want to challenge the claims that narratology and its key concepts are indeed paradigm examples of traveling theories and concepts, and that they have made significant contributions to the development of narrative medicine and other interdisciplinary research fields that have recently emerged. Although the ongoing development and proliferation of ever more narratologies (see Herman 1999; Alber and Fludernik 2010) does indeed seem to support the view that "narratology is increasingly appealed to as a master discipline" (Fludernik 2005, 47), a closer look at the history and state-of-the-art of 'narrative research across the disciplines' (see Heinen 2009) suggests that what we are faced with is, more often than not, various more or less independent trajectories of scholarship in different disciplines that have more or less independently displayed sustained interest in narrative. All of the disciplines within the humanities and social sciences that are usually mentioned in recent overviews and histories of narrative theory, e.g. linguistics, media studies, historiography, anthropology, philosophy, psychology and psychoanalysis, medicine, political science, economics as well as law and legal discourse (see Fludernik 2005, 47–48; Heinen 2009, 193; Klein and Martínez 2009), have their own and very rich disciplinary tradition of narrative research. Moreover, though there are many different theoretical frameworks and context- or culture-sensitive interpretations of individual narratives in many of these disciplines, the great interest has largely been multidisciplinary rather than inter- or transdisciplinary in nature. With regard to the interface between narrative theory as developed largely in literary studies, and narrative research in the social sciences and narrative medicine, there has been relatively little interdisciplinary traffic or traveling of concepts.

So what we are faced with is not so much a case of narrative and narratogical tools as 'traveling concepts,' but rather a complex co-emergence of interest in the forms, role, and functions of narrative and storytelling in a wide array of disciplines. Each of these fields has developed its own research traditions, paradigms, and concepts, not many of which are narratological in either nature or origin, suffice it to say that any story about either narratology or narrative research across the disciplines can ever hope to offer is just one "of the countless possible plots" in a field that has been "a garden of forking paths" (Onega and García Landa 1996, 36) for some time, but that has recently even turned into a highly complex landscape, or labyrinth, characterized by divergent tendencies, numerous trajectories, and peaceful co-existence of diverse disciplinary traditions that have often failed to meet and profit from one another's work.

One might thus even go so far as to argue that the metaphor of traveling may be misleading. To take but two examples: the rich tradition of narrative research developed in historiography and the theory of history that has been dubbed the 'narrativist school of historiography' and that includes such luminaries as David Carr, Arthur Danto, Jörn Rüsen, and Hayden White was developed largely independently from narratology, although there are important go-betweens equally well-versed in both fields, most notably Philippe Carrard (1992; see also Jaeger 2002). Another case in point of such fruitful co-existence, or co-emergence, of interest in narrative in two largely unrelated fields is the equally rich tradition of narrative psychology that is associated with the work of Jerome Bruner, Jens Brockmeier, Michele Crossley, Donald Polkinghorne, Theodore Sarbin, Jürgen Straub, and many other researchers (for overviews, see Echterhoff 2002; Crossley 2005), and that has also displayed little if any interest in narratology. The same holds true for narrative research in other disciplines in the humanities and social sciences, including medicine, political science, economics, and law or legal discourse (for very good overviews, see the articles in Klein and Martínez 2009).

On the whole, the notion of a co-emergence of interest in narratives in many disciplines seems a more appropriate way of conceptualizing the manifold developments in cross-disciplinary narrative research in general, and the peaceful coexistence of narratology and narrative medicine in particular. Moreover, as excellent recent volumes that chart current trends in narratology serve to show, illness, medicine, and health are not yet among the most important areas or directions into which cross-disciplinary narrative research has been developing in the last decade or so. As Monika Fludernik and Greta Olson (2011) have shown, the emphasis lies rather on cognitive approaches, transgeneric, transmedial, and interdisciplinary narrative study, and in attempts at reconstructing local and national research traditions in narratology itself (see the essays in the volumes edited by Ryan 2004; Meister 2005; Heinen and Sommer 2009; Olson 2011). While there have been sophisticated attempts at mediating cognitivist and culturalist approaches in other interdisciplinary fields like metaphor theory (see, for example, Fludernik, Freeman, and Freeman 1999), narratology has to date largely continued to shy away from the study of pressing cultural and social concerns in general, and health and medicine in particular.

There have, of course, been laudable exceptions, most notably Mieke Bal, Monika Fludernik (1999, 2007), and Wolfgang Müller-Funk (2012), but not many have followed their context-sensitive work on the relation between cultural contexts and narratives, or heeded Mieke Bal's clarion-call "from narratology to cultural analysis" (1999), but even these and other well-known narrative theorists have displayed little if any interest in the health benefits of narrative and storytelling. While practitioners of such new approaches as feminist narratology, postcolonial narratology, or intercultural narratology have begun putting the analytic toolkits of narratology "to the service of other concerns considered more vital for cultural studies" (Bal 1990, 729), narratology has so far largely failed to explore what the functions of narratives are and what the cultural work that they do consists in. Bal was the first narratologist to ask a question which sounds very simple, but which is as important as it is invaluable for anyone interested in gauging the functions, uses, and usefulness of narratives and narratology: "what's the point?" (1990, 729). If narrative theory managed to come to terms with the health benefits of narratives, it would certainly be in a much better position to demonstrate what "The Point of Narratology," as Bal's article is tellingly entitled, might be.

However, there is one domain or emerging research field in which the important role that narratives play for health and illness has been explicitly acknowledged and explored. We are, of course, referring to interdisciplinary studies on the role of stories of health and illness, often subsumed under the umbrella term of 'medicine and narrative' (Hydén 2005), or just 'narrative medicine' (Charon 2008). Scholars working in this "narrative field of health, illness, and culture" (Hydén and Brockmeier 2008b, 10), have mainly explored illness narratives, i.e. stories told by patients or relatives trying to make sense of their experiences, symptoms and the presumed origins of their health problems, and narratives about illness. While illness narratives present paradigm examples of 'broken narratives' (see Nünning and Nünning 2016), narratives about illness are among the central means of medical illness-, self-, and worldmaking (see Hydén 2005). The latter are an important "means, especially for medical doctors, of assembling and integrating information from various sources, and articulating and communicating clinical knowledge" (Hydén 2005, 295). Studies in the field of narrative medicine look at the ways in which narratives and stories contribute to the personal, cultural, and institutional constructions of health and illness, often focusing on the role of narrativity and broken narratives in accounts of suffering and healing (see Becker 1997), and on "narrative as a clinical tool" (see Hydén 2005, 296).

Three salient examples of the kind of work done in this field are the volumes *Narrative and the Cultural Construction of Illness and Healing* (see Kirmayer 2000; Mattingly and Garro 2000), and *Health, Illness and Culture: Broken Narratives* (Hydén and Brockmeier 2008a), and, most notably, Rita Charon's magisterial overview of the conceptual and practical underpinnings of narrative medicine. In his pioneering essay "Broken Narratives: Clinical Encounters and the Poetics of Illness Experience" (2000, 154), Laurence J. Kirmayer not only shows how "identity can become fragmented through ruptures in narrative." One of the many interesting insights of his analysis of the poetics and pragmatics of clinical storytelling is that broken narratives typically display certain stylistic signs of incoherence, discontinuity, and fragmentation, and that these signs can be interpreted as textual manifestations of "threats to the narrative coherence of the self" (2000, 155). Though Kirmayer does not venture a definition or explication of the key term of broken narratives, he does provide a valuable catalogue of "the many ways that narratives are broken" (2000, 169) in clinical encounters, rightly emphasizing that such clinical narratives display distinctive features that set them off from storytelling in other scenarios and, even more so, from literary narratives.

For Charon (2008, 17), narrative medicine is, first and foremost, "a very practical undertaking" that "not only describes an ideal of health care but also provides practical methods to develop the skills needed to reach that ideal" (2008,

10). As the emphasis on the ethical obligation in the subtitle of her book, *Honoring the Stories of Illness*, already serves to indicate, she uses the term "to mean medicine practiced with these narrative skills of recognizing, absorbing, interpreting, and being moved by the stories of illness" (2008, 4). According to Charon, narrative medicine is thus "medicine practiced with narrative competence" (2008, 10), while "narrative ways of knowing and experiencing the world and self are held in common by health care professionals and patients" (2008, 39).

Proceeding from the observation that narratives and storytelling are much more crucial for health care and medicine than most of its practitioners usually realize, Charon is one of the few scholars to emphasize "that narrative *does* things for us" (2008, 39), thus making an unwitting reference to the title and topic of the volume at hand. Although she does not systematically pursue the question of what it is that narrative *does* for us, she stresses that narrative is an irreplaceable "instrument for self-knowledge and communion" (2008, 40). Moreover, Charon is also one of the few researchers working in narrative medicine who make more than just some passing reference to narrative theory. More specifically, she outlines and discusses "five narrative features of medicine – temporality, singularity, causality/contingency, intersubjectivity, and ethicality" (2008, 39).

As this all-too-brief summary may have served to show, there are obvious parallels of concern between narrative medicine, on the one hand, and narratology and salutogenesis, on the other, but they clearly differ in terms of aims, emphasis, frameworks, and scope. Narrative medicine is not so much a theoretical project or a narratologically informed analysis or study of the stories of health and illness, but revolves around a very practical concern, i.e. "developing narrative competence" (Charon 2008, 105), in order to make tangible improvements in health care and effective treatment for patients. Moreover, though Charon's monograph is one of the relatively rare examples of work in narrative medicine that features some references to canonical works in narratology (see 2008, 14, 40–41, 49, 61), it is not as informed by state-of-the-art concepts in narratology as one might wish as a narrative theorist. As the list of the five narrative features of medicine that she singles out for discussion demonstrates, she is much more interested in the ethicality and intersubjectivity of storytelling in the singular contexts in which they occur in the health-care system than in the formal description of the features of narratives or their functions over and beyond general notions of narratives as ways of meaning-making and of "knowing and experiencing the world and self" (2008, 39). Moreover, while the emphasis in narrative medicine is generally on stories of illness or pathographies, a salutogenetic narratology as outlined in the next section is more interested in exploring the importance of narratives for staying healthy and well.

The multidisciplinary co-emergence of interest in the role and functions of narratives in various disciplines outlined in this section raises the question of how the exchange of concepts and ideas between narrative theory and the study of health and illness could be fostered. Taking stock of some of the key concepts of these two and exploring conceptual overlaps between them might be a useful starting-point for charting a trajectory from recent developments in narrative medicine to the kind of salutogenetic narrative theory that we envisage and attempt to outline.

3 From Narrative Medicine to a Salutogenetic Narrative Theory: Conceptual Overlaps between Salutogenesis and Narratology

Let us now turn our attention to the two interfaces between the main research fields that this essay is mainly concerned with: narrative theory, or cross-disciplinary narrative research, and narrative medicine and salutogenesis, or the study of health. Although these two fields have a number of parallels of concern, narratology has not yet heeded the call that Charon made almost ten years ago: "Narrative theory and practice hold out the promise of a set of solutions of the hobbling isolation and divisions that currently plague and weaken our medicine" (2008, 198). If scholars working in the fields of narrative theory and analysis had managed to display as much interest in health, illness, medicine, the conceptual underpinnings of these fields, and of salutogenesis, as scholars like Rita Charon have in narrative theory, then they might have managed to overcome their own hobbling isolation and the divisions that currently plague and weaken the competing approaches in classical and postclassical narratology.

A brief exploration of some of their key concepts may be a useful starting point to show why narrative medicine and salutogenesis, on the one hand, and narrative theory and analysis, on the other, can mutually benefit from each other. Although the respective approaches have largely been developed independently from each other, the conceptual overlap between them is striking. As Charon has convincingly demonstrated, medicine is not only "a more narratively inflected enterprise than it realizes" (2008, 39); it also has narrative features that were for a long time largely unacknowledged. While singularity and intersubjectivity pertain mainly to the particularities and specificities of storytelling scenarios in the health-care system and in medicine at large, temporality, causality, contingency, and ethicality are among the concepts that have also been fully elaborated in narrative theory. Charon even goes so far as to argue that her "new philosophy of medical knowledge is a narrative one" (2008, 39).

There are also other concepts and concerns that provide even more common ground for fruitful collaboration. These include the concepts of narrative knowledge, narrative competence and such genuine narratological terms like narrator, point of view, and narrative perspective. Sharing interest in the narrative quality of knowledge, both narrative medicine and narratology conceive of narrative as a mode of knowing that enables people to make sense of their experiences and cognitive processes. Conceiving of narratives and stories as 'tools for thinking' (see Herman 2003), one can reasonably assume that narrative competence plays an important role in people's sense of well-being. One of the key aims of the project of narrative medicine is "developing narrative competence," as part three of Charon's book is tellingly entitled. It is reasonable to assume that a more sophisticated knowledge of the forms, structures, and functions of narratives are as important for the development of narrative competence as experience in close reading (the topic of chapter 6 of Charon's book), the refinement of attention, the ability to truly listen to the narratives that others tell, and to honor their stories of crises, health, illness, and redemption.

What the latter involves is, of course, the ability to adopt the point of view of others (see Charon 2008, 174), i.e. a complex process of cognitive and emotional activities that is dubbed 'perspective-taking' in narrative theory and cognitive psychology. There is an impressive amount of empirical evidence by now that reading fiction enhances people's empathy and their ability to take the perspective of others (see V. Nünning 2014, Ch. 5). Given the cognitive similarities between comprehending human beings and human-like fictional characters, fictional narratives can function as a privileged means of simulation, the more so because they are usually concerned with specific events and provide contexts for the understanding of characters and their actions. In narrative fiction, aesthetic devices of foregrounding and of inducing perspective-taking guide readers' attention to the specificities of the characters' emotions, thought-processes, and interactions. As fictional stories provide more information about characters than is usually available in personal interactions, they even make it possible to take the perspectives of strangers and characters with unfamiliar backgrounds. Readers can follow the mental processes of unfamiliar others, thus practising extraordinary ways of thinking that are beyond their usual repertoire of cognitive processes in oral communication and other natural narratives. Fictional narratives often "require their readers to inhabit alien spheres and to adopt and respect contradictory points of views" (Charon 2008, 212). Reading fiction can thus serve to practise and hone the kind of perspective-taking that is also required with regard to narrative competence in medical contexts.

In addition to these conceptual overlaps between narrative medicine and narrative theory, Aaron Antonovsky's (see 1991, 1997, 1998) key term for the definition and understanding of salutogenesis, i.e. the concept of a 'sense of coherence,' is not only a or even the crucial factor for people's sense of mental and physical well-being; it is also almost certainly connected to narrative competence and the reading of fictional, and factual, narratives. According to the salutogenesis model developed by Antonovsky and refined by many scientists working in his tradition (see Schüffel et al. 1998; Wydler 2000), this sense of coherence is a central prerequisite for mental and physical health.

The model illustrates that the concept of a 'sense of coherence' is constituted by three dimensions or factors which can be mapped onto concepts and concerns in narrative theory. First of all, 'comprehensibility' involves the degree to which internal and external stimuli can be interpreted in ways which not only make it possible to understand experiences and events, but it also enables human beings to make plans for the future. As research on narrative comprehension has convincingly demonstrated, narrative is among the crucial ways in which human beings comprehend what is happening in their lives and what is going on around them by creating mental models of the characters, contexts, events, and settings that constitute a story (see Emmott 1997).

Second, 'manageability' refers to the feeling or conviction that one has the necessary resources for coping with challenges, crises, problems, and stressful situations. This means that storytelling and the acquisition of narrative authority (see Lanser 1992; Dawson 2013) is an effective way not only of coming to terms with one's conflicting emotions and experiences; it is also a way of coping with crises and problems, enhancing one's sense of manageability. There can be little or no doubt, for instance, that especially in such fields as stories of illness and 'trauma studies,' broken narratives not only typically delineate "disrupted lives" (Becker 1997); they also serve to reintegrate disruptive experiences and re-establish a sense of coherence. In *Disrupted Lives*, Gaylene Becker explores how people (mainly Americans) deal with the increasingly disjunctive nature of the forms of life in late (post)modernity and how they try to cope with situations in which expectations about the course of life are no longer met, but are radically challenged. Becker examines "the major elements of a disrupted life – the disruption itself, a period of limbo, and a period of life reorganization" (1997, 2). In broken narratives and disrupted lives it is especially pertinent that their narrators make a sustained effort at reconstructing some kind of coherence and continuity, and that storytelling itself is an important means of regaining some sense of manageability and coherence.

The third aspect that defines one's sense of coherence, i.e. 'meaningfulness,' which refers to the ability to experience life as emotionally meaningful, is even more closely connected to narrative and narrative competence in that storytelling is a crucial tool for the creation of identities, meaning, and selves (see Eakin 1999, 2008). One of the central points of convergence shared by the different narrativist approaches which have been developed in many disciplines across the humanities and social sciences is the insight that narratives are one of the most important cultural ways of meaning-making. Explaining the choice of the title of one of his seminal monographs, the narrative psychologist Jerome Bruner (1990, xii) emphasizes the performative quality that storytelling has as an act of making meaning: "I have called it *Acts of Meaning* in order to emphasize its major theme: the nature and cultural shaping of meaning-making, and the central place it plays in human action." Charon describes the potential of narrative fiction to foster meaning-making in similar terms:

> Fiction's critical and irreplaceable consequences are to force readers to recognize the storied shape of reality, to understand in the most basic way that we create meaning by weaving the fragments of life into plot. (2008, 212)

The concept of coherence, as defined and used in textlinguistics and narratology, can be used as a convenient foil against which the specificity of narratives as a crucial way of enhancing a person's sense of coherence can be gauged. Characteristic elements that are regarded as essential to narrative coherence include "general expectations of unity, continuity and perseveration" (Toolan 2014 [2009], 66). As we have tried to demonstrate elsewhere (see Nünning and Nünning 2016), broken narratives not only disrupt narrative coherence on the story level, but also on the level of discourse, more often than not even challenging this cherished narratological binarism altogether. Like stories of illness, broken narratives constitute departures from the norms associated with the notion of coherence, typically defying conventional "expectations about time, intention, goal, causality, and closure" (Toolan 2014, 66). Following the distinctions made in textlinguistics between certain "main subtypes of coherence, such as temporal, causal, and thematic coherence" (Toolan 2014, 66), one can characterize stories of illness and other kinds of broken narratives as a deviation from, or even a violation of, all these subtypes of coherence: they "disrupt the ceaseless linear continuity of time" (Tamboukou 2010, 74), they suspend or question the belief in causal coherence, and they are characterized by abrupt thematic discontinuities, both within and between topics (see Armstrong 2002, 21). Conceptualizing broken narratives and stories of illness in terms of a deviation from narrative coherence thus not only sheds additional light on their features, it also serves to underline the close conceptual link that exists between narrative and narrative theory on the one hand, and medicine and salutogenesis, on the other. The key concept of a sense of coherence underscores the default notions of coherence, linearity, progression, and meaningfulness that we associate with stories of health and well-being.

Although the project of trying to combine narrative theory with the study of mental and physical health is still in its infancy, the interdisciplinary field of narrative medicine has not only shown how fruitful an assessment of the narrative features of medicine can be; it has also paved the way for developing an analogous project for what we have tentatively christened a salutogenetic narrative theory.

4 How to Do Things with Narrative – and What Narratives Can Do for Us, or: Reflections on the Salutogenetic Power of Narratives

On the basis of the conceptual underpinnings outlined in the previous section, we should now like to explore the question of why narratives are arguably very important for maintaining good health and fostering well-being. Although the pioneering work done in the field of narrative medicine has occasionally touched upon this issue, the salutogenetic power or potential of narratives have not been systematically explored. Another of Rita Charon's clarion-calls has largely gone unheeded, namely her salutogenetic effort to alert "doctors of all considerations that might help or hinder patients from [...] becoming true partners in achieving and maintaining the best health within their reach" (2008, 27).

The obvious reference to John L. Austin's foundational work of speech act theory, *How to Do Things with Words* (1962), in the title of the present volume highlights the performative quality of narratives, drawing attention as it does to the cultural, social, and political functions that speech acts and narratives fulfil. The title *How to Do Things with Narrative* presupposes that human beings do something when they tell stories, i.e. that narratives have a performative dimension analogous to what Austin defined as performative speech acts. It is not only people who do things with narrative, however, but narratives also do things for human beings. Taking our cue from both the title of this volume and from

Charon's felicitous observation "that narrative *does* things for us" (2008, 39), we should like to discuss some of the things that human beings do with narratives, while also taking into consideration that narratives do important things for us. Before we zoom in on the health benefits of narratives, we should first like to take a look at the performative power of narratives (see Nünning and Sommer 2011), i.e. address the question of what people can actually do with narrative.

Narratives, and by extension also narratology, are of special interest for an understanding of the performative quality of speech acts because narratives or storytelling are important cultural ways of self-, identity-, and worldmaking (see Goodman 1992 [1978]; Nünning, Nünning, and Neumann 2010). Narratives and narrative forms are not only related to culture and subject to historical variation, but are also bearers of meaning in their own right, cognitive tools and cultural ways of worldmaking that bestow sense and identity. In the introduction to *Making Stories*, Bruner emphasizes the performative quality that narrative and storytelling have as an act of meaning- and even worldmaking (see 2002, 8). The insight into the performative power of narration makes clear how great the interdisciplinary value of narratology for the study of health could be. If telling stories is a basic anthropological need felt by human beings, and if narratives are a central medium of creating identities, making worlds and fostering the sense of coherence that is so crucial for maintaining good health, then the theory of narrative could not only occupy centre stage in literary and cultural theory but also become a starting point of interdisciplinary research into health, illness, and salutogenesis.

In order to come to terms with the performative quality of narratives, narrative theory, however, needs to extend its aim and scope from the mere description of the features and forms of narratives to the cultural and psychological functions that narratives can fulfil. Instead of restricting its focus largely to narrative as a literary form or a macro-genre, an interdisciplinary narrative theory should rather extend its scope in such a way that it includes the broad range of forms and functions of narratives as cultural ways of self-, community-, sense-, and worldmaking across media. In order to get to grips with the complexities involved in narrative self- and worldmaking, narrative theory could greatly benefit by fostering the dialogue with narrative research in other disciplines, especially the social sciences and narrative medicine. Although such a claim may be misinterpreted as another case of "'narrative imperialism,' the impulse by students of narrative to claim more and more territory, more and more power for our object of study and our ways of studying it" (Phelan 2005, 206), we are convinced that narrative theory could, and should, shed more light on the performative power of narratives as important cultural ways of identity-, self-, coherence-, health-, and worldmaking. More specifically, this hypothesis is an answer to a question raised by Paul John Eakin in a rejoinder to Phelan's essay on narrative imperialism: "Should *Narrative* [the journal] stick to narrative narrowly conceived as a literary form or forms, or should it entertain a more adventurous approach to narrative as something to do with society, with identity, with the body?" (Eakin 2006, 186).

Rather than conceiving of such an "expansionist impulse" (Phelan 2005, 206) as a case of 'imperialism' or as another 'colonizing project' (see Phelan 2005, 206.), we should like to suggest that narrative theory would be better served by reframing such a move in terms of interdisciplinary collaboration and the notion of "travelling concepts," as launched by Mieke Bal (2002) and developed further in a volume entitled *Travelling Concepts for the Study of Culture* (Neumann and Nünning 2012) and recently applied to the study of narrative by Matti Hyvärinen, Mari Hatavara, and Lars-Christer Hydén (2013). In contrast to the kind of multidisciplinary co-emergence of interest in narrative in largely unrelated disciplines as described in section 2, a salutogenetic narrative theory would, however, have to be a truly inter- or even transdisciplinary project with a genuine export, import, and exchange of concepts that really do travel from one field to the other. Extending the aims and scope of narrative theory to include all the instances of narrative self- and worldmaking, especially factual narratives in the context of health-care and medicine, is not a strategic move but an acknowledgement of such a crucial role in many domains over and beyond literature, film, and the arts in general.

Since studying narrative self- and worldmaking, however, is a genuinely inter- or transdisciplinary project, literary narrative theory should foster a more sustained dialogue with narrative research in the social sciences (see Mildorf 2010). The credit for redirecting narrative theory to the issues of worldmaking probably goes to David Herman (see 2009) and his pioneering work on the topic at hand. It was also Herman who emphasized that "no one area of study can come to terms with the multidimensional complexity of narrative worldmaking" (Herman 2011, ix). If we want to come to terms with the forms, modes, and media involved in narrative worldmaking, we should heed Herman's reminder and follow in the footsteps of those colleagues who have not just advocated the interdisciplinary expansion of narrative studies, but also successfully engaged in collaborative ventures with the kind of narrative research done in the social sciences. As the essays in the volume tellingly entitled *Narratology in the Age of Cross-Disciplinary Narrative Research* (2009), edited by Sandra Heinen and Roy Sommer, for instance, demonstrate, narrative theory stands lots to gain by taking into consideration the rich tradition of narrative research in the social sciences and such emerging fields as narrative medicine (see Charon 2008; Frank 1995, 2010).

Although there is a broad consensus by now that narratives are of great importance for the ways in which we make sense of our experiences and the world, narrative theory has not yet been much concerned with either the ways in which narratives serve to make events, stories, and fictional or real worlds (see Nünning 2010), nor with the functions that narratives and narrative worldmaking can fulfil in various cultural, social, and political contexts. Narratives are at work in such processes as identity formation, forging of communities and nations, negotiating and disseminating norms and values, and fabricating storied versions of 'the world': "narrative, including fictional narrative, gives shape to things in the real world and often bestows on them a title to reality" (2002, 8), as Jerome Bruner aptly observed.

The constructivist notions which provide the epistemological underpinnings of Nelson Goodman's pioneering approach pertain to a wide range of different domains of worldmaking, including the making of stories of health and illness. The performative quality of narratives range all the way from creating identity (see Eakin 2008; Neumann, Nünning, and Pettersson 2008; Holler and Klepper 2013) and *Making Selves* (1999), to borrow the subtitle of Eakin's seminal book over the making of events and crises (see Nünning 2010, 2012b) to worldmaking in such domains as politics, law, medicine, and economics. The question of ways of worldmaking is particularly important in the case of narrative fiction, as well as other literary genres and artistic media in that literature and the arts function as world-building institutions, projecting alternatives to the world-models that we generally regard as 'reality.' In addition, narrative fictions often self-reflexively foreground and explore many of the epistemological and ontological questions involved in worldmaking, playing an important role as media of cultural self-observation and critique (see Butter 2007).

While there is quite a lot of research in studies of autobiography and life-writing on the ways in which narratives serve as one of the most important means of self-making, narrative theory has not been much concerned with the performative power that storytelling exerts in many domains beyond narrative fiction and autobiography. Narratives, for instance, also contribute to what may be called 'community-making,' with genres and culturally available plots serving as the main interfaces between the making of selves and the making of communities, which plays a key role for maintaining a sense of coherence. Moreover, narratives can be endowed with performative power, actively moulding, constructing, or even creating the cultural and ideological conflicts that they purport merely to reflect or represent. Instead of merely referring to actual conflicts, metaphors and narratives play an active role in generating them and in producing a hegemonic discourse that serves to interpret events in a particular way and to shape a shared cultural understanding of the world as projected in the hegemonic narrative. Several notable exceptions (see Salmon 2007; Klein and Martínez 2009; Bietz 2013) notwithstanding, narrative theory has yet to fully come to terms with such influential and ubiquitous narrative ways of worldmaking as "The News" (see de Botton 2014), the so-called 'social' networking services like Facebook, and the forms and functions of storytelling in organizations, politics, law, economics, and medicine. Let us just single out one example: As Alain de Botton shrewdly observes in his highly readable book *The News*: "The news […] fails to disclose that it does not merely report on the world, but is instead constantly at work crafting a new planet in our minds in line with its own often highly distinctive priorities" (2014, 11).

As we have tried to show in this section so far, human beings can do a lot of different things with narratives, but narratives also do important things for us like creating a coherent sense of who we are, or believe to be, in the first place. Against this general backdrop of the performative quality of storytelling in different contexts, we will round off this section by addressing the question of what people do with narrative in order to achieve and maintain the best health within their reach, and what narratives can do for us to stay healthy and well. Given the general neglect of the performative quality of narratives, it does not come as a big surprise that narrative theory has not yet displayed much interest in the role that narratives play for staying healthy and well. So what can people do with narrative in order to achieve and maintain the best health within their reach, and what can narratives do for us?

Both questions can, of course, be approached from a variety of different angles, depending, for instance, on what kinds of narratives are taken into consideration, whether the focus is on storytelling or reading narratives, and who the 'we' and 'us' are who do things with narratives and for whom stories do something. Since any attempt at providing a comprehensive account of the complex topic at hand would be doomed to failure, we will focus our reflections on the salutogenetic power of narratives on two areas: research on the health benefits of storytelling and the beneficial effects that reading narratives can have. Since we can only cover a fraction of the research done on these issues in such fields as cognitive science, cognitive and narrative psychology, and narrative medicine, we have singled out a number of recent publications that directly address the nexus between narratives and possible health benefits.

There is impressive evidence, for instance, that the processes of forming, narrating, and writing stories is beneficial for mental and physical health. As James W. Pennebaker and Janel D. Seagal have demonstrated in several experiments described in an article published in the *Journal of Clinical Psychology*, "writing about personal experiences in an emotional way brings about improvements in mental and physical health" (1999, 1243). Although they do not make any explicit references to the concepts of salutogenesis, the explanations they provide of the processes involved in forming a story could easily be mapped onto the three dimensions of a sense of coherence elaborated above: the process of constructing or forming a story

> allows one to organize and remember events in a coherent fashion while integrating thoughts and feelings. In essence, this gives individuals a sense of predictability and control of their lives. Once an experience has structure and meaning, it would follow that the emotional effects of that experience are more manageable. (1999, 1243)

It is certainly no coincidence that the health benefits are ascribed to forming a story. Storytelling is key to enhancing an individual's sense of coherence, which is so crucial for staying healthy and being well. In other words, the salutary effects that narratives evidently have on physical and mental health are explained in terms of the three factors that constitute the concept of a sense of coherence: 'comprehensibility,' i.e. the degree to which experiences can be interpreted in ways which make it possible to understand the events; 'meaningfulness'; and 'manageability,' i.e. the feeling that one has the necessary resources for coping and being in control. Although Pennebaker and Seagal freely admit that it is not clear what the underlying mechanisms responsible for the health benefits they describe in some detail are, their research suggests that "health gains appear to require translating experience into language" and that by integrating thoughts and feelings in the format of a story, "the person can construct more easily a coherent narrative of the experience" (1999, 1248).

These findings underscore the key hypothesis of this essay that storytelling and salutogenesis are closely intertwined, i.e. that narratives and a sense of coherence mutually reinforce each other. One of the most important insights of much recent work in narrative psychology is that narratives not only serve to make sense of critical events and disturbing experiences, but that putting them into stories also serves to provide some kind of explanation and "a sense of resolution" (Pennebaker and Seagal 1999, 1248). Moreover, there is a direct correlation between mastering the art of storytelling and "the development of a coherent emotional life" (1999, 1244): "A constructed story, then, is a type of knowledge that helps to organize the emotional effects of an experience as well as the experience itself" (1999, 1249).

Research on the role of narratives in emotion-focused therapy also confirms the hypothesis that storytelling can have salutary effects on mental and physical health. As the subtitle of their book *Working With Narrative in Emotion-Focused*

Therapy: Changing Stories, Healing Lives (2011) already serves to indicate, Lynne E. Angus and Leslie S. Greenberg manage to show that shaping personal experiences into narratives or stories is one of the most important meaning- and sense-making devices that human beings have at their disposal:

> Our sense of security develops when we can, with the help of others, regulate our affect and weave a coherent account of our emotional experience with others. When we become narrators of our own stories, we produce a selfhood that joins us with others and permits us to look back selectively to our past and shape ourselves for the possibilities of an imagined future. (2011, 3)

Although there is no direct reference to the work done in salutogenesis, the conceptual parallels to the dimensions that make up the sense of coherence are, again, quite obvious: While weaving a coherent account and producing a sense of selfhood joined with others ensures comprehensibility and meaningfulness, becoming narrators of our own lives is key to fostering a sense of manageability. Drawing on Jerome Bruner's seminal work, Angus and Greenberg not only emphasize that narratives are an indispensable means of self-, sense-, and meaning-making, they also point out that working with stories in their kind of emotion-focused therapy is likely to have similar health benefits to those described by Pennebaker and Segal in that emotion-focused therapy "promotes heightened personal agency" and "an enhanced sense of coherence and well-being in life" (2011, 7).

There is even more evidence that reading narratives, especially literary fiction, can have at least as many health benefits as telling and writing stories. The salutary effects of reading fiction include an enhancement of several cognitive and emotional abilities, especially an improvement of empathy, Theory of Mind, perspective-taking, and thus the ability to understand other human beings. Reading narrative fiction and being immersed in storyworlds can also hone narrative competence and serve as a privileged means of acquiring cognitive, affective, and social skills (see V. Nünning 2014). As the title of their paper in the widely read scholarly journal *Science*, "Reading Literary Fiction Improves Theory of Mind" (2013), boldly announces, the psychologists David Comer Kidd and Emanuele Castano have demonstrated that reading quality fiction, e.g. polyphonic novels by such writers as Charles Dickens and Téa Obreth, can enhance readers' ability to understand other people's emotions, improving empathy, and Theory of Mind. Given the fact that the ability to adopt other people's perspectives and to look at the world from different points of view "is a crucial skill that enables the complex social understandings that characterize human societies" (2013, 377), it is reasonable to assume that the engagement with narratives which foster such crucial skills will also have salutary effects for mental and physical health and general well-being.

These assumptions are corroborated by a host of recent research in the cognitive sciences. In a review article dating from August 2016, the renowned Canadian psychologist Keith Oatley, who has made some of the most original and important contributions to research in this field himself, provides a concise and very informative overview of the most important findings and insights. According to Oatley, the salutary effects of reading fiction on readers' cognitive abilities described in the previous paragraph are "due partly to the process of engagement in stories, which includes making inferences and becoming emotionally involved, and partly to the contents of fiction, which include complex characters and circumstances that we might not encounter in daily life" (2016, 618). As the title of his review article, "Fiction: Simulation of Social Worlds," serves to highlight, narrative fictions open up the possibility to augment and foster readers' everyday cognition and social understanding because they essentially simulate the complexity of characters interacting in imaginary social worlds: "Fiction is the simulation of selves in interaction" (2016, 618; see also Hakemulder 2000, who has felicitously called fiction a "moral laboratory"). Since empathy and understanding other minds in social contexts are not just desirable social graces, but rather essential abilities for successful communication and for leading meaningful lives, one can reasonably assume that narrative fictions that serve to enhance these cognitive skills will also foster a sense of coherence and thus have salutary effects on readers' mental and physical health.

Beyond the research in narrative psychology and the cognitive sciences briefly reviewed above, there are many other scattered developments and indications that seem to underline our assumption that human beings seem to do lots of interesting things with narratives that can have beneficial effects for their or others' health and well-being. In a book published in German in 2015, the English title of which would be *Reading as Medicine: The Wondrous Effect of Literature*, Andrea Gerk has given a fascinating overview of a great variety of movements and scholarly findings, including narrative medicine, that all suggest that reading is much more than just a pleasurable pastime, in that engaging with literature and particularly narratives can have various tangible health benefits. Whether or not the claim that e.g. bibliotherapy or poetry therapy really do have healing effects may be open to question or debate, some of her observations and reports on the salutary effect of reading are certainly grist to our mill, underscoring as they do our key hypothesis that narratives and salutogenesis are more closely linked than is suggested by the fact that its respective practitioners have so far preferred to ignore each other.

5 Why Narratives are Important for Staying Healthy and Well: Open Questions and Suggestions for Further Research for a Salutogenetic Narrative Theory

What all of the conceptual observations and empirical findings delineated in the previous sections suggest is that narrative theory and salutogenesis not only share some theoretical assumptions and underpinnings, they could also greatly enrich each other through the exchange of concepts and methods. What we hope to have shown is that narratives and storytelling are very important and perhaps even indispensable for achieving and maintaining good health and well-being. Rita Charon has rightly emphasized "the redemptive force of narrative itself to heal" (2008, 80), a force about which we still know relatively little.

The evidence that we have tried to discuss above that there is an as yet largely unexplored link between narratives and health, and between narrative theory and salutogenesis is just too compelling and interesting for anyone interested in narrative theory to continue ignoring it.

Much more work, however, needs to be done before we can really come to terms with the complex ways in which narratives and salutogenesis are interrelated and in which their respective conceptual frameworks can be fruitfully combined, to the benefit of both. For narrative theory such an alliance could be an important opportunity to demonstrate that narratology can help to understand issues that are important for human interests, but one needs to further clarify the relation between narratives and mental and physical health. This endeavor includes the study of the connection between narrative and what has been called 'cognitive reserve,' and the link between resilience, narrative competence, and fictional and factual narratives. In addition to the outstanding questions listed in Oatley (2016, 625), there are other challenges and open questions that a salutogenetic narrative theory, or a narratively oriented salutogenesis, for that matter, will have to address and deal with.

The list of open questions includes, but is by no means limited to, the following: first, which narratological concepts, over and beyond those discussed above, could be especially useful for fostering a better understanding of the salutogenetic potential of narratives and storytelling? And which other concepts that have recently been proposed by scholars working in interdisciplinary frameworks (e.g. connectivity, embeddedness, and entanglement, see Mehl-Madrona 2007, 102–120; hindsight, see Freeman 2010; turning-points, see Abbott 1997, Nünning and Sicks 2012) could be fruitfully employed in a narrative salutogenetic framework? Second, how can a salutogenetic narrative theory accommodate the insights of contextualist narratologies (see Sommer 2007; Nünning 2009, 2012a) and of narrative approaches to cultural psychology (see McAdams 2013), i.e. take into consideration the fact that narratives and metaphors are shaped by cultures just as much as they serve to shape them (see Grabes, Nünning, and Baumbach 2009), and that stories of health and illness "are embedded in families and cultures of which we need to make sense" (Mehl-Madrona 2007, 87)? Third, how can a salutogenetic narrative theory that attempts to integrate the conceptual frameworks developed by classical and postclassical narratologies with those from narrative studies in the social sciences and in narrative medicine incorporate recent insights into the embeddedness, entanglement, "connectivity and interrelatedness of all things" (Mehl-Madrona 2007, 87–88), which narratives in general and stories of health and illness in particular emphasize, with an analysis of salient phenomena in the respective cultural, institutional, and social contexts in which storytelling occurs? Fourth, how will the remarkable pace of developments in digital technologies, which are currently leaving their mark on our brains and mind, as the renowned British neuroscientist Susan Greenfield (2014) has shown, change and influence not just our notions of self and identity, but also of health, relationships, storytelling, and of what constitutes a good life in the digital age (and will the impact of the digital media be primarily salutary or detrimental for our mental and physical health and well-being)? Given the fact that the ways in which different cultures (and periods, for that matter) define health, illness, healing, and a good life differ remarkably, it would be important for scholars working within the framework of a salutogenetic narrative theory to take the time to explore the plethora of such cultural "stories that differ from the one with which we are most familiar" (Mehl-Madrona 2007, 93).

The challenging questions raised by Lewis Mehl-Madrona in *Narrative Medicine: The Use of History and Story in the Healing Process*, which presents a fascinating account of indigenous uses of narratives and storytelling as an important healing modality, not only serve to show that there are many other interesting issues that a salutogenetic narrative theory will have to address, but also indicate that the further development of such an integrated narrative theory is a truly interdisciplinary project that involves collaboration with the so-called life sciences: "But what if health is a matter of equilibrium? What if disease and misfortune are related to disharmony? What if nature is pliable and plastic and molds to our intent and wishes? What if intent really does change material processes? What if it is all just story and some stories no longer fit as well as they once did?" (Mehl-Madrona 2007, 86).

If a salutogenetic narrative theory wants to come to terms with these questions surrounding stories of health and illness, but also with such proliferating kinds of narratives as crisis narratives, broken narratives (see Nünning and Nünning 2016), and new forms of fictional storytelling like "fragmented novels" (Gioia 2013), then it needs to question some of its premises, extend the scope of its concepts, and engage in more interdisciplinary dialogue with the variety of approaches and methodologies for the study of narrative that have been developed in the social sciences, narrative medicine, and other disciplines. The further development of such a salutogenetic narrative theory involves "the necessity of integrating diversity and multiple perspectives into the practice of medicine, thereby enabling it to transcend its current limitations" (Mehl-Madrona 2007, 82). Jerome Bruner's observation that "turning points need more study" (1991, 74) pertains equally well to stories of health, illness, and well-being. They also need much more study, both as interesting objects of study in their own right and because of the new light they can shed on the limits of many of the concepts of narratology that are not very well suited to explore such forms of slow change (see Jullien 2010 [2009]) as ageing, evolution, climate change, mind change as a result of the impact of digital technologies (see Greenfield 2014), illness, extinction of species and other stories without actors, events, actions, and plot which seem to defy classical narratological analysis.

A salutogenetic narrative theory which attempts to be context- and culture-sensitive could certainly benefit from taking into consideration some of the valuable insights of Gay Becker's seminal monograph *Disrupted Lives*, which has shed more light on the functions of broken narratives and on *How People Create Meaning in a Chaotic World*, as the felicitous subtitle has it, than any other publication. In her illuminating analyses of a broad range of 'narratives of disruption' (1997, 10–11, 111), she manages to show that broken narratives and disrupted stories indicate "that cultural notions of normalcy can be contested" (1997, 46), calling into question and rejecting as they do dominant discourses, widely accepted values, and the hegemonic version of normalcy. Both a great part of the value of stories of illness and narratives of disruption, and the need for more research on this topic, reside in the fact that such narratives of disrupted lives challenge what she so aptly calls the "moral force of normalizing ideologies" (1997, 111, 134, 191) as well as the norms and values attached to the master narratives of the age that we all too often accept at face value and take for granted: "Continuity is an illusion. Disruption to life is a constant in human experience," Becker rightly maintains, adding an observation that pertains equally well to stories of illness and other broken narratives as the paradigmatic articulation of disrupted lives: "The study of disrupted lives enables us to look at the disparity between cultural notions of how things are supposed to be and how they are, a disparity that is highlighted by disruption" (1997, 190). The metaphorical notion of 'brokenness' is perfect to point out that seeing "oneself as 'broken' goes against the current of contemporary North American culture" (Frank 1995, 149). Deviating as they do from "the cultural ideal" (Becker 1997, 85) and going against the grain of dominant "cultural ideologies" (1997, 108), narratives of disruption can thus be read as "a refusal to engage in normalizing ideologies" (1997, 95) and as brave attempts to "create a sense of continuity after a disruption" (1997, 122), to retrieve meaning and to reorganize life. Demonstrating "unrelenting perseverance in the face of adversity" (1997, 151), stories of disruption – like those written up and juxtaposed in George Packer's *The Unwinding: An Inner History of the New America* (2013) – and broken narratives serve to reinterpret experience and explain one's life and world in innovative ways that challenge hegemonic discourses, "well-entrenched ideologies" (1997, 110), widely accepted values, and "cultural expectations about turning a life into a success story" (1997, 166). If the "stories that people grow up on are unchosen," then broken narratives can constitute important new "templates for experience" (Frank 2010, 25), providing viable alternatives to the culturally available plots that revolve around well-made, linear, and teleological success stories. Studying broken narratives and stories of disruption can thus not only enable "us to examine the wellsprings of many core tenets of U.S. society and to explore how deeply these core tenets are embedded in the cultural contours of people's lives" (Becker 1997, 7); it can also shed much light on the cultural discourses on normalcy and on the respective predominant cultural expectations, ideologies, and values from which stories of disruption and broken narratives deviate in significant ways. These are also some of the many reasons why narratives in general and broken narratives in particular, just like crisis narratives and fragmented novels, are such a rich topic and why they merit much more narratological and interdisciplinary attention than they have hitherto received.

We should, however, like to leave if not the last words, then the second but last paragraph of this essay, to Monika Fludernik, who has arguably done more than anyone else working in the fields of narrative theory and analysis not only to enhance our understanding of narratives and narratology, but also to extend the aims and scope of narrative theory in a variety of interesting ways. Although her many important contributions to the field(s) cannot be adequately appreciated in a single paragraph, or even in a full-length review-essay, we should at least like to mention four of the many reasons for why her work has prepared the ground for what we have attempted to do in this essay, albeit perhaps unwittingly so. First, her seminal and award-winning monograph *Towards a 'Natural' Narratology*, especially her radical redefinition of narrativity in terms of the narrative schemata of experientiality, i.e. "the quasi-mimetic evocation of 'real-life experience'" (Fludernik 1996, 12), has paved the way for an appreciation of the experiential and subjective quality of narratives, i.e. for a hitherto unduly neglected quality without which their healing and salutary, or salutogenetic, effects could hardly be gauged, let alone be conceptually grasped. Second, her astute observations on cognitive parameters (see esp. 1996, 43–52) could greatly enhance our understanding of the narrative features of medicine and the complexities involved in the story-telling scenarios that we encounter in real-life contexts. Third, her recent work on the possible ways of distinguishing between fictional and factual narratives, and her pioneering work on various kinds of factual narratives, mark a trajectory for future research in interdisciplinary narrative theory from which studies in the fields of narrative and medicine, and possibly also the project of a salutogenetic narrative theory, could greatly benefit. And last, but certainly not least, her recent and current projects on the wonderful German notion of *Muße*, which implies more (and perhaps also less) than just idleness, could be another promising way of staying healthy and well with narratives.

If the central hypothesis and the conceptual reflections outlined above about the importance of narratives and storytelling for staying healthy and well hold up to closer scrutiny, then that would certainly be good news for scholars working in the fields of narrative theory and analysis. Although it may be open to debate whether theorizing about narratives and studying fictional and factual narratives are as conducive to fostering health and well-being as telling stories and reading narratives, one can reasonably assume that a sustained interest in narratives correlates with a strong sense of coherence. Whether or not reading fiction or studying narratives makes you a better person may be an open question, but recent research into the association of book reading with longevity has shown that "book readers experienced a 20% reduction in risk of mortality over the 12 years of follow up compared to non-book readers" (Bavishi, Slade, and Levy 2016, 44), which is nothing to be sneezed at. On an equally optimistic note, Pennebaker and Seagal conclude their article in a way that confirms our hypothesis that doing things with narratives can be an important means of staying healthy and fostering well-being: "Regardless of how narratives get formed, they serve a critical function in people's lives that have important implications for health and general well being" (1999, 1252). All of this seems to suggest that we have good reasons to be optimistic that we may hopefully be able to read, and learn from, many more publications from a scholar who has raised narratological inquiry to a new level of sophistication, and to whom we should like to wish the best of health and well-being, our renowned colleague and esteemed friend Monika Fludernik.

References

Abbott, Andrew. 1997. "On the Concept of Turning Point." *Comparative Social Research* 16: 85–105.
Alber, Jan, and Monika Fludernik, eds. 2010. *Postclassical Narratology: Approaches and Analyses*. Columbus: Ohio State University Press.
Angus, Lynne E., and Leslie S. Greenberg. 2011. *Working With Narrative in Emotion-Focused Therapy: Changing Stories, Healing Lives*. Washington: American Psychological Association.
Antonovsky, Aaron. 1991. *Health, Stress and Coping*. San Francisco: Jossey-Bass.
---. 1997. *Salutogenese: Zur Entmystifizierung der Gesundheit*. London: DGVT: Deutsche Gesellschaft für Verhaltenstherapie.
---. 1998. Unraveling the Mysteries of Health: How People Manage Stress and Stay Well. San Francisco: Jossey-Bass.
Armstrong, Judith G. 2002. "Deciphering the Broken Narrative of Trauma: Signs of Traumatic Dissociation on the Rorschach." *Rorschachiana* 25.1: 11–27.
Bal, Mieke. 1990. "The Point of Narratology." *Poetics Today* 11.4: 727–753.
---. 1999. "Close Reading Today: From Narratology to Cultural Analysis." In *Grenzüberschreitungen: Narratologie im Kontext/Transcending Boundaries: Narratology in Context*, edited by Walter Grünzweig and Andreas Solbach, 19–40. Tübingen: Narr.
---. 2002. *Travelling Concepts in the Humanities: A Rough Guide*. Toronto: University of Toronto Press.
Bavishi, Avni, Martin D. Slade, and Becca R. Levy. 2016. "A chapter a day: Association of book reading with longevity." *Social Science & Medicine* 164: 44–48.
Becker, Gaylene. 1997. *Disrupted Lives: How People Create Meaning in a Chaotic World*. Berkeley, Los Angeles, and London: University of California Press.
Bietz, Christoph. 2013. *Die Geschichten der Nachrichten: Eine narratologische Analyse telemedialer Wirklichkeitskonstruktion*. Trier: WVT.
Bruner, Jerome. 1990. *Acts of Meaning*. Cambridge and London: Harvard University Press.
---. 1991. "Self-Making and World-Making." *Journal of Aesthetic Education* 25.1: 67–78.
---. 2002. *Making Stories: Law, Literature, Life*. Cambridge and London: Harvard University Press.
Butter, Stella. 2007. *Literatur als Medium kultureller Selbstreflexion: Literarische Transversalität und Vernunftkritik in englischen und amerikanischen Gegenwartsromanen aus funktionsgeschichtlicher Perspektive*. Trier: WVT.
Carrard, Philippe. 1992. *Poetics of the New History: French Historical Discourse from Braudel to Chartier*. Baltimore and London: The Johns Hopkins University Press.

Charon, Rita. 2008. *Narrative Medicine: Honoring the Stories of Illness*. New York and Oxford: Oxford University Press.
Crossley, Michele L. 2005. "Narrative Psychology." In *Routledge Encyclopedia of Narrative Theory*, edited by David Herman, Manfred Jahn, and Marie-Laure Ryan, 360–362. London and New York: Routledge.
Dawson, Paul. 2013. *The Return of the Omniscient Narrator: Authorship and Authority in Twenty-First Century Fiction*. Columbus: Ohio State University Press.
De Botton, Alain. 2014. *The News: A Reader's Manual*. London: Pantheon.
Eakin, Paul John. 1999. *How Our Lives Become Stories: Making Selves*. Ithaca and London: Cornell University Press.
---. 2006. "Narrative Identity and Narrative Imperialism: A Response to Galen Strawson and James Phelan." *Narrative* 14: 180–187.
---. 2008. *Living Autobiographically: How We Create Identity in Narrative*. Ithaca and London: Cornell University Press.
Echterhoff, Gerald. 2002. "Geschichten in der Psychologie: Die Erforschung narrativ geleiteter Informationsverarbeitung." In *Erzähltheorie transgenerisch, intermedial, interdisziplinär*, edited by Vera Nünning and Ansgar Nünning, 265–290. Trier: WVT.
Emmott, Catherine. 1997. *Narrative Comprehension: A Discourse Perspective*. Oxford: Clarendon Press.
Fludernik, Monika. 1996. *Towards a 'Natural' Narratology*. London: Routledge.
---. 1999. "'When the Self is an Other': Vergleichende erzähltheoretische und postkoloniale Überlegungen zur Identitäts(de)konstruktion in der (exil)indischen Gegenwartsliteratur." *Anglia* 117.1: 71–96.
---. 2005. "Histories of Narrative Theory (II). From Poststructuralism to the Present." In *A Companion to Narrative Theory*, edited by James Phelan and Peter J. Rabinowitz, 36–59. Oxford: Blackwell.
---. 2007. "Identity/alterity." In *Cambridge Companion to Narrative Theory*, edited by David Herman, 260–273. Cambridge: Cambridge University Press.
Fludernik, Monika, Donald C. Freeman, and Margaret H. Freeman. 1999. "Metaphor and Beyond: An Introduction." *Poetics Today* 20.3: 383–396.
Fludernik, Monika, and Greta Olson. 2011. "Introduction." In *Current Trends in Narratology*, edited by Greta Olson, 1–34. Berlin and New York: De Gruyter.
Frank, Arthur F. 1995. *The Wounded Storyteller: Body, Illness and Ethics*. Chicago and London: The University of Chicago Press.
---. 2010. *Letting Stories Breathe: A Socio-Narratology*. Chicago and London: The University of Chicago Press.
Freeman, Mark. 2010. *Hindsight, The Promise and Peril of Looking Backward*. New York and Oxford: Oxford University Press.
Gerk, Andrea. 2015. *Lesen als Medizin: Die wundersame Wirkung der Literatur*. Berlin: Rogner & Bernhard.
Gioia, Ted. 2013. "The Rise of the Fragmented Novel." *fractious fiction*, 17 July. Accessed 30 November 2016. Web.
Goodman, Nelson. 1992 [1978]. *Ways of Worldmaking*. Indianapolis: Hackett.
Greenfield, Susan. 2014. *Mind Change: How digital technologies are leaving their mark on our brains*. London: Penguin.

Grabes, Herbert, Ansgar Nünning, and Sibylle Baumbach, eds. 2009. *Metaphors Shaping Culture and Theory*. REAL: Yearbook of Research in English and American Literature 25. Tübingen: Narr.
Hakemulder, Jèmeljan. 2000. *The Moral Laboratory: Experiments Examining the Effects of Reading Literature on Social Perception and Moral Self-Concept*. Amsterdam and Philadelphia: John Benjamins.
Heinen, Sandra. 2009. "The Role of Narratology in Narrative Research across the Disciplines." In *Narratology in the Age of Cross-Disciplinary Narrative Research*, edited by Sandra Heinen and Roy Sommer, 193–211. Berlin and New York: De Gruyter, 2009.
Heinen, Sandra, and Roy Sommer, eds. 2009. *Narratology in the Age of Cross-Disciplinary Narrative Research*. Berlin and New York: De Gruyter.
Herman, David, ed. 1999. *Narratologies: New Perspectives on Narrative Analysis*. Columbus: Ohio State University Press.
---. 2003. "Stories as a Tool for Thinking." In *Narrative Theory and the Cognitive Sciences*, edited by David Herman, 163–192. Stanford: CSLI Publications.
---. 2009. "Narrative Ways of Worldmaking." In *Narratology in the Age of Cross-Disciplinary Narrative Research*, edited by Sandra Heinen and Roy Sommer, 71–87. Berlin and New York: De Gruyter.
---. 2011. "Editor's Column: Principles and Practices of Narrative Worldmaking." *Storyworlds* 3: vii–x.
Herman, David, Manfred Jahn, and Marie-Laure Ryan, eds. 2005. *Routledge Encyclopedia of Narrative Theory*. London and New York: Routledge.
Holler, Claudia, and Martin Klepper, eds. 2013. *Rethinking Narrative Identity. Persona and Perspective*. Amsterdam and Philadelphia: Benjamins.
Hühn, Peter, John Pier, Wolf Schmid, and Jörg Schönert, eds. 2014 [2009]. *Handbook of Narratology*. 2 Vol. Berlin and New York: De Gruyter.
Hydén, Lars-Christer. 2005. "Medicine and Narrative." In *Routledge Encyclopedia of Narrative Theory*, edited by David Herman, Manfred Jahn, and Marie-Laure Ryan, 293–297. London and New York: Routledge.
Hydén, Lars-Christer, and Jens Brockmeier, eds. 2008a. *Health, Illness and Culture: Broken Narratives*. New York: Routledge.
---, and Jens Brockmeier. 2008b. "Introduction: From the Retold to the Performed Story." In *Health, Illness and Culture: Broken Narratives*, edited by Lars-Christer Hydén and Jens Brockmeier, 1–15. New York: Routledge.
Hyvärinen, Matti, Mari Hatavara, and Lars-Christer Hydén, eds. 2013. *The Travelling Concepts of Narrative*. Amsterdam and Philadelphia: John Benjamins.
Jaeger, Stephan. 2002. "Erzähltheorie und Geschichtswissenschaft." In *Erzähltheorie transgenerisch, intermedial, interdisziplinär*, edited by Vera Nünning and Ansgar Nünning, 237–263. Trier: WVT.
Jullien, Francois. 2010 [2009]. *Die stillen Wandlungen: Baustellen I*. Berlin: Merve.
Kidd, David Comer, and Emanuele Castano. 2013. "Reading Literary Fiction Improves Theory of Mind." *Science* 342: 377–381.
Kirmayer, Laurence J. 2000. "Broken Narratives: Clinical Encounters and the Poetics of Illness Experience." In *Narrative and the Cultural Construction of Illness and Healing*, edited by Cheryl Mattingly and Linda C. Garro, 153–180. Berkeley: University of California Press.
Klein, Christian, and Matías Martínez, eds. 2009. *Wirklichkeitserzählungen: Felder, Formen und Funktionen nicht-literarischen Erzählens*. Stuttgart and Weimar: Metzler.

Kreiswirth, Martin. 1995. "Tell Me a Story: The Narrativist Turn in the Human Sciences." In *Constructive Criticism: The Human Sciences in the Age of Theory*, edited by Martin Kreiswirth and Thomas Carmichael, 61–87. Toronto: University of Toronto Press.
---. 2005. "Narrative Turn in the Humanities." In *Routledge Encyclopedia of Narrative Theory*, edited by David Herman, Manfred Jahn, and Marie-Laure Ryan, 377–382. London and New York: Routledge.
Lanser, Susan Sniader. 1992. *Fictions of Authority: Women Writers and Narrative Voice*. Ithaca and London: Cornell University Press.
Mattingly, Cheryl, and Linda C. Garro, eds. 2000. *Narrative and the Cultural Construction of Illness and Healing*. Berkeley: University of California Press.
McAdams, Dan P. 2013. *The Redemptive Self: Stories Americans Live By*. Oxford: Oxford University Press.
Mehl-Madrona, Lewis. 2007. *Narrative Medicine: The Use of History and Story in the Healing Process*. Rochester: Bear & Company.
Meister, Jan Christoph, ed. 2005. *Narratology beyond Literary Criticism: Mediality, Disciplinarity*. Berlin and New York: De Gruyter.
Mildorf, Jarmila. 2010. "Narratology and the Social Sciences." In *Postclassical Narratology: Approaches and Analyses*, edited by Jan Alber and Monika Fludernik, 234–254. Columbus: Ohio State University Press.
Müller-Funk, Wolfgang. 2012. *The Architecture of Modern Culture: Towards a Narrative Cultural Theory*. Berlin and New York: De Gruyter.
Nash, Christopher, ed. 1990. *Narrative in Culture: The Uses of Storytelling in the Sciences, Philosophy, and Literature*. London and New York: Routledge.
Neumann, Birgit, and Ansgar Nünning, eds. 2012. *Travelling Concepts for the Study of Culture*. Berlin and New York: De Gruyter.
Neumann, Birgit, Ansgar Nünning, and Bo Pettersson, eds. 2008. *Narrative and Identity: Theoretical Approaches and Critical Analyses*. Trier: WVT.
Nünning, Ansgar. 2009. "Surveying Contextualist and Cultural Narratologies: Towards an Outline of Approaches, Concepts and Potentials." In *Narratology in the Age of Cross-Disciplinary Narrative Research*, edited by Sandra Heinen and Roy Sommer, 48–70. Berlin and New York: De Gruyter.
---. 2010. "Making Events – Making Stories – Making Worlds: Ways of Worldmaking From a Narratological Point of View." In *Cultural Ways of Worldmaking: Media and Narratives*, edited by Vera Nünning, Ansgar Nünning, and Birgit Neumann, 191–214. Berlin and New York: De Gruyter.
---. 2012a. "Narrativist Approaches and Narratological Concepts for the Study of Culture." In *Travelling Concepts for the Study of Culture*, edited by Ansgar Nünning and Birgit Neumann, 145–183. Berlin and New York: De Gruyter.
---. 2012b. "Making Crises and Catastrophes: Metaphors and Narratives Shaping the Cultural Life of Crises and Catastrophes." In *The Cultural Life of Catastrophes and Crises: Facts, Forms, Fantasies*, edited by Carsten Meiner and Kristin Veel, 59–88. Berlin and New York: De Gruyter.
Nünning, Ansgar, and Vera Nünning, eds. 2002. *Erzähltheorie transgenerisch, intermedial, interdisziplinär*. Trier: WVT.

---. 2016. "Conceptualizing 'Broken Narratives' from a Narratological Perspective: Domains, Concepts, Features, Functions and Suggestions for Research." In *Narrative im Bruch: Theoretische Positionen und Anwendungen*, edited by Anna Babka, Marlen Bidwell-Steiner, and Wolfgang Müller-Funk, 37–86. Göttingen: Vienna University Press.

Nünning, Ansgar, and Kai Sicks, eds. 2012. *Turning Points: Concepts and Narratives of Change in Literature and Other Media*. Berlin and New York: De Gruyter.

Nünning, Ansgar, and Roy Sommer. 2011. "The Performative Power of Narrative in Drama: On the Forms and Functions of Dramatic Storytelling in Shakespeare's Plays." In *Current Trends in Narratology*, edited by Greta Olson, 200–231. Berlin and New York: De Gruyter.

Nünning, Vera. 2014. *Reading Fictions, Changing Minds: The Cognitive Value of Fiction*. Heidelberg: Winter.

Nünning, Vera, Ansgar Nünning, and Birgit Neumann, eds. 2010. *Cultural Ways of Worldmaking: Media and Narratives*. Berlin and New York: De Gruyter.

Oatley, Keith. 2016. "Fiction: Simulation of Social Worlds." *Trends in Cognitive Science* 20.8: 618–628.

Olson, Greta, ed. 2011. *Current Trends in Narratology*. Berlin and New York: De Gruyter.

Onega, Susana, and José Ángel García Landa, eds. 1996. "Introduction." In *Narratology: An Introduction*, 1–41. London and New York: Longman.

Packer, George. 2013. *The Unwinding: An Inner History of the New America*. New York: Farrar, Straus & Giroux.

Pennebaker, James W., and Janel D. Seagal. 1999. "Forming a Story: The Health Benefits of Narrative." *Journal of Clinical Psychology* 55.10: 1243–1254.

Phelan, James. 2005. "Who's here? Thoughts on Narrative Identity and Narrative Imperialism." *Narrative* 13: 205–210.

Phelan, James, and Peter J. Rabinowitz, eds. 2005. *A Companion to Narrative Theory*. Oxford: Blackwell.

Ryan, Marie-Laure, ed. 2004. *Narrative across Media: The Languages of Storytelling*. Lincoln and London: University of Nebraska Press.

Salmon, Christian. 2007. *Storytelling : La machine à fabriquer des histoires et à formater les esprits*. Paris: La Découverte.

Schüffel, Wolfram, Ursula Brucks, and Rolf Johnen, eds. 1998. *Handbuch der Salutogenese: Konzept und Praxis*. Wiesbaden: Ullstein Medical.

Sommer, Roy. 2007. "'Contextualism' Revisited: A Survey (and Defence) of Postcolonial and Intercultural Narratology." *Journal of Literary Theory* 1: 61–79.

Tamboukou, Maria. 2010. "Broken narratives, visual forces: Letters, paintings and the event." In *Beyond Narrative Coherence*, edited by Matti Hyvärinen, Lars-Christer Hydén, Maarja Saarenheimo, and Maria Tamboukou, 67–85. Amsterdam and Philadelphia: John Benjamins.

Toolan, Michael. 2014 [2009]. "Coherence." In *Handbook of Narratology*, vol. 1, edited by Peter Hühn, John Pier, Wolf Schmid, and Jörg Schönert, 65–83. Berlin and Boston: De Gruyter.

Wolf, Werner. 2011. "Narratology and Media(lity): The Transmedial Expansion of a Literary Discipline and Possible Consequences." In *Current Trends in Narratology*, edited by Greta Olson, 145–180. Berlin and New York: De Gruyter.

Wydler, Hans. 2000. *Salutogenese und Kohärenzgefühl: Grundlagen, Empirie und Praxis eines gesundheitswissenschaftlichen Konzepts*. Weinheim and München: Juventa-Verlag.

Benjamin Kohlmann
Muße, Work, and Free Time: Nineteenth-Century Visions of the Non-Alienated Life

This essay recommends a new linguistic import into the contemporary vocabulary of cultural and literary analysis. The German term *Muße*, I suggest, can help us to describe activities that cut across the binary divisions – work vs. free time, heteronomous vs. autonomous labor – which are typically invoked in order to position nineteenth-century literature in relation to its socioeconomic contexts. The word *Muße* suggests a retreat from public activity and social obligation, and it is frequently associated with the private comforts of nonworking time. At the same time, *Muße* is crucially distinct from both leisure and idleness: unlike idleness, *Muße* does not bear the social stigma of unproductivity; and unlike leisure, it is not restricted exclusively to the sphere of free time. Instead, *Muße* signifies both a set of socioeconomic factors and a particular mental disposition: it implies the structural division into working and nonworking time characteristic of modern societies but it also crucially refers to a particular mood or state of mind.

Theodor W. Adorno and others have noted that the linguistic history of *Muße* can be traced to the aristocratic elite culture of medieval Europe. In this historical context, the term – like its Old and Middle High German roots, *muoza* and *muoze* – referred to a state of leisured ease that is removed from the realm of economic necessity and that opens up a space for the enjoyment of non-material pleasures.[1] In Adorno's influential formulation, aristocratic *Muße* "denoted the privilege of an unconstrained, comfortable life-style" that could be devoted to self-determined pursuits (1991 [1969], 162).[2] As Monika Fludernik (2014) has recently pointed out, *Muße* never completely shed these connotations of status and class and, as such, it has continued to act as a marker of social distinction. In what follows, I will pursue Fludernik's cue in order to trace the discursive afterlife of *Muße* in the nineteenth century and to map some of the narrative effects associ-

---

All unattributed translations in this essay are mine.

[1] *Muoza* and *muoze* are etymologically related to the modal verb "müssen" whose older meanings include a "condition of possibility enabling a person to do certain things" (Kluge 2011, n. pag.).

[2] For a classical account of the historical differentiation of middle-class and aristocratic attitudes towards time 'management,' including *Muße* practices, see Norbert Elias 1998 [1939], 1, 105–124.

DOI 10.1515/9783110569957-012

ated with representations of *Muße*. As regards the broader cultural argument outlined here, I argue that the history of *Muße* in nineteenth-century Germany and England is best understood as a complex series of discursive appropriations through which this formerly aristocratic term became associated, first, with the rise of the bourgeoisie, and later in the century, with the fledgling working-class movement. The features of *Muße* hinted at above – *Muße* as freedom from economic constraint and *Muße* as a marker of social distinction – were carried over from one stage of this process to the next, but they also underwent crucial transformations and triggered specific narrative effects. As I suggest, the remarkable portability of the term *Muße* – and of the set of experiences which it denotes – stems from its ability to mediate the systemic tensions of modernizing societies, most importantly the structural split between work and free time.[3] This essay identifies two tectonic shifts in the semantic and social field demarcated by the term *Muße*. First, I argue that bourgeois *Muße* expressed the dream of an existence liberated from the economic pressures of hyper-productivity while also projecting the image of a harmonious reintegration of work and free time. Second, I indicate that in the context of the working-class movement of the 1880s and 1890s *Muße* came to be identified as a work-like but crucially unalienated activity. *Muße*, according to this second account, enabled narratively mediated visions of a future life in which the alienating effects of industrialized modernity were temporarily suspended, if not fully resolved.

1 Bourgeois *Muße* Between Work and Free Time

Jeremy Bentham's educational treatise *Chrestomathia* (1816) contains one of the most striking illustrations of the dangers of free time in early nineteenth-century Britain. Featuring the designs for a utilitarian day school, Bentham's work warns against the risks of not using one's time wisely.[4] It is easy to reject Bentham's

---

[3] The polysemy of the term *Muße* indicates that we can classify it among the group of terms Barbara Cassin has called "untranslatables." As Emily Apter points out in the preface to her translation of Cassin's *Dictionary of Unstranslatables*, "untranslatables" such as *bildung*, mimesis, or *kitsch* convey a "density of richness of color or tone in the source language [that] seems so completely to defy rendering into another language that we would just as soon not try." "Untranslatables," on Apter's account, "signify not because they are essentialist predicates […] with no ready equivalent in another language, but because they mark singularities of expression that contour a worldscape" (2014, xiv–xv).

[4] The ancient Greek "chrestomathia" translates as "desire for learning."

plans for the school (which never came to fruition) as a blueprint for the kind of oppressive educational institution depicted in Charles Dickens's *Hard Times* (1854). However, as I want to suggest, such dismissals run the risk of ignoring the constructive side of Bentham's enterprise as well as his attempt to remedy what he regarded as the ills of early nineteenth-century social organization.

Chrestomathia concludes with a cautionary tale about "the Effects of Ennui," what Bentham calls "the Disease of an unfurnished Mind, illustrated by an example" (1816, 85). Bentham derived his story from the obituary of a clerk, John Beardmore, who died in 1814, not long after "withdr[awing] himself entirely from business." "From the hour in which he quitted business," Bentham writes in *Chrestomathia*,

> he grew insensibly more and more the victim of listlessness and *ennui*. With high animal spirits – with a mind still active, and a body still robust – with confirmed health, independent property, an amiable wife, numerous friends, a plentiful table, and a social neighbourhood, Mr. B. was no longer '*at home*', as it were, in his own house. The main spring of action was now stopped. In all his pleasures, in all his engagements [...] he was conscious of a *vacuum*. Want of customary application brought on relaxation of activity; want of exercise, languor of body, and depression of spirits; a train of evils ensued, comprising loss of appetite, nervous affections debility, mental and corporeal – decay, pain, and death. (1816, 85–86)

C. K. Ogden, who glosses Bentham's passage in his *Theory of Fictions*, points out that Mr Beardmore's fatal disease, which Ogden memorably dubs "Mr Beardmore's Blues," is "restlessness in retirement" (1932, cxlv). Bentham observes that Mr Beardmore's "customary application" has been limited exclusively to the sphere of work. He consequently lacks the resources to organize his free time in a way that will offer him both rest *and* purposive activity. Lacking such purpose Mr Beardmore's retirement activities give rise to an empty and unproductive "restlessness," or "ennui," which fails to lead to genuine repose. In Bentham's text, this social diagnosis has observable narrative consequences: because Mr Beardmore is constitutively incapable of any form of agency that would generate forward-directed narrative momentum, his appearance in the book is limited to the form of a brief characterological vignette, a minimalistic cautionary tale that is sealed off from its surrounding textual environment by the definitiveness of its ending ("decay, pain, *and death*").

I want to dwell for a moment on the broader cultural implications of Bentham's vignette. Ogden notes that Mr Beardmore's restlessness results from "insufficient intellectual stimulus in youth, maturity, and middle age" (1932, cxlv). As a lower-middle-class clerk who has worked his way up from humble origins, Beardmore lacks the subjective disposition that would enable him to transform free time into the leisurely activity of *Muße*. "Beardmore's Blues" is thus indicative of a historical constellation in which the distribution of cultural skills, including the ability to exercise *Muße*, remains tied to social stratification. Anticipating the increase of available free time in the wake of industrialization and mechanization, Bentham's Chrestomathic schools were intended to provide members of the lower middle class with the *bildung* required to forestall the "*désoeuvrement*" that threatens "him whose mind unoccupied [...] is on the lookout for pleasure" (Bentham qtd. in Greiner 2012, 65). Bentham's account of Beardmore's Blues shows that while *Muße* is primarily associated with nonworking time, it refers to an active and purposeful use of that free time. But Bentham's story also points to the deeper socioeconomic tensions which necessitated the transferral of *Muße* practices to the middle class in the first place. The increasingly rigid split between work and free time under the historical conditions of commercialization and industrialization, Bentham argues, has led to an impoverished understanding of what counts as a good life. Purposeful activity has become restricted to the sphere of economically productive working time while free time has been degraded to the status of mere recreation.[5] *Muße*, by contrast, cuts across this division as it points to a set of self-determined activities that take place outside work. The cultural construction of middle-class *Muße* thus involves the attempt to delimit activities that are exempt from the productive imperatives of work even as they retain a residually purposive structure.

The intentional structure of *Muße* can be difficult to distinguish from forms of rational recreation in which leisure-time is used to cultivate behavior conducive to work.[6] However, rather than subsuming *Muße* activities under the label of rational recreation, I want to propose that we reserve the term *Muße* for a set of phenomena that are self-consciously marked out as leisure activities. These activities possess a purposive structure, but they are also defined by their distance from work itself. Like the middle-class ideal of "comfort," which Franco Moretti has recently explored at some length, *Muße* is located in "proximity to work" without simply being a substitute for it. *Muße* offers personal "well-being" that is unattainable during work, "but one that doesn't seduce you away from your calling, because it remains too sober and modest to do so" (2013, 49).

So what types of social practices and personal dispositions are included in bourgeois *Muße*? The term *Muße* originated in a German-language context, and

---

[5] On the split between working and nonworking time, see Voth 2000.
[6] Instances of rational recreation include workers who teach themselves to read and write or who engage in physical exercise that restores their physical health and labor power. The standard account of rational recreation in nineteenth-century Britain is Bailey (1978).

a few textual examples can help us to illustrate the cultural (as well as some of the more narrowly narrative) functions which the word came to acquire in its German-language environment. As far as the German context is concerned, all my examples will be drawn from the popular family magazine *Die Gartenlaube* (1853–1937). Geared towards a bourgeois audience and featuring prose narratives as well as edifying poetry, *Die Gartenlaube* dominated the German market for periodicals in the second half of the nineteenth century with circulation figures estimated at up to five million issues per year. The magazine's title, the German word for 'garden arbor,' calls up the quintessential image of bourgeois privacy and repose. The magazine's header featured the iconic image of an arbor occupied by a group engaged in the quintessential communal *Muße* activity of magazine-reading (see Ill. 1).

Fig. 1: Header of *Die Gartenlaube. 1853.*

The illustration reveals some of the ideological work that was performed by *Muße* in this distinctly bourgeois context. Most notably, the heterogeneity of the group points to *Muße*'s capacity to create social harmony between generations (ranging from the grandfatherly figure who reads aloud to the grandchildren flocking around the table), between classes (the maid, while peripheral to the scene, is significantly included in the image), between the sexes, as well as between work and leisure. In defusing potential conflicts between individuals (and between the social groups and classes which these individuals represent), *Muße* thus emerges as the powerful fantasy of a rising middle class which saw itself as a pacifying force at the center of society. In this respect, *Muße* corresponds precisely to the socioeconomic position of the nineteenth-century bourgeoisie. Unlike the older aristocracy, members of the bourgeoisie took care to show that they engaged in *Muße* activities which were both leisurely *and* useful. At the same time, the socioeconomic position of the middle class transcended the precarious existence of the industrial proletariat, dominated as it was by material necessity, in favor of 'higher' intellectual and aesthetic pursuits.

Muße figures prominently in the prose and poetry which fill the issues of *Die Gartenlaube*, and these texts illustrate the ways in which *Muße* negotiates the seemingly opposed spheres of productivity and non-productivity as well as of freedom and necessity. One of these stories, entitled "Der gute Bürger ["The Good Citizen" or "The Good Bourgeois"]," takes the form of a real-life home-story featuring the "self-made man" Classen Kappelmann, "son of a petit bourgeois [*Kleinbürger*] from the small Rhenish town of Sinzig, who came to Cologne at age sixteen" (Anon 1865, 363). Like Mr Beardmore, Kappelmann has risen from humble beginnings to become a respectable manufacturer – "solely through his own energy," as *Die Gartenlaube*'s reporter is keen to emphasize (1865, 363). Kappelmann manages to avoid Beardmore's Blues by using his free time in a manner that is both leisured and purposeful:

> Gegen Mittag besteigen wir den Wagen, der uns hinaus auf's Dorf führt, wo das Landgut und die Wollspinnerei sich befinden. Trotz der heute gewiß besonders knapp bemessenen Zeit findet der Fabrikant neben der Erledigung seiner kaufmännischen Arbeiten doch noch Muße, ein Stündchen in seinem Garten zuzubringen; denn er ist mit Begeisterung Landwirth, cultivirt persönlich alle möglichen neuen Erscheinungen auf dem Gebiete des Garten- und Ackerbaues und liefert den meistens schwerfälligen Bauern in seinem Versuchsgarten Beweise von der Nützlichkeit des Fortschritts. [...] Dies Privatissimum, diese bescheidene Clause ist die Werkstatt für größere literarische Arbeiten. Wie wir selbst gesehen haben, bleibt auf dem Hauptcomptoir in der Stadt keine Muße; hier auf dem Lande wird sie den andern Beschäftigungen abgekargt. (1865, 365–366)

[Around noon we mount the cart which brings us out to the village where [Mr Kappelmann's] estate and the wool spinning mill are located. Even though his free time is scarce owing to his commercial business, the manufacturer finds some *Muße* to spend a short hour in his garden; he is a passionate horticulturalist, and he is personally involved in testing all sorts of new cultivating methods in gardening and agriculture. By means of this experimental garden the peasants, who are generally less eager to learn new tricks, are taught the usefulness of progress. [...] [Mr Kappelmann's study] is a place of private retreat, a humble room which he uses for substantial literary enterprises. We have seen with our own eyes that the office leaves [Mr Kappelmann] no time for *Muße*; here, in the country, he manages to spare some time from his other occupations.]

The passage indicates that Mr Kappelmann's *Muße* involves a form of directed, purposive activity that resists complete identification with either idling or work. Instead, it combines elements of both in an attempt to harmonize the structural antagonism between working and nonworking time. Mr Kappelman's "constant harmonious mood [*die stets harmonische Stimmung seines Inneren*]", the article notes, "keeps all dissonances [*Dissonanzen*] at bay" (1865, 366). The passage thus suggests that the reconciliation of the socioeconomic tensions between work and free time is supported by the subjective disposition which the individual experiences while immersed in *Muße*.

The case of Mr Kappelmann indicates that *Muße* avoids the empty time of idleness while also steering clear of the utilitarian means-ends logic of work. In *Die Gartenlaube*, as in many other nineteenth-century German texts, *Muße* is typically embedded in grammatical constructions that point to its peculiar suspension of intentionality ("*Muße haben zu ...*" or "*Muße haben, um ...*"). Let us take the following passage from "Jagderinnerungen aus dem Gebirge ["Memories of a Hunt in the Mountains"]," which focuses on the isolated male figure of a hunter:

> War ich geraume Zeit vor Sonnenuntergang, um durch späteres Kommen nichts rege zu machen, hinausgeschritten an die Grenze, um mich dort anzustellen, so blieb mir volle Muße – bei aller Vorsicht für etwa eintretende Eventualitäten – mich der Betrachtung der mich umgebenden herrlichen Natur hingeben zu können. (Hammer 1863, 325)

> [Having arrived long before dusk so as not to stir up wildlife, and stepping out to the treeline and assuming the position of the hunter, I had sufficient *Muße* – while remaining wary of any eventualities that might come to pass – to give myself over to a contemplation of the majestic nature which surrounded me.]

Muße here enables an aesthetic contemplation of the grandeur of nature which forces the plot-driven movement of the hunting narrative to a halt and which temporarily replaces the text's focus on external events with an internal, psychological dynamic. Similar to the scenes of sublime nature depicted by the Romantic painter Caspar David Friedrich, "Jagderinnerungen aus dem Gebirge" invites the reader to share in the protagonist's contemplative musing – an identificatory narrative procedure which serves to foreground the intentional structure of *Muße*.

This intentional structure remains a constant feature of *Muße* across a wide range of discursive concretizations, and it means that *Muße* (unlike the state of external stasis and decomposition associated with Mr Bearsmore) is capable of initiating an incipient forward-directed narrative momentum. Consider, for example, the following description of an old house in Levin Schücking's story "Der gefangene Dichter ["The Imprisoned Poet"]":

> Dies Haus wird als eine Merkwürdigkeit den Fremden gezeigt; das heißt, wohlverstanden, denjenigen Fremden, welche darnach fragen sollten […]; denn wer in unserer vielbeschäftigten Zeit hat so viel Muße übrig, um sich der Betrachtung alter Häuser hinzugeben, und seine Theilnahme haften zu lassen an Mauern und Wänden, die höchstens wohl „Ohren", aber leider keinen Mund besitzen, womit sie erzählen könnten, was sie einst Alles vernommen und erlauscht haben! (Schücking 1858, 73)
>
> [This house is considered a quaint oddity and this is how it is presented to visitors; by "visitors" I mean those educated travelers who might happen to make inquiries about it […]; for who, in this busy time of ours, has enough *Muße* to give himself over to a contemplation of old houses and to give heed to old walls which have "ears" but, alas!, no mouth with which to relate the things they have seen in their time.]

By the 1850s, the link between *Muße* and aesthetic experience had become a literary cliché. In fact, both Schücking and the author of "Jagderinnerungen" use identical phrases (*Muße, ... um sich hinzugeben*) to describe the essential aesthetic dimension of *Muße*. Given the stereotypical nature of this link, it is easy to miss the intentional structure which underlies these different instantiations of *Muße* and which invariably turns it into a form of free but un-idle time.

Muße, then, is a surprisingly busy time that can be used for any number of active pursuits. As *Die Gartenlaube* author Felix Dahn noted in his poem "Ferien!": "Wohl dem, der wie aus Arbeit sich zur Muße, / Aus Muße sich zu seiner Arbeit sehnt! [Blessed be those who desire *Muße* while working and who long for work while enjoying *Muße*]" (1875, 541). Dahn's narrative poem indicates that, for most middle-class writers, *Muße* retains a covert affinity with the instrumental logic of work, but it also hints that the nineteenth-century middle-class discourse of *Muße* was closely bound up in the language of commodity exchange. *Muße*, as Dahn reminds his readers in "Ferien!," needs to be "well earned" (*wohlverdient*) before it can be consumed (*gekostet*). Other German writers of the period agreed. Friedrich Wilhelm Riemer, Goethe's erstwhile secretary and author of the frequently reprinted *Mittheilungen über Goethe* (1841), regretted that the old Goethe had taken up the "subaltern job" of administrator at the Jena and Weimar libraries instead of using his "*verdiente Muße*" to engage in new literary projects (1841, 93). Similarly, the protagonist of *Die Schwiegermutter* [*The Stepmother*] by the popular novelist Henriette Hanke looked forward to a retirement filled with "*verdiente Muße*" (1842, 45). These textual samples suggest that while *Muße* was regarded as an activity which typically takes place outside work, its discursive logic continued to be bound up with a bourgeois ethos that threatened to subordinate

Muße either to the logic of labor or which treated it as a commodity earned in return for physical exertion. It is important to grasp *Muße*'s links to the twinned ideologies of bourgeois productivism and consumerism in order to measure the distance which the concept had traveled from its aristocratic origins. Having severed its ties to earlier forms of aristocratic leisure as a completely "unconstrained lifestyle," *Muße* now paradoxically signified a release from work while also remaining tied to it.

2 Working-class *Muße* and Unalienated Labor

Because *Muße* played such a central role in the construction of bourgeois identity, it is easy to misread it as a form of false consciousness, i.e. as an aestheticizing retreat from the deep structural contradictions – between work and free time – of socioeconomic modernity. Similarly, by inscribing the male bourgeois subject firmly at the heart of this discursive constellation, the contemplative inwardness typically associated with *Muße* appears to act as a screen against questions of gender and class. Because the mystificatory potential of bourgeois culture is now so obvious to us, the more difficult task faced by an inquiry into the functions of nineteenth-century *Muße* consists in taking *Muße* seriously – that is, it consists in asking how we might recuperate it as a counterhegemonic formation capable of performing a critique of social conditions. One starting point for such an investigation of *Muße* is the recognition – first articulated in Adorno and Horkheimer's *Aspects of Sociology* from 1965 – that false consciousness is not a fiction which takes the place of reality but a distorted perception of reality. To put it another way: false consciousness, including the "*stets harmonische Stimmung*" created by *Muße*, contains elements of a social vision which resists hegemonic social protocols and which can be activated when *Muße* practices are appropriated into a new class context (Adorno and Horkheimer 1972, 198–199).[7] When we consider *Muße* from this perspective, it is possible to see it not simply as a falsely harmonious (or aestheticized) view of work and free time, but as a potentially utopian experience which does not (yet) have a real-life correlate under the divided conditions of life pertaining in industrialized societies. In the non-bourgeois class contexts

---

[7] Fredric Jameson glosses this critical recuperation of false consciousness as follows: "Adorno's philosophical procedure does not involve the destruction of older, sometimes even false categories (and the projection of some new hitherto non-existent utopian philosophical terminology or language), but rather a playing through them which mobilizes even their untruth to project its opposite" (2007 [1990], 203).

considered below, *Muße* implies not a prevailing sense of nostalgia for what has vanished, nor is it simply a conservative celebration of aristocratic repose. Rather than signifying a truth *or* an illusion, *Muße* becomes the object of an ideological struggle – it becomes the very site where socioeconomic transformations are contested.

In what follows, I want to outline a second transformation which *Muße* underwent in the second half of the nineteenth century. Following its bourgeois rearticulation as a form of purposive free-time activity, in the second half of the nineteenth century bourgeois *Muße* practices began to be co-opted by the working class. If *Muße* is considered exclusively or even primarily as a form of false consciousness, this adoption of *Muße* practices by the working class will appear as a step in the gradual deradicalization and (self-)domestication of the British proletariat. However, as I want to suggest, *Muße* could also be appropriated in a more radical fashion. Most importantly, working-class discourses reimagined *Muße* as a fundamentally unalienated and emancipated activity that offered a utopian foil to the regime of estranged labor under Victorian capitalism.

Many literary and visual artefacts from the period poignantly contrast the labor conditions of the working class with (non-alienated) *Muße* activities (see Ill. 2). Examples of such *Muße* practices prominently include the spread of allotments which afforded members of the lower classes the opportunity to spend their free time cultivating their gardens. While working-class gardening seems to resemble the horticultural activities pursued by *Die Gartenlaube*'s Mr Kappelmann, it would be wrong to see it merely as an emulation of bourgeois *Muße* practices. Instead, as Margaret Willes (2014) has recently reminded us, working-class gardening had a long history in Britain, and it was often seen as a microcosm of the class-bound nature of British society. Since the working classes were usually only able to cultivate land which was not their own, the occupation of land by workers carried radical implications. This political dimension came to the fore in the 1880s and 1890s when many radicals – including the poet Edward Carpenter, the evolutionary thinker Alfred Russel Wallace, and the economist Henry George – reactivated an older popular radicalism in their calls for land nationalization (Howkins 2002; Taunton 2011). This reinvigoration of popular radicalism was further spurred by the translation of works by Russian revolutionaries such as Peter Kropotkin who suggested that the cultivation of land constituted a potentially emancipatory practice.

Fig. 2: A Spitalfield weaver spinning alongside his family. The window offers a glimpse of the family's garden and their pet, a bird in a cage. In: *Queen*, 21 September 1861; reprinted in Willes 2014, 110.

The *Muße* associated with working-class horticulture should not be regarded as merely fraudulent or as a screen for the covert affirmation of hegemonic values. This is borne out by the reflections on land ownership which came to dominate Carpenter's works of the early 1880s. In an essay entitled "Private Property" (1886), Carpenter argues that "property" is bound up with the question of an owner's "proper" relationship to his land. The essay opens with an anecdote about a "gentleman who owned a large property" but who turns out to be ignorant of the natural properties of his estate when questioned by a visitor. "In what sense did that gentleman own that land?," Carpenter asks. If "[t]o own means to confess, to recognise, to acknowledge," this landlord, though legally entitled to call the land his own, cannot be said to "own" it in a way that could make it the site of future *Muße* (1887, 115). Carpenter's essay contrasts the landowner's alienation with the working-class cultivator's intimate knowledge of the land:

> While the people about him and working on the land are continually thinking (as I have often had occasion to notice) what can be done for the land, how they can best do justice to it – spending affection and thought upon it – and indeed grieving when they see it neglected, when they see it undrained or insufficiently manured, or allowed to run to waste and dishevelment – even though these matters are as the saying is "not their concern," and make no difference to their pockets. While, I say, the common people spend this love and affection on the land, the legal owner, as a rule is thinking concerning it of only one thing – and that is how much money he can get out of it. (1887, 116)

Unlike the self-interested *homo economicus* of classical political economy who seeks to maximize the financial gain he can extract from the land, Carpenter advocates an attitude of custodial care and concern, of "affection and thought," that is independent of legal entitlements.

Carpenter's essay contrasts false (commercial) and true (affective) proprietorship, and in doing so marks out a discursive site where the reappropriation of bourgeois *Muße* practices by the working class becomes possible. The *Muße* experienced by Classen Kappelmann, Carpenter might say, is only an extension of his workaday life: Kappelmann's literary projects ("*größere literarische Arbeiten*") are merely a continuation of the work he pursues for a living (his "*kaufmännische Arbeiten*"). By contrast, the *Muße* experiences enabled by working-class horticulture signify a form of self-determined activity that contrasts with the unskilled wage labor of the factories. Carpenter's essay distinguishes between two forms of "property" by deploying the same rhetorical move he had used to unearth the hidden meanings of "ownership":

> We may now pass on to a consideration of what property really means. If legal ownership is a negative thing, is there some reality of which it is, as it were, the shadow – which it has at some time or other vainly tried to represent? [...]
> Can we get anything out of the word Property itself? [...] That which is 'proper' to a thing. What are the properties of brimstone — its essential characteristics, qualities, relations to other things? What is the property of chalk as distinguished from cheese? What are the properties of vegetable life, of animal life? What is the essential Property of Man?
> This last is the question of questions. Amid all the shows and illusions, is it possible that the reality which we seek is hidden here? What if material property is only a symbol and indication of it? All the scrambling after calculable wealth, all the delusions and illusions, all the bog-floundering and fatuous wisp-catching are not in vain, if they lead us to find an answer to *that*, if they show us at last the wealth which is truly incalculable. (1887, 119–121)

Carpenter presents his interrogation of "property" as a form of etymological recovery work which retrieves the signifying core of a word that has been emptied of real meaning through legalistic overuse. Carpenter's idiosyncratic linguistic procedure allows him to invest his analysis of existing social and economic structures with a utopian charge that points forward to a utopian reordering of existing relations. While "property" – as a source of economic value and as the guarantor of civic rights (including the right to vote) – is deeply rooted in bourgeois society, true proprietorial right foregrounds ethical questions of tact and "propriety," i.e. the question of the owner's "proper" relationship to the soil. Carpenter's rhetorical procedure is significant because it allows him to find shards of a different social order in the present, rather than rejecting existing social arrangements out of hand. In analogous fashion, we should not dismiss the *Muße* experienced by gardening workers as an ideological delusion or as a ploy of bourgeois ideology that channels the desire for political change into a set of non-disruptive social practices. Instead, we should understand Carpenter's recasting of the bourgeois idea of "property" and of bourgeois *Muße* practices as an attempt to imagine forms of activity that are fundamentally disalienated.

The co-optation of *Muße* by members of the working class continued to draw on the set of general characteristics that I discussed towards the beginning of this essay. We should therefore expect to find some overlap between bourgeois and working-class figurations of *Muße*. For example, in countless working-class autobiographies from the second half of the nineteenth century, *Muße* practices operate as a marker of social prestige vis-à-vis workers whose uncultivated restlessness brings about, to recall Bentham's term, moral and physical "*désoeuvrement*." These autobiographies feature many examples of *Muße* activities that bear a clearer resemblance to work than, say, casual gardening or the writing of poetry. For example the autobiography written by former factory-worker Charles Manby Smith attacks the "tide of lazy and filthy vagabonds, professedly of various trades, but virtually living without work, or the intention of working, flow[ing] lazily through the kingdom from one end of it to the other" (1854, 25). The passage goes on to suggest that the best way to remedy the *désoeuvrement* brought about by idling is to engage in *Muße*-like activities. Smith, who had become a teacher after years of factory labor, recalls the problems which his new job brought with it, in particular the difficulties of making good use of free time:

> My new vocation [...] afforded me much more leisure than had heretofore been at my command. But I cannot say that I ever thoroughly enjoyed this leisure. The instinct 'to be doing,' the result of the habits of my life, twelve hours a day of which had been passed in constant labor from my childhood, drove me continually to some manual occupation; and I tried my

hands at all sorts of contrivances – such as cobbling my boots and clothes, binding my books, and manufacturing musical instruments, with little better results than quieting the reproaches of my handicraft conscience, which would not suffer me to rest without the attempt, at least, at producing something real and tangible. (1854, 116–117)

Smith's autobiography points out that the best way to safeguard against the rot of *désoeuvrement* is to allow particular kinds of work ("cobbling my boots, binding my books, manufacturing musical instruments") to colonize free time. It may seem a stretch to group these work-like activities under the label of *Muße*, but it is important to recognize that all of these free-time activities are self-chosen and, to this extent, non-alienated.

Another important continuity between bourgeois and working-class conceptions of *Muße* can be found in the idea that *Muße* is an acquired skill. The fatal restlessness of Mr Beardmore had stemmed from his inability to transform his free time into *Muße*, and as a remedy Bentham had proposed the establishment of Chrestomathic schools which would teach lower-class individuals how to cultivate *Muße*. Bentham's proposal indicates that *Muße* came to signify a particular form of cultural *bildung*. While radicals of the 1880s and 1890s were receptive to this view, they gave it a critical twist by stressing that genuine *bildung* needed to revert the stunting effects brought about by professionalization and specialization. Professionalization and specialization were held to be characteristic of modern societies, and, as Kristin Ross has recently shown, they were often seen to enforce a dystopian regime of alienated labor. Ross traces socialist arguments that attempted to counter these historical developments by advocating an "integral, polytechnic education" as opposed to "the harnessing of a child prematurely into a particular trade" (2015, 41–43). Such schemes included Charles Fourier's utopian plans for communal living in so-called "phalanstères" and the experimental pedagogies touted during the Paris Commune of 1871. Many socialists hoped that such new forms of "integral" education would repair the human lives that had been broken on the iron grid of capitalism with its binary division into work and free time.

In the British context, the belief that *Muße* might offer utopian glimpses of a reformed social order found its fullest expression in William Morris's *News from Nowhere* (1890). Within the limits of this article, it is not possible to engage in an extended discussion of the novel.[8] Instead, I want to invoke Morris's utopian fiction only briefly in order to suggest that, in a socialist context, *Muße* could be

---

[8] For a discussion of *News from Nowhere* in relation to late nineteenth-century languages of work and leisure, see Kohlmann 2014, 205–211.

presented as the model for a whole way of life rather than as the exclusive pursuit of the leisured classes. Victorian society, Morris's narrator notes,

> pinched 'education' for most people into a niggardly dole of not very accurate information; something to be swallowed by the beginner in the art of living whether he liked it or not, and was hungry for it or not: and which had been chewed and digested over and over again by people who didn't care about it in order to serve it out to other people who didn't care about it. (1994, 97)

Because in Morris's utopia *Muße* is imagined to encompass a whole praxis of living, educational institutions of the type imagined by Bentham are no longer required. This fact also explains why *News from Nowhere* is best described as a utopian bildungsroman in which William Guest, Morris's time traveler, learns to experience *Muße* simply by virtue of participating in the life of the utopians. To put this another way: *Muße* practices are effortlessly integrated into Morris's narrative precisely because they involve an active component, i.e. a form of purposeful agential 'doing' which lends itself easily enough to narrativization. Describing Ellen, Guest's love interest and the symbol of this new life-to-come, Morris writes:

> She smiled with pleasure, and her lazy enjoyment of the new scene seemed to bring out her beauty doubly as she leaned back amidst the cushions, though she was far from languid; her idleness being the idleness of a person, strong and well-knit both in body and mind, deliberately resting. (1994, 209)

Ellen's "deliberate resting" points to an activity which is directed and purposeful but which is not circumscribed by narrowly utilitarian considerations. In this respect, it resembles the bourgeois *Muße* I described earlier. But in *News from Nowhere* such leisurely *Muße* activities come to include instances of non-alienated and *Muße*-like work:

> We came just here on a gang of men road-mending, which delayed us a little; but I was not sorry for it; for all I had seen hitherto seemed a mere part of a summer holiday; and I wanted to see how this folk would set to on a piece of real necessary work. They had been resting, and had only just begun work again as we came up [...]. There were about a dozen of them, strong young men, looking much like a boating party at Oxford would have looked in the days I remembered, and not more troubled with their work. [...] A half-dozen of young women stood by watching the work or the workers, both of which were worth watching, for the latter smote great strokes and were very deft in their labour, and as handsome clean-built fellows as you might find of in a summer day. They were laughing and talking merrily with each other and the women. (1994, 82)

Guest presents the back-breaking work of "road-mending" as a test case for the status of non-alienated labor. He discovers that the utopians consider "resting" and "work" to be equally pleasurable, as the structural division into work and free time is obliterated by radically democratized forms of *Muße*. As such, Morris's descriptions of *Muße* activities point beyond the limits of the present: they generate a narrative momentum that extends beyond the narrower confines of the text and into the world of the reader. In doing so, Morris's vision goes beyond the demands floated by other socialists around 1900 (e.g. calls for a living wage and an existential minimum): such reformist measures, Morris recognized, failed to break with the alienating logic of wage labor and they ran the risk of ignoring the deeper structural problems that beset capitalist societies. In this respect, Morris's novel offers one of the last glimpses of a buried strand of nineteenth-century working-class writing: a utopian imaginary that aimed not at the increase of disposable free time, but at the realization of *Muße* as an entire way of life.

References

Adorno, Theodor W. 1991 [1969]. "Free Time." In *The Culture Industry: Selected Essays on Mass Culture*, edited by Jay Bernstein, 162–170. London: Routledge.

Adorno, Theodor W., and Max Horkheimer. 1972 [1965]. *Aspects of Sociology* [*Soziologische Exkurse*]. Boston: Beacon Press.

Anon. 1865. "Der gute Bürger." *Die Gartenlaube* 23: 363–366.

Apter, Emily. 2014. "Preface." In *Dictionary of Untranslatables: A Philosophical Lexicon*, edited by Barbara Cassin, vii–xv. Princeton: Princeton University Press.

Bailey, Peter. 1978. *Leisure and Class in Victorian England: Rational Recreation and the Contest for Control, 1830–1885*. Toronto: Toronto University Press.

Bentham, Jeremy. 1816. *Chrestomathia, Being a Collection of Papers Explanatory of the Design of an Institution [...]*. London: Payne and Foss.

Carpenter, Edward. 1887 [1886]. "Private Property." In *England's Ideal and Other Papers on Social Subjects*, 115–138. London: Swan Sonnenschein.

Dahn, Felix. 1875. "Ferien!" *Die Gartenlaube* 32: 541.

Elias, Norbert. 1998 [1939]. *Über den Prozess der Zivilisation*. 2 vols. Frankfurt am Main: Suhrkamp.

Fludernik, Monika. 2014. "The Performativity of Idleness: Representations and Stagings of Idleness in the Context of Colonialism." In *Idleness, Indolence and Leisure in English Literature*, edited by Monika Fludernik and Miriam Nandi, 129–153. London: Palgrave-Macmillan.

Greiner, Rae. 2012. *Sympathetic Realism in Nineteenth-Century Fiction*. Baltimore: Johns Hopkins University Press.

Hammer, Guido. 1863. "Jagderinnerungen aus dem Gebirge." *Die Gartenlaube* 21: 325–328.

Hanke, Henriette. 1842. *Die Schwiegermutter*. Hannover: Hahn.

Howkins, Alun. 2002. "From Diggers to Dongas: The Land in English Radicalism, 1649–2000." *History Workshop Journal* 54: 1–23.

Jameson, Fredric. 2007 [1990]. *Late Marxism: Adorno or the Persistence of the Dialectic*. London: Verso.
Kluge, Friedrich, ed. 2011. *Etymologisches Wörterbuch der deutschen Sprache*. Accessed 13 October 2015. Web.
Kohlmann, Benjamin. 2014. "Versions of Working-Class Idleness: Non-Productivity and the Critique of Victorian Workaholism." In *Leisure, Idleness and Indolence in British Literature*, edited by Monika Fludernik and Miriam Nandi, 195–214. Basingstoke: Palgrave-Macmillan.
Moretti, Franco. 2013. *The Bourgeois: Between History and Literature*. London: Verso.
Ogden, C. K. 1932. *Bentham's Theory of Fictions*. London: Kegan & Paul.
Riemer, Friedrich Wilhelm. 1841. *Mittheilungen über Goethe, aus mündlichen und schriftlichen, gedruckten und ungedruckten Quellen*. Vol.1. Berlin: Duncker und Humblot.
Ross, Kristin. 2015. *Communal Luxury: The Political Imaginary of the Paris Commune*. London: Verso.
Schücking, Levin. 1858. "Der gefangene Dichter." *Die Gartenlaube* 6: 73–76.
Smith, Charles Manby. 1854. *The Working-Man's Way in the World: Being the Autobiography of a Journeyman Printer*. New York: Redfield.
Taunton, Matthew. 2011. "Cottage Economy or Collective Farm? English Socialism and Agriculture between Merrie England and the Five-Year Plan." *Critical Quarterly* 53.3: 1–23.
Voth, Hans-Joachim. 2000. *Time and Work in England, 1750–1830*. Oxford: Oxford University Press.
Willes, Margaret. 2014. *The Gardens of the British Working Class*. New Haven: Yale University Press.

Kerstin Fest
The Intermediate State between Good and Bad Company: Managing Leisure in Frances Brooke's *The Excursion*

In 2014 Monika Fludernik published – together with Miriam Nandi – the first comprehensive study to provide transhistorical perspectives and critical analyses of the subject of leisure in the form of the edited volume *Idleness, Indolence and Leisure in English Literature*. This publication and Fludernik's highly influential role in the founding of and continuous engagement in the Freiburg Collaborative Research Centre 1015 "Otium/Leisure: Concepts, Spaces, Figures" are more than proof of her significance for the study of leisure in literary, cultural, and semantic contexts. In her project in the Collaborative Research Centre – "'Performing Idleness': British Theatre in the Eighteenth Century as a Space of Leisure, Idleness and Otium" – Monika Fludernik analyzes the eighteenth century as a significant era for concepts such as leisure and *otium* especially when seen in a broader social context as she locates a lowering of the "threshold to the society of leisure" as the possibility of experiencing leisure spread from the upper class to the middle class and new leisure activities and sites emerged (133, 2017). This, however, also highlights the ambivalence of the term of leisure which can be conceived positively as time free from obligations in which one can pursue interests that lie outside the mundane realm of everyday life or negatively as morally dubious indolence and frivolity. This article will discuss this ambivalence with a special focus on how leisure and society are intertwined.

Frances Brooke (1724–1789) was a prolific figure in the cultural scene of eighteenth-century London. She was a playwright, a librettist, a theatre manager, a journal editor, and a novelist.[1] She is the author of the first Canadian novel, *The History of Emily Montague* (1769), which is also the work that has garnered the most critical attention.[2] In the context of theater history, she is known as an adversary of David Garrick: wishing for a career as a playwright she submitted a

---
[1] Frances Brooke, née Moore, was born as the daughter of a clergyman in 1724. As a young woman, she moved to London to start a literary career. In her thirties, she married the Rev. John Brooke whom she followed to Quebec, where he was the chaplain of the British garrison. After her return to England in 1768, she continued her career in literature. In 1985, a crater on Venus was named after her. For Brooke's biography see McMullen 1983.
[2] *The History of Emily Montague* is an epistolary novel about the experiences of a retired English army officer in Canada. Apart from a love story, the novel also offers the reader vivid descriptions

DOI 10.1515/9783110569957-013

manuscript of a play entitled *Virginia: A Tragedy* only to have it turned down by David Garrick who was already planning a production of very similar material. Frances Brooke never forgave him and included a vicious caricature of him in *The Excursion* (1777) in which the young heroine, Maria Villiers, is snubbed by an old, arrogant, and foolish theater manager.[3] Very often it is this scene and the real-life reactions to Brooke's unflattering portrayal of the by then retired venerated David Garrick that is considered the central element of *The Excursion*. Katherine J. Charles, for instance, reads the entire novel in the light of Brooke's position in the London theater world (2014).

However, Maria's run-in with the theatre patriarch composes only one episode in this at times picaresque novel about a young woman's adventures in the alluring yet dangerous metropolis. At the beginning of the novel, Maria and her twin sister Louisa lead a peaceful but somewhat monotonous life with their indulgent uncle in the countryside. Not satisfied with this, spirited and ambitious Maria leaves her well-meaning yet naive uncle Col. Dormer and her more domestic twin sister behind to try her luck in London from where she plans to return "after an absence of two or three months with a ducal coronet on her coach" (1997, 10). However, she regards London not simply as a promising marriage market but also as a site where she will be able to enjoy herself, and, last but not least, fulfil her professional ambitions as a writer as she sets out with "a novel, an epic poem and a tragedy" (1997, 16) in her portmanteau, confident that her work will also be of financial use. Having arrived in London, a series of unfortunate incidents and her own naiveté lead her into fashionable yet not entirely respectable society. Maria, while clever, beautiful, and good, is soon out of her depth both emotionally and financially.

It comes as little surprise that criticism on *The Excursion* tends to focus on its engagement with questions of gender and femininity, often in the context of the

---

of the Canadian landscape and touches on religious and political issues in the Canadian colonies.

3 *Virginia: A Tragedy* was never staged but published in print in 1756. Brooke's vitriolic portrayal of Garrick in *The Excursion* more than twenty years later drew mostly negative reactions in the English press. The *Monthly Review* of August 1777, for example, writes about "the aspersions Mrs Brooke has unjustly cast on our old friend ROSCIUS" and wishes to defend him "not because he is the best actor in the world, but because we think him a worthy man too" (Anon. 1777, 141). Garrick himself wrote in a letter to his friend Frances Cadogan: "I hope you have seen how much I am abus'd in yr. Friend Mrs. Brook's new Novel? – she is pleased to insinuate that [I am] an excellent Actor, a so so writer, an Execrable Manager and a Worse Man – Thank you good Madame Brookes [sic]" (1963, 1172). In her second edition, Brooke tones down her caricature of Garrick.

genre of the sentimental novel. Frances Brooke's biographer (and staunch supporter) Lorraine McMullen considers the novel as a *bildungsroman* in which a young woman "is educated in the ways of the world" (1983, 169). Janet Todd puts Brooke firmly into the camp of sentimental novelists and more or less dismisses her as "typical of the new woman novelist and [...] utterly respectable" (1989, 177); possible ironic elements employed by Brooke and similar authors are according to Todd "overwhelmed by the sentimental tone" as there "is no real alternative to the sentimental construction of femininity" (1989, 178). Other critics offer more differentiated readings: Katherine Rogers reads Brooke's sentimentality in a feminist context (1978, 170) and Betty A. Schellenberg similarly argues that Brooke's awareness of and engagement with political, cultural, and social questions inform her writing (2005, 145). Emily Smith also argues that Brooke writes against a neat gendered separation of private and public spheres (2007, 171).

This article, however, moves away from the topics of sentimentality and gender and focuses on the concept of leisure instead. As leisure becomes a social marker in the eighteenth century it is worthwhile to make it the focus of the analysis of a novel so concerned with social contexts and mores as *The Excursion* is. Leisure also lends coherence to the narrative. It appears in different forms and in various contexts, provides momentum for the novel's *bildungsroman* plot and propels it towards the inevitable happy ending. This article provides an exploration of leisure as a motif. However, it is fair to say, that leisure also has a considerable narrative function.

The article will discuss how two versions of leisure are juxtaposed in Brooke's text: one is associated with the countryside and the other with the fashionable city. At first glance, leisure in the country appears as morally superior and more 'natural' than the hedonistic pursuit of sensual pleasures in the city. Yet, similar aspects of leisure appear in both contexts and are equally ambiguous in both settings. This is especially true for the relation between leisure and love on the one hand, and leisure and money on the other. These aspects are presented as flashy and extravagant in the city: love is an idle game of intrigue or chasing the most alluring courtesan; money is associated with reckless gambling and characters indulge in their various pleasures. Each of these elements, however, has its equivalent in the countryside: love is a genteel ritual that eventually leads to marriage; money is not talked about but is still necessary to create 'good' leisure and people are also in danger of being ruled by their, albeit rather harmless, pleasures. What is considered good or bad leisure is thus relative and rather a question of degrees than of absolutes. Leisure becomes part of a cultural capital that can either be accrued by more or less reckless high-risk investments in the city or prudent saving and long-term investments in the countryside. It is a "state between good and evil" Maria, but also the other characters, have to achieve. Tied to this is the question of how to properly "manage" and cultivate one's leisure as to not being overwhelmed and becoming controlled by it. In presenting idleness and leisure as highly ambivalent, *The Excursion* is typical of the eighteenth century; Sarah Jordan for instance argues that "idleness was a subject of intense anxiety in eighteenth-century Britain" (2014, 107). The beginning of the novel presents the two different kinds of leisure mentioned above. *The Excursion* starts with a scene of prototypical rural leisure, describing how Maria and her sister

> were leaning over the terrace wall of their uncle's garden, admiring the radiant lustre of the setting sun, the mixed gold and azure which played on a rustic temple belonging to a neighbouring villa, praising the heart-felt pleasures of retirement, and the tranquil joys of a rural life. (Brooke and Backscheider 1997, 5)

The extremely overt authorial narrator, however, almost immediately undercuts this idyll by repeating almost the entire phrase within significantly ironic inverted commas when talking about Maria's attitude towards her peaceful life at her uncle's estate.[4] Watching an upper-class acquaintance driving off in "a superb carriage" (1997, 5), Maria "sighed; her bosom beat with an emotion unknown before; she forgot the radiant lustre of the setting sun [...] the tranquil joys of country life." Instead Maria "felt, for the first time, the poison of ambition in her heart" (1997, 5). Unlike her placid sister Louisa, who "fancied Happiness reposed on roses in the shade," Maria "sighed to pursue the fugitive goddess through the brilliant mazes of the world" (1997, 7). In short, Maria is not inclined and perhaps not even able to appreciate the rural leisure of her close family and her ambitiousness sets her apart from Louisa. She will not be satisfied with the heir of a humble country squire, and is sure that she will return to Belfont within a few months "with a ducal coronet on her coach" (1997, 10).[5]

The life she dreams of is one of glamor and pleasure in the city. Her wish to move to the capital is triggered by her friendship with the young vivacious widow Mrs Herbert who, while being one of the positive characters in the novel, is submerged in an urban life of leisure that is as much about enjoyment as it is about

---

[4] Schellenberg connects the narrative voice in *The Excursion*, "whose self-consciously cynical tone is darker and more all-pervasive" than in Brooke's other writing with the depiction of the countryside as "self-consciously stylized and represented with irony" (2005, 67).
[5] A duke is the highest rank below the monarch; a squire refers to a local dignity, ranking above a gentleman and below a knight.

status and appearances. She "doated [sic] on the Opera and Ranelagh because there were no two places where people looked so well; and abjured the Pantheon, not because it was *triste*, but because it was unbecoming" (1997, 10).[6] Things, however, do not go smoothly once Maria has arrived in London. Mrs Herbert is abroad and so Maria is catapulted into London's leisure society without a chaperon or guide. She ends up in a shady demi-monde led by Lady Hardy, a former dairymaid whose late husband, a baronet who "very generously made her an honest woman" after a turbulent fifteen-year on-off relationship (1997, 18). The narrator archly calls this social class "*a certain set*" (printed in telling italics throughout the novel) that consists of "a heterogeneous mass of unknown gentlemen, self-made captains, demireps, neglected coquets, antiquated virgins, and dowagers *sur le retour*" (1997, 20). What makes this group *a certain set* is "its ever-open gate [which] stands ready to admit all who, for whatever cause, are either utterly rejected, or coldly received, in more estimable society" (1997, 20). The *certain set* is also mostly about appearances:

> If fortunes, if dress, if diamonds, if equipage, if even title alone, abstracted from all regard to character, or to the qualities of the head and heart, could constitute good society, *a certain set* would undoubtedly merit the name. (1997, 20)

The *certain set* thus becomes the foil to Maria's seemingly boring circle of family and friends in the countryside. However, the *certain set* and the community at Belfont have in common that both of them know how to negotiate their particular version of leisure. Each member of these radically different groups knows the rules and rituals of their performance and how to achieve the cultural capital of leisure; Maria, on the other hand, still needs to find her place.

Money is central in *The Excursion* and it is connected to leisure and idleness in an often problematic way. An idle life in London requires both having money and displaying one's wealth. Here Brooke, on the one hand, takes up the trope of performative leisure so typical of Restoration drama where "naughty idleness [is] a marker of social indolence" (Fludernik 2014, 129). Wealth, on the other hand, is

---

[6] The reference to the Opera can be read as a tongue-in-cheek allusion to Brooke herself who, together with Mary Ann Yates, became manager of the King's Theatre in the Haymarket which was known as the Opera House. Ranelagh, opened to the public in 1741, was an extremely popular pleasure where masquerades, concerts, and fireworks took place. It was considered as more fashionable than its middle-class competitor Vauxhall Gardens. The Pantheon had been designed by Henry Wyatt and was located in Oxford Street. Horace Walpole referred to it as a "winter Ranelagh" (1844, 291). One can speculate that Mrs Herbert finds the indoor lighting less flattering than the gaslights on balmy summer evenings in Ranelagh. On pleasure gardens see Bending 2013, Borg and Coke 2011, and Fest 2015.

also potentially morally dubious. In fashionable London, it often comes from questionable sources such as gambling, being the mistress of a wealthy man, or marrying for money. The urban leisure society is thus both based on and threatened by money. However, also the 'good' life of leisure in the country is based on money albeit not as visibly as in the city.

The performance of leisure in this context turns out to be a social and moral marker: 'good' characters are able to perform a genteel leisure without drawing undue attention to the material basis of their existence or the performativity of their only seemingly natural behavior; morally dubious characters – like those from London's demi-monde – perform their leisure and wealth ostentatiously and consciously. In both contexts, however, leisure is the result of money used in an advantageous way: in the city, money must be inserted into a constant cycle of winning and losing in which risks must be taken and debt is seen as a means to achieve social status and the pleasures coming with it; in the country, money must be prudently saved and invested to ensure a peaceful life of leisure in the long run.

Money in the city is mostly linked to gambling.[7] Gambling is presented as a highly ambivalent activity that simultaneously rejects and requires money. George Bataille argues in "The Notion of Expenditure" that gambling is a sign of an elevated social group who can sacrifice money in "unproductive social expenditure" (Botting 1998, 175) that displays the gambler's wealth through his lack of concern about financial loss. Bataille celebrates this as "generous, orgiastic and excessive" and laments the decline of this attitude as a symptom of the bourgeoisie's ascendancy: "The representatives of the bourgeoisie have adopted an effaced manner; wealth is now displayed behind closed doors, in accordance with depressing and boring conventions" (Bataille 1997, 175).[8]

The scene Maria is confronted with at her first visit at Lady Hardy's house appears on the surface like the aristocratic nonchalance Bataille describes, but the gamblers in *The Excursion* are ambiguous when it comes to social standing. Lady Hardy's *certain set* is in no position to blithely enjoy their games without thinking about their financial situation. They are neither Bataille's aristocrats nor do they belong to the thrifty bourgeoisie. On the contrary: they are constantly

---

[7] For gambling in the eighteenth century see Markley 2006, Molesworth 2010, Rosenthal 2015, and Astbury 2000.
[8] Evans uses Bataille's notion of aristocratic gambling and bourgeois frugality for a non-chronological view of attitudes towards gambling in England as he talks about "the Carolean carnival that followed the Cromwellian lent" (Evans 2002, 2). By Brooke's time, the pendulum had obviously swung back again.

aware of the need to perform as well as of the necessary financial underpinnings of their performance. The narrator also indicates that Lady Hardy's routs are not about "matching nubile men and women with each other" (Schneider 1993, 6). The gamblers are devoid of any concerns or alliances beyond gambling: "[The gambler] is of no *sex*; as he is of no *age*, no *country*, no *party*, no *religion*" (1997, 22). Maria, of course, does not see through this. She only sees the pseudo-aristocratic performance and wishes to be part of what she thinks is the upper class. On her first night at Lady Hardy's, "she sat down without having dared to enquire into the stake, and was surprised at being asked for twenty guineas to put into the pool" (1997, 22).

That Maria is soon faced with financial difficulties comes as no big surprise. Not only does she frequently lose at cards but she also overspends at Lady Hardy's advice: "[Y]ou must have a house, servants, carriage, and a thousand necessary *et ceteras*, without which you will ever be regarded as one whom nobody knows" (1997, 54). Maria seems unable to see the connections between the life of leisure she aspires to, the necessity of money and the question of where to get it. Unlike the members of the *certain set*, she does not realize that these things should be considered as investments that will ensure their purchaser's entrance to the *certain set* and the subsequent possibilities of winning money or snaring a wealthy husband or lover there. Maria simply wants to own these props of a fashionable life of leisure and she purchases them straightforwardly and foolishly as an exasperated narrator points out: "Behold her then on the eve of appearing [...] with a carriage and two footmen, on an income of less than a hundred pounds a year" (1997, 55). She also does not know how to invest and strategically use her financial and cultural capital in order to appear wealthy, carefree, and desirable. When her hairdresser reminds her of her unpaid bills, she reacts honorably but rashly: "Both her own temper, and the education given her by Col. Dormer, had inspired her with the laudable pride of disdaining to be in debt. She therefore paid him, however inconvenient, and found she had only twenty pounds remaining" (1997, 88–89).[9] Maria's appealing to Lady Hardy, whom she thinks a friend, for a loan is another point in case: money, to Maria, is only a means to an end while Lady Hardy is weighing up Maria's value in relation to her own social standing and finally decides against helping her. While Maria expects Lady Hardy to

---

9 Also, Maria's certainty that she will be able to make extra money by selling her literary works illustrates Maria's touchingly naive attitude towards financial matters extremely well: "She also considered that, if necessary, she had a considerable sum in bank in her portmanteau: she estimated her epic poem at 500l., her novel at 200l., and her play, including the copy, at 500l." (1997, 55).

act as a friend, the latter behaves in a business-like way, coolly deciding on what serves her best.

When it comes to romance, Maria is also disastrously unaware of the strategies and calculations of the *certain set*. The key incident supporting this claim is Maria's infatuation with Lord Melvile, a dashing young nobleman, with whom she falls in love at first sight. The narrator deftly exposes Maria's inexperience by juxtaposing her rapture with Melvile's nonchalance: after their first meeting, Maria writes an ecstatic letter to her sister informing her that she has met her future husband and could have "filled a folio sheet in this Pindaric style" (1997, 26). The narrator describes Lord Melvile as follows:

> We should be happy if that scrupulous regard for truth [...] would permit us to say that, this wonderful sympathy was as strong on the side of Lord Melvile: but the plain fact is, he went from Lady Hardy's to Arthur's, played deep, won a very considerable sum, retired home at two, in all the pride of triumphant success, to Mademoiselle Dorignon [his live-in French mistress], and forgot, before he reached Grosvenor-street, that there existed such a being as Miss Villiers. (1997, 27)

Lord Melvile is a perfect creature of urban leisure. Although the narrator repeatedly points out that he is not a complete villain, he is certainly spoilt and lax in his morals. His household, for example, is a tableau of idle and risqué frivolity ruled by his mistress Mademoiselle Dorignon who perfectly performs her role of a charming figure of idleness:

> The divine creature! What engaging vivacity! What fire! What *piquantes caprices*! What were a thousand [Marias] to the enchanting Dorignon! [...] Her sallies were sometimes a little eccentric, but did not those very sallies stamp a greater value on her paroxysms of good humour? (1997, 30)

Unlike Maria, of course, Mademoiselle Dorignon knows exactly what she is doing and is precisely calculating how long to retain Melvile and when to move on to another benefactor. She eventually snares a clueless nabob who has just returned to England and who "knows about as much of the world as a country school-boy of thirteen" (1997, 103).

In Maria's mind, however, there is no calculation when it comes to love and anything but marriage is unimaginable to her. This is used to create a comic effect in an episode about a meeting between Melvile and Maria in which he wants to discuss the terms of setting her up as his "favourite sultana" (1997, 63) and she is convinced that the subject of their conversation is their pending marriage. In their short exchange, the discourses of love and money become ambiguous and fused with each other: Melvile offers Maria "*carte blanche* in respect to settlement" but Maria's "idea of the word settlement differed very essentially from his lordship's" and she answers that "she had the most lively sense of his lordship's generosity and nobleness of sentiment; but that she loved him for himself alone, and was indifferent to every other consideration" (1997, 91). This is indeed a "romantic misunderstanding of the market" (Richard 2011, 193).

Unlike Maria, Melvile considers taking on Maria as his "declared mistress" as an investment in his social status:

> As vanity was the predominant passion of his soul, he could not resist the triumph his imagination promised him, in producing (as soon as decency after marriage allowed) so much beauty, as his property, to the world. (1997, 77)

Melvile is here reminiscent of Bataille's aristocratic gambler, his ability to flaunt his enjoyment without the shackles of middle-class values such as frugality and faithfulness only adds to his allure. While the gamblers at Lady Hardy's only act as if they were able to carelessly lose their money, Melvile is in no position to make decisions about his private life independently from any other consideration. In fact, he has just agreed with his dissolute father, who, at ten in the morning, is "in an elegant *dishabille*, reclining on a sopha, reading a political pamphlet with a dish of chocolate in his hand," that he will have to marry a rich heiress whose father "has offered [...] eighty thousand pounds down" for which, so Melvile's father, "we have great present occasion" (1997, 45). Concisely, Melvile has to 'sell' himself to the, at this stage, unknown daughter of a rich man to keep up his and his father's leisurely lifestyles.[10]

Good investments, both financially and in regards of social status, are also tantamount when it comes to rural leisure. The good education of Maria and her sister, for instance, is the result of their uncle's financial generosity:

> [Col. Dormer] had gone beyond the bounds of his little fortune to procure them, as far as his remote situation and retired manner of living made possible, those external accomplishments [...]; or, in the words of a late noble writer, to give them "the Graces." (1997, 6)[11]

---

[10] In an ironic twist intended by Brooke, Miss Harding turns out to be not only rich but pretty and accomplished as well. Melvile is both surprised and enchanted. Also, her parents' house turns out to be the perfect place for a life in leisure and luxury as it is "furnished with all the splendour of the East": the table is "covered with every costly delicacy of the world" and Miss Harding appears as "rather an Asiatic queen than the daughter of an English private gentleman" (1997, 106). The connection between money and leisure is obvious here.

[11] This is a reference to Philip Dormer Stanhope's (1694–1773) *Letters to His Son* about the importance of good breeding in a young gentleman (Brooke 1997, 156).

Maria's apparently natural charms on which she relies so much at the beginning of the novel are thus to a certain extent a commodity acquired by her uncle by wise husbandry.

Col. Dormer has also very consciously chosen to invest in the possibility of a life of (good) leisure in the countryside:

> [H]e had bought a small house, with an estate of about five hundred pounds a year, at Belfont, a delightful village in Rutland; where, as the human mind must always have a pursuit, he acquired a passion of gardening; a passion which filled up those hours which might have lain heavy on his hand, and chased the monster *Ennui*, to avoid whose chilling embrace, men turn rakes, heroes, gamesters, politicians, and hunt Folly through her ever-varying circle. (1997, 6)

The result of Col. Dormer's investment is a leisurely existence which is presented as genteelly productive:

> An enthusiastic neatness, elegance, were the characteristics of his little domain: delicate in his choice, attentive in his culture, his flowers bloomed more fair, his fruit had a more delicious flavour, than those of his more opulent neighbours. (1997, 8)

This pleasant state, however, is potentially as precarious as the gamblers' luck in the city as the narrator hints at the somewhat limited funds of Col. Dormer. And while he is primarily lauded for his management of the estate, his natural inclination towards tranquility and idleness has its darker side, too: when Maria begs him to let her go to London, the narrator concedes that the most obvious solution would be for him to accompany her to the city. Yet, "he pleaded his decline of life, his indolence of temper, his delicate health, his disgust of the world, his love of tranquillity and retirement" (1997, 13). At this point, rural leisure is not presented as entirely positive. Taken to the extreme, here in the form of Maria's uncle's excessive passion for gardening, it is actually damaging to Col. Dormer's responsibility towards his ward:

> At another season he would not have hesitated a moment; but to leave his garden during the three most important months of the year – his early flowers, his hyacinths then ready to blow, his tulips, his anemonies, his articulas; his lovely new polyanthus [...] all the blooming hope of the genial spring, the floral pride of the rising year – all, all, would too probably perish, if he left the tender nurselings, or (to speak in technical terms) the *babes*, at this critical juncture. (1997, 13)

As the narrator points out, his "ruling passion" has "throw[n] a veil over [his] reason" (1997, 13) and the consequence is the almost fatal neglect of his human "nurseling" Maria, although she too is in her youthful prime and thus as vulnerable as the flowers. Like Maria, Col. Dormer has to find a way to control his performance of leisure to arrive at true happiness in the end.[12]

Col. Dormer's mostly appropriate performance of rural leisure is mirrored in Maria's sister Louisa who, unlike her sister, has been wishing for a peaceful life in the country with the eldest son of a neighboring squire all along. While this might be considered dull in comparison to Maria's romantic and financial turmoil in the city, it is also prudent and, as it turns out, financially advantageous. Pleased by his son's proposal to Louisa, Squire Montague reveals that he has already prepared for his son's future happiness:

> Determined to guard my son against the misery of selling himself to keep the family estate together, I have always had this moment in view. My estate is three thousand pounds a year, of which I have laid by half ever since I was married; that I might become rich enough to make my children happy, without retrenching my own expenses. (1997, 130)

Again, leisure in the country (the Squire has also already purchased "a pretty house" [1997, 130] for his son) is the result of sound financial planning that has happened behind the scenes. The Squire, who has been disparaged at the beginning of the novel for his unrefined tastes, thus proves to be the far better father than Lord Melvile.

As the loose ends of the novel are tied up towards the end, the narrator takes the restoration of "good" rural leisure to an ironic extreme: Maria is saved from moral and financial disaster by well-meaning friends, moves back to her uncle's estate and finds herself drawn to the upright and dependable Col. Herbert. As the narrator remarks: "In short, she was the Maria of Belfont, not of Berner's-street [her address in London]" (1997, 143).

Interestingly, elements that have been depicted as tempting yet dangerous in the city reappear as parts of genteel peaceful country life, well managed rather than indulged in by the characters involved: playing cards, for instance, turns into an innocent occupation that allows Maria to ponder her newly found tender feelings for Col. Herbert. She no longer associates gambling with Lady Hardy's overwhelming routs where she was desperately trying to impress Lord Melvile

---

[12] Interestingly, it is Maria's placid sister Louisa and her love interest, Mr Montague, who master the art of balanced harmony right from the beginning. Mr Montague is a sophisticated Eton and Cambridge alumnus but also "walked, rode, played cricket, and shot flying" and thus combines the best of both worlds: "He was easy, courteous, attentive, well-bred; but without the high Parisian varnish" (1997, 35).

while frantically calculating how much money she could afford to lose. As the following quotation verifies, the opposite is actually the case:

> Miss Villiers had never observed [Col. Herbert] so attentively before: the fire of his eyes, the spirit of his whole countenance, formed such a contrast with the maukish [sic], unmeaning, uninformed, macaroni faces about town, as could not fail to strike very forcibly a woman of her turn of mind.
> He was certainly not so handsome as Lord Melvile – O! not a thousandth part so handsome –
> And yet she knew not how – but he was more interesting – had more soul – (1997, 145)

At the very end of *The Excursion*, the return to social harmony is also rewarded by a stroke of pure luck. Col. Dormer receives a letter informing him that he has inherited the fortune and the title of an Earl from a distant and estranged relative. Upon receiving the letter, Col. Dormer informs the company that he has been aware of this possible inheritance for quite some time but has refrained from telling his nieces because he did not want to raise their hopes in case it should end in disappointment (1997, 151). Once again, Col. Dormer was able to 'manage' leisure wisely and not speculate and rely on a possible future outcome. At this point, he wants to invest his fortune in his nieces' future:

> I have more money than I know how to make use of myself: I therefore present each of you with twenty thousand pounds, and leave it to yourselves to bestow it as you please. (1997, 151)

What he plans is to enable his friends and family to lead a quiet life of leisure as he wishes "to form a neighbourhood of persons endeared to each other by the most tender ties" (1997, 152). This 'airy project' is diametrically opposed to Lady Hardy's *certain set*: the people in it have secure social standings and roles, they are well provided for and most importantly, they are carefully chosen. Col. Dormer has clearly learnt to manage his leisure well and is now also able to see the necessity of balance as he plans to also have a house in London where all his friends will be welcome to stay.

This *deus ex machina* ending is certainly in the tradition of the sentimental novel but also ironically and gently questions the somewhat clichéd message of the novel, namely that 'good' leisure can be earned. In the end, rural leisure, or at least Col. Dormer's ideal, despite all its well-managed performances and investments, requires simple good luck to be realized.[13] Thus, this ending, which is

---

13 Col. Dormer himself remarks: "And now who will say that Fortune, though in herself contemptible, does not sometimes contribute to happiness?" (1997, 153).

almost exaggeratedly happy and whose message is almost too pat, once again reaffirms the ambivalence of leisure which is neither good nor bad and is as likely to be achieved through prudent investment as by gambling.

References

Anon. 1777. "The *Excursion*. A Novel by Mrs. Brooke, Author of Julia Mandeville and Emily Montague." *The Monthly Review, Or, Literary Journal* 57: 141–145.
Astbury, Katherine. 2000. "Games in the Moral Tale: A Reflection on Changing Tastes in the 1760s." In *French Social History/Games in the Eighteenth Century/Happiness in Duclos and Rousseau*, edited by Anthony Strugnell, 161–167. Oxford: Voltaire Foundation.
Bending, Stephen, ed. 2013. *A Cultural History of Gardens in the Age of Enlightenment*. London: Bloomsbury.
Borg, Alan, and David Coke. 2011. *Vauxhall Gardens: A History*. New Haven: Yale University Press.
Botting, Fred, ed. 1998. *Bataille: A Critical Reader*. Oxford: Blackwell.
Brooke, Frances, and Paula R. Backscheider. 1997 [1777]. *The Excursion*. Lexington: University Press of Kentucky.
Charles, Katherine G. 2014. "Staging Sociability in The Excursion: Frances Brooke, David Garrick, and the King's Theatre Coterie." *Eighteenth-Century Fiction* 27.2: 257–284.
Evans, James E. 2002. "'A Sceane of Uttmost Vanity': The Spectacle of Gambling in Late Stuart Culture." *Studies in Eighteenth-Century Culture* 31: 1–20.
Fest, Kerstin. 2015. "Strumpets and Nightingales: The Amusement Parks of London." In *Der Garten im Fokus Kultureller Diskurse im 18. Jahrhundert*, edited by Peter Wagner et al., 101–114. Trier: WVT.
Fludernik, Monika. 2014. "The Performativity of Idleness: Representations and Stagings of Idleness in the Context of Colonialism." In *Idleness, Indolence and Leisure in English Literature*, edited by Monika Fludernik and Miriam Nandi, 129–153. New York: Palgrave Macmillan.
---. 2017. "Spectators, Ramblers and Idlers: The Conflicted Nature of Indolence and the Eighteenth-Century Tradition of Idling." *Anglistik* 28.1: 133–154.
Fludernik, Monika, and Miriam Nandi, ed. 2014. *Idleness, Indolence and Leisure in English Literature*. New York: Palgrave Macmillan.
Garrick, David. 1963. *The Letters of David Garrick. Letters 816–1362*. Cambridge: Belknap Press of Harvard University Press.
Jordan, Sarah. 2014. "Idleness, Class and Gender in the Long Eighteenth Century." In *Idleness, Indolence and Leisure in English Literature*, edited by Monika Fludernik and Miriam Nandi, 107–128. New York: Palgrave Macmillan.
Markley, A. A. 2006. "Aristocrats Behaving Badly: Gambling and Dueling in the 1790s Novel of Reform." *European Romantic Review* 17.2: 161–168.
McMullen, Lorraine. 1983. *An Odd Attempt in a Woman: The Literary Life of Frances Brooke*. Vancouver: University of British Columbia Press.
Molesworth, Jesse. 2010. *Chance and the Eighteenth-Century Novel: Realism, Probability, Magic*. Cambridge: Cambridge University Press.

Richard, Jessica. 2011. *The Romance of Gambling in the Eighteenth-Century British Novel*. New York: Palgrave Macmillan.
Rogers, Katharine M. 1978. "Sensibility and Feminism: The Novels of Frances Brooke." *Genre* 11: 159–171.
Rosenthal, Richard J. 2015. "Gambling." In *Dostoevsky in Context*, edited by Deborah A. Martinsen and Olga Maiorova, 148–156. Cambridge: Cambridge University Press.
Schellenberg, Betty A. 2005. *The Professionalization of Women Writers in Eighteenth Century Britain*. Cambridge: Cambridge University Press.
Schneider, Matthew. 1993. "Card-Playing and the Marriage Gamble in *Pride and Prejudice*." *Dalhousie Review* 73.1: 5–17.
Smith, Emily. 2007. *Triumphant Bodies: Sexual Political Conquest in Women's Published Writing, 1660–1763*. Newcastle: Cambridge Scholars.
Todd, Janet M. 1989. *The Sign of Angellica: Women, Writing and Fiction, 1660–1800*. New York: Columbia University Press.
Walpole, Horace. 1844. *Letters of Horace Walpole, Earl of Orford, to Sir Horace Mann*. Philadelphia: Lea & Blanchard.

Margarete Rubik
Out of the Dungeon, into the World: Aspects of the Prison Novel in Emma Donoghue's *Room*

1 *Room* as a Prison Novel

When Emma Donoghue's novel *Room* was published in 2010, it was greeted with glowing reviews and was shortlisted for the Man Booker Prize. It was praised as "taut, devastating and gripping" (blurb), but also extolled as "affecting and uplifting" (blurb), "absorbing, truthful and beautiful" (Barr 2010) – adjectives that may seem surprising at first, given the book's subjects of kidnap, forcible rape, and false imprisonment. In fact, the novel's plot was inspired by a sensational real-life crime case: Josef Fritzl kept his own daughter prisoner in the cellar of his house for twenty-four years and fathered several children on her, one of whom finally fell so ill that she had to be taken to hospital, which led to the discovery of the victims. *Room* deals with a similar scenario, although Donoghue left out the aspect of incest: a young woman is kidnapped and incarcerated in an escape-proof garden shed for seven years, together with her son, the product of frequent sexual assaults, to whom she gave birth during her imprisonment. To save the boy from traumatization and perpetual frustration about his captivity, she tells him that they are the only people on earth, that outside their room there is outer space, and that the films he sees on television, the books they read together and the stories she tells him are mere fiction, with no reference to reality. She also tries to shield him from awareness of her constant sexual violation by hiding him in the wardrobe during the kidnapper's nightly visits. Mother and son finally trick the kidnapper into believing the boy is dead, so that the man carries the supposed corpse outside, from where the child can escape and call help. The second part of the novel then deals with the aftermath of their jail-break and the difficulties both encounter in adapting to the world outside their prison.

For all its lurid subject matter, *Room* "has no intention of trafficking in the sexual charge of abduction thrillers" (Charles 2010) and avoids the "prurience of so much crime fiction" (Gibbs 2010), eliminating all fascination and voyeuristic identification with the criminal, because the events are narrated through the eyes of the five-year-old child, who has never been outside of the eponymous room and does not understand what his mother is going through. Readers have no access to the woman's mind – or rather, only indirect access through empathetic projection [1] – and certainly understand more about the woman's ordeal than the child listening to the sounds of the kidnapper's nightly visits in his wardrobe: "When Old Nick creaks Bed, I listen and count five on my fingers, tonight it's 217 creaks" (Donoghue 2010, 46). The author's focus, thus, is not on the fate of the abused woman, but on the world view little Jack has pieced together under these extraordinary circumstances, the way he tries to make sense of his existence, his inevitable cognitive constraints and knowledge gaps, and his later gradual schema adjustments after their escape. The novel, however, is not only a fascinating study of cognitive development, but can also be read as a prison novel,[2] complete with a climactic jailbreak and a return of the victims to what at least we as readers would consider to be the normal world. *Room* is unique also in the context of the genre of prison literature because it adopts a unique point of view on the prison experience: pre-schoolers, of course, are not generally thrown into prison, and few prison novels are even told from the narrative perspective of juvenile delinquents who have reached adolescence.[3] Jack's naive perspective thus provides a new angle on the genre, first and foremost because he is not aware that he is incarcerated and does not conceive of the small shed as a prison. Not that the boy does not know what a prison is; indeed, he has two prison schemas: through Dumas's *Count of Monte Cristo* (1844–1846) and the legend of St. Paul's rescue from prison he is familiar with the idea of unjust captivity at the hands of tyrants, and through TV crime series he is aware of imprisonment as a punitive

---

[1] When such an *externalist perspective*, which "stresses those aspects that are outer, active, public, social, behavioral, evident, embodied, and engaged" (Palmer 2010, 39) is employed, readers will construct character consciousness on the basis of a "bare minimum of information" (2010, 10) by bringing "real-world cognitive frames to bear" (2010, 49) on the narrative and deducing mental attitudes from a character's body language, tone of voice, or behavior.

[2] As Fludernik (2005a, 2) points out, prison settings have become rare in non-ethnic, non-immigrant novels ever since the Modernist period, though they frequently feature in African-American and postcolonial fiction and in movies.

[3] Examples are, for instance, Alan Sillitoe's "The Loneliness of the Long Distance Runner" (1959), the last part of DBC Pierre's *Vernon God Little* (2003), Walter Dean Myers's *Lockdown* (2010), or Shanon McKay's *Prison Boy* (2015), though in the latter novel a seven-year-old child is incarcerated, too. The Japanese-Canadian girl interned with her family during the Second World War in Shizuye Tanashima's *A Child in Prison Camp* (1971) is eleven, thus also considerably older than Jack. Like Louis Sacher's *Holes* (1998), set in a boys' boot camp, it is children's fiction and not a prison novel in the true sense of the word.

measure, although for him all these narratives are purely fictional, bearing no relation to any outside reality. What he lacks is an appropriate schema for what freedom is.

The prison which is Jack's home, of course, is not a penitentiary or corrective institution in the traditional sense; it is an oubliette built to give the kidnapper access to the sexual services of the mother and to prevent her from fleeing. As Jack is unaware of these circumstances, it is not immediately obvious to the reader on the first few pages of the text that mother and son are incarcerated. Undoubtedly, we may experience a certain estrangement and puzzlement due to Jack's way of narrating (Caracciolo 2014, 199–200) – in particular his penchant of referring to Room, Wardrobe, Bed, or Lamp with capital letters and without an article (because, as we find out later, he regards them as friends and unique, being unaware that many objects of the same kind exist out in the world). However, the very first sentence of the novel – "Today I'm five" (Donoghue 2010, 3) – offers an appropriate frame for readers to naturalize some of the oddities by interpreting them as childish ways of expression,[4] quite in line with his naivety when pondering about his age: "Was I minus numbers? [...] Up in Heaven." (Donoghue 2010, 3). Since the novel so conspicuously draws attention to the narrator's age at the beginning, readers are likely to anticipate a fallible narrator, to use Olson's term,[5] and will be ready to make allowance for his naive world-view. We certainly do not expect a child's world knowledge, interests, and emotional reactions to concur with ours.

As in all novels with child-narrators, the gap between a naive and an adult reader's understanding opened up by the choice of such a point of view is "a territory of emotional power" (Bender 2010), but precludes *narratorial implicature*, a term coined by Bortolussi and Dixon as a counterpart to H. P. Grice's *conversational implicature*, or in other words, it does not allow readers to make "inferences licensed by the assumption that the narrator is cooperative" (Bortolussi and Dixon 2003, 72–73). We cannot expect a child narrator to follow Grice's co-

---

[4] In fact, the beginning of the novel is a showcase of both the way readers will employ naturalization (Culler 1975, 137), i.e. they try to find plausible explanations for textual oddities, for instance in a narrator's cognitive or mental problems, and of the primacy effect in a literary text, i.e. the tendency "that the reader retains the meanings constructed initially *to what ever extent possible*" (Perry 1979, 57), which is why it takes him or her so long to realize that a five-year-old should be incarcerated.

[5] Olson (2003) distinguishes between fallible and untrustworthy narrators, who elicit different audience responses ranging from understanding for the failings of the former to exasperation with the dispositional unreliability of the latter.

operative principle. Jack never lies intentionally, but his world knowledge is completely awry, and at least in the beginning he also does not give sufficient or relevant enough information for readers to orient themselves. If we use Phelan's classification (2005, 51), Jack both misinterprets his situation and underreports, which requires the reader to reconstruct the true state of affairs from circumstantial evidence, and to supplement information the boy fails to understand or considers too normal to merit mentioning. Although some of his strange notions and beliefs run counter to "the reader's pre-existing conceptual knowledge of the world and standards of normality" (Nünning 2005, 105), the reader is unlikely to draw on a schema of imprisonment to account for such anomalies. Thus, when Jack tells us that last night he fell asleep in Wardrobe and woke up in Bed, we note the non-standard English, but are more likely to focus on trying to explain his sleeping habits as a childish tantrum, or as rather cruel punishment – after all, Harry Potter was made to sleep in the cupboard under the stairs.

So any reader who is not aware that the novel is modeled on the Fritzl case is unlikely to suspect from the beginning that the setting is, in fact, a modern dungeon and that the two characters are kidnap victims. No bars, shackles, or chains – icons of incarceration[6] – are visible, and only much later do we learn that the whole structure is surrounded by a chain-link fence. Readers will probably originally attribute Jack's homebirth to premature labor, or extreme poverty, or a secret pregnancy, and the man's nightly visits to a secret amour. Indeed, Jack's proclivity for exaggerations ("the thousand chocolates we got the time Christmas happened" [Donoghue 2010, 5]) and his supposedly busy life ("We have thousands of things to do every morning" [2010, 10]), are likely to put readers on the wrong track, and it is only when he asserts that "dogs are only TV" (2010, 10) and it transpires that they have to beg the man who comes at night for provisions instead of shopping themselves that we slowly realize that they are confined in the room. The most astonishing information in the first few pages is not the setting but the fact that the mother still breastfeeds the boy at the age of five, and that Jack's hair comes down to his waist. By the time we have figured out his true fate and circumstances, the novel has firmly established a narrative perspective that Phelan (2007) conceptualizes as bonding unreliability, and readers have moved from confusion at the boy's strange behavior to compassion and sympathy with the narrator, indeed to admiration for his resilience, courage, and intelligence.

---

6 For a list of typical metonymic paraphernalia of prisons see Fludernik 2005a, 16.

2 The Portrayal of the Prison

Let us look at the prototypical features of literary descriptions of prisons which Fludernik has perceptively defined (see Fludernik 2004, 2005a, 2005b, 2008) and see how they are realized in this novel. As mentioned above, the eponymous Room is not immediately recognizable as a jail. Their 11x11 foot habitation is poorly furnished, but has electric light and heating, a bathroom (without door, thus providing no space of withdrawal), a small oven, a bed, a wardrobe and some boards, and a rug. What we only learn much later is that it is situated within a garden shed made of vinyl-coated steel insulated by foam and a layer of sheet lead to kill all sound, and it is accessible only through a security door which can be opened with an electronic code (Donoghue 2010, 106). The light comes in through a soundproof skylight secured by a polycarbonate mesh. Hence, like prisoners in a dungeon with windows too high to reach, they cannot see their surroundings, only the sky, and Jack therefore has no idea of what the world actually looks like.

As the child-narrator has no personal sense of being incarcerated and hence no wish to escape, the door, generally the focus of a prisoner's fear and longing since it provides ingress and egress to the cell (Fludernik 2008, 49), affords him little interest. He prefers to play with other objects in the room, though he occasionally fiddles with the electronic buttons of the keypad randomly to make them beep. The "constitutive opposition between an inside and an outside" (Fludernik 2008, 68), so characteristic of prison literature, also exists in *Room*, but with an uncommon valuation: as Jack believes that outside of their room there is outer space, and the world shown on television is a mere invention, leaving Room is not really attractive to him and he does not realize that he has a natural habitat quite different from the dingy shed. He has, however, learned to be apprehensive of the electronic beeps of the door which announce Old Nick's arrival at nine o'clock in the evening, by which time he must hide in the wardrobe. Sometimes he wishes to peep outside on these occasions: "I bet I could see right into the stars and the spaceships and the planets and the aliens zooming around in UFOs, I wish I wish I wish I could see it" (Donoghue 2010, 59).

In their small room, their space of movement is severely limited – as is typical of the prison experience (Fludernik 2004, 147; 2008, 52). Nonetheless, they regularly do all kinds of physical exercises and gymnastic games to keep themselves fit. Jack, as we have seen, surprisingly does not feel any boredom as his mother keeps him busy with creative games, all kinds of stories, reading the nine books they possess again and again, or watching television. The matter is, of course, entirely different for Ma. Throughout the novel, two different experiences and perceptions of imprisonment clash: Jack regards the shed as normality, as his home, indeed, as a safe haven, a metaphorical second womb which he is reluctant to leave even when his mother undeceives him about the true state of affairs.[7] For the mother, obviously, the room must be a horrible dungeon, a torture chamber which cuts her off from her family and her former life, although she tries to hide her despair and tedium for Jack's sake. The reader, however, can decipher her true feelings much better than the child and gauge her boredom when she makes a face at having to read him the picture book of *Dylan the Digger* once again (Donoghue 2010, 21). Jack is not insensitive to her mood swings, but attributes them to the wrong cause: "She gets sick of things fast, it's from being an adult" (2010, 49). "I can't stand Dylan," she confesses on another occasion, "I've read it too many times" (2010, 68) – but to make him happy, she reads on. Occasionally, however, she is overwhelmed by depression and does not stir from bed for a whole day; when she is thus "Gone" (2010, 74), the boy has to prepare his own food and play by himself, assuming that Ma is troubled by a particularly severe spell of toothache.

Their room of detention partakes of the worst aspects of both the old prison type and the modern Benthamite or Foucauldian institution (see also Fludernik 2008, 44). Like in the old dungeon, the prisoners are in the hands of a cruel and arbitrary jailor, who regularly rapes the mother[8] and can gain access to her cell at any time, though he generally visits only at night. He beats and throttles the woman at any sign of disobedience and brutally broke her wrist when she tried to attack him in order to flee. On the other hand, their complete isolation from contact with relatives and friends, who indeed think that the woman is dead since she vanished without trace, is a feature reminiscent of the new prison. No sound from the outside world comes into the shed, and the prisoners fail to make themselves heard.

> After nap we do Scream every day but not Saturdays or Sundays. We clear our throats and climb up on Table to be nearer Skylight, holding hands not to fall. We say "On your mark, get set, go," then we open wide our teeth and shout holler howl yowl shriek screech scream the loudest possible. (Donoghue 2010, 50)

---

[7] In the novel the womb/tomb equivalence (Fludernik 2005a, 9) typical of prison literature does not apply to any ambiguity in Jack's attitude to Room, but it may well be applied to the juxtaposed perceptions of their place of detention on the parts of son and mother.

[8] Fludernik draws attention to the fact that safety from rape and violent attack increasingly can no longer be guaranteed in modern American penal institutions either (2004, 164).

Jack is, of course, unaware that their screaming game is meant to attract the notice of neighbors or passers-by when Old Nick is out of the house – all to no avail – and that the light signals his mother sends at night are, in fact, a distress alert in Morse code. At least they have television, and, most importantly, they have each other. However, the kidnapper originally kept the victim in solitary confinement, with serious psychic effects, as will be discussed below. Now, however, they are together, and the horrible "chilliness of prison life" (Fludernik 2005, 7; 2008, 54) has been replaced by an intense bonding, which helps the woman to survive her ordeal.

Despite their complete sealing-off, wildlife – often a sentimental harbinger of freedom in older prison literature (see Fludernik 2008, 53–55) – sometimes finds its way into the shed, but Ma squashes the mosquito (which Jack takes for a vampire sucking his blood), cleans away the spider web, and, much to Jack's dismay, also stops up the hole of a mouse, the biggest animal he has ever seen, which he hoped to make friends with like Alice in Wonderland. While the boy is thus fascinated by these live creatures, Ma makes short shrift of vermin for hygienic reasons – and possibly also because its existence threatens to call into question her fabrication about outer space beyond the door of their room.

Besides physical violence, the criminal-turned-jailor uses the "strategic physical deprivation" and a "deliberate infliction of physical discomfort" (Fludernik 2010, 61) used in modern corrective institutions to force his victim into compliance. She must thus hide her frustration and anger – both in front of the kidnapper and in front of the boy. Instead, she has to thank the man for the goods he brings them and refrains from screaming at him, lest she antagonize her captor and call forth some of his sadistic punitive measures. Despite her helplessness vis-à-vis her abuser, the birth of a child has given her back some agency of educating and protecting Jack from the criminal, yet her motherly love also renders her vulnerable to his manipulation. Thus she invites him into her bed to distract his attention from Jack, whom, she fears, he might also molest, and thus confirms Old Nick's belief that she actually enjoys her sexual degradation. Indeed, Old Nick sarcastically calls her "the boss" and himself just "the grocery boy" (Donoghue 2010, 45) and cynically reconfigures his violation of her body into something she ought to feel grateful for – considering that he could also have incarcerated her in an underground vault:

> I don't think you appreciate how good you've got it here... Aboveground, natural light, central air, it's a cut above some places, I can tell you. Fresh fruit, toiletries... Plenty girls would thank their lucky stars for a setup like this, safe as houses. Especially with the kid---. (2010, 86)

In reality, however, he only provides them with the bare necessities. Their clothes are ragged, the food is of low quality, mostly frozen or in cans, the cheapest he can get. Shockingly, when Jack was a baby, "Ma used to chop and chew up my food for me" (2010, 20) because, the reader guesses, she did not have proper baby food. The lack of vitamins may be one of the reasons why she still breastfeeds him. The insufficient nutrition has left him thin and undersized, so that the media after their rescue unflatteringly refer to him as a "bonsai boy" (2010, 269). The kidnapper also does not give them access to proper medication (a threatening scenario for anyone who has read John Fowles' *The Collector* [1963]): he buys Ma some cheap pain killers for her rotting teeth and broken wrist, but he refuses to take Jack to hospital though he is made to believe that the child is seriously ill. Even such modern amenities as electric lighting and heating are contingent upon his spleen: to punish their supposed misbehavior, he switches off the electricity for days, with the effect that their frozen food spoils and cannot be cooked, and they are in danger of starving and freezing to death. These life-threatening disciplinary measures by which he means to prove his power, however, finally motivate the mother to make one last attempt to flee.

Spectacular flights from jails are rare in contemporary prison literature (Fludernik 2008, 51) and rather a feature of adventure stories and action thrillers. After Old Nick's vengeful cutting off the electricity, however, Ma decides they must make a desperate bid to escape, lest he try the same game again, with more lethal results. Also, he has confessed that he lost his job, which means that he may no longer be able to afford their maintenance and decide to murder them. Hence she must undeceive her son about their true situation and prepare him for a daring venture. However, it proves more difficult than she has estimated to undo the web of lies she has spun. Jack will not believe that his own mother was ever "in Outside" (Donoghue 2010, 104) and once lived with her own parents. "I shake my head. '*You're* the mother.' [...] Why she's pretending like this, is it a game I don't know?" (2010, 103). And he mixes up the new reality she enlightens him about with the story worlds of his books.

At the beginning of her captivity, she tells him, she tried some of the traditional strategies to flee: screaming for help when her abductor opened the door, beating the criminal over the head with a toilet lid and holding a knife to his throat. But he refused to tell her the code opening the door, beat her up and broke her wrist. Digging a tunnel also failed. To her exasperation, for Jack, these exploits are no more realistic than the stories he has read:

> "I pried up the cork, but the wood took me a while. Then the lead foil and the foam were easy enough, but you know what I found then?"
> "Wonderland?"

Ma makes a mad sound so loud I bang my head on Bed [...].
"What I found was a chain-link fence." (2010, 119)

Their final route of escape is more unconventional than the woman's previous jailbreak attempts, but has a literary model in Dumas's *Count of Monte Cristo*. As the kidnapper refuses to take Jack to a hospital when he pretends to be seriously ill – they have heated up his face with hot water bags – Ma persuades the child to pretend to be dead and let himself be wrapped in the rug. Once Old Nick throws the supposed corpse on his pick-up and drives away to bury it, he is to jump down and call for help. Jack, however, is not keen on flight; he prefers to put it off. "'Don't you want to escape?' 'Yeah. Only not really. [...] Let's just stay'" (2010, 140). Indeed, for Jack his identity is so inextricably linked to Room that he wonders, when Old Nick does carry him outside: "I'm not in Room. Am I still me?" (2010, 172).

That the mother actually asks her five-year-old child to perform this daredevil rescue is an indication of just how desperate and near breaking point she is. Blissfully Jack does not realize how hazardous this plan is. There is no guarantee that the man will not bury the body immediately in the garden, and given his fear of detection and brutality he is likely to kill the boy if he discovers the deception. He has developed no emotional relationship whatsoever with his son, callously assuming the boy to be retarded or misshapen, since his mother keeps him hidden away – indeed, he refers to Jack as a thing: "It speaks" (2010, 45). The central scene – in the middle of the novel – when the terrified boy is actually carried out of the shed by the criminal, wriggles out of the rug, escapes, and manages to have the police notified, indeed has all the potential of a thriller, but also exerts a powerful pull of empathy in the reader by making us privy to his fear of the infuriated kidnapper, who for him turns into an ogre "coming to tear me in half" (2010, 175), to his confusion at the unknown surroundings, and to his frustration when the pedestrian he seeks help with and the police officers take a long time to make sense of his confusing statements. After his heroic adventure, it comes as a shocking anti-climax to both the freed mother and the reader that now he wants to return to his familiar habitation:

"I've seen the world and I'm tired now."
"Oh Jack," she [his mother] says, "we're never going back [to Room]." [...]
I'm crying so much I can't stop. (2010, 193)

3 The Psychological Effects of Imprisonment

As Jack's surprising wish to return to Room suggests, Jack was a truly happy prisoner (to adapt Brombert's term of a "happy prison" [1978, Ch. 5]), remarkably contented and even-tempered, despite the secluded environment he grew up in and the violence going on around him. Generally, children faced with direct or indirect violence often develop severe psychological problems; they "cope with a complex array of feelings that may include fear, anger, love, guilt, and animosity" and are "more likely than other children to exhibit a variety of behavioural, emotional, social and cognitive problems" (Siegel 2011, 80; 90), including anxiety, depression, withdrawal, low self-esteem, sleep disorders, and aggression (2011, 91). His mother, however, shields him from knowledge of the abuse she is subjected to, so that Old Nick for him is at first merely a vague figure of apprehension: "he's not human like us. He only happens in the night, like bats" (Donoghue 2010, 22), a sort of zombie, vampire, or ogre, or indeed a frightful Medusa, since the mother does not want Old Nick even to look at the boy. Once he realizes, however, that the supposed dirt smudges on his mother's throat are, in fact, the marks of the man's fingerprints, this naturally arouses an impotent wish for revenge: "I'm going to kick Old Nick till I break his butt" (2010, 77), and when his mother weeps and confesses downright that she is afraid, this naturally scares the boy all the more. Also, convincingly, though he does not really want to leave, as soon as he is told that there is a fascinating world waiting for him outside, he feels frustrated and confined in his jail: "Before I didn't even know to be mad that we can't open Door…I don't think the Easter Bunny knows where Room is, anyway we don't have bushes and trees, they're outside Door" (2010, 126–127). Mother and child thus escape just in the nick of time, before Jack becomes traumatized and develops the symptoms listed above. The flight itself, when he has to pretend to be dead, is almost suffocated by the rug, is about to be snatched back by the kidnapper, and is terrified that Old Nick may murder his mother in revenge before the police can rescue her, is doubtless traumatic, and Jack has frequent nightmares and panic memories even after the kidnapper is arrested.

Although he has spent all his short life in a prison, his cognitive development and emotion regulation are much better than one might expect in view of his social isolation. Psychologists agree that infants need to build a strong relationship to a caregiver (Siegel 2011, 35)⁹ and that "the quality of parent-child interactions is one of the most powerful environmental influences on child development" (Jeon, Peterson, and DeCoster 2013, 258), which is actually used to predict developmental risks (Maccoby 1983, 49). Jack's fate is so unique that it is difficult to compare him to real-life children studied by psychologists. A survey conducted by Goshin, Bryne, and Blanchard-Lewis, for instance, suggests that a prison environment itself does not harm infants, but "may confer resilience to anxious/depressed behaviour problems in the preschool period" (2014, 142) if it involves a close contact to the mother. Indeed, infants who were cared for by their imprisoned mothers in prison nurseries showed secure attachment rates (2010, 147) and had "significantly lower mean anxious/depressed and withdrawal behaviour scores than children who were separated from their mothers in infancy or toddlerhood because of incarceration" (2010, 147), though obviously a lot depends on the quality of the environment and context. Unlike neglected children or feral children growing up outside of society, Jack has a devoted mother, who – during their imprisonment – gave him her attention twenty-four hours a day and showered all her love on him.

Because of this extremely close – indeed "claustrophobic" (Tonkin 2010) – relationship between mother and son, however, Jack has not broken the primal bond to his mother and, in a way, still regards himself as part of her. When the psychiatrist who is examining him after the escape tries to convince him that he belongs only to himself, Jack secretly objects: "He's wrong, actually, I belong to Ma" (Donoghue 2010, 261), and later he muses, "maybe I'm a human but I'm a me-and-Ma as well. I don't know a word for us two. Roomers?" (2010, 342). As a result, he develops severe separation anxiety once they are outside of their prison, where they were constantly in each other's sight. He does have an understanding of object permanence – he knows very well, for instance, that his mother is still imprisoned in the shed when he has escaped from Old Nick to call help, or that his old ramshackle playthings are still in Room. But after their rescue he is jealous of sharing his mother's attention with others and throws a tantrum when she wants to leave the room or even take a shower. He cannot understand why she wants to read the paper instead of going to bed with him, why she wants a separate room to herself, and why she now has things belonging exclusively to her, though they shared everything when they were locked up in Room. When his

---

9 In order to stress the importance of the mother-child relationship, the novel includes references to Harry Harlow's experiments in the 1950s: he showed that baby monkeys removed from their mothers and receiving no nurture developed pathological behavior patterns, although they were properly fed.

mother tries to commit suicide and he has to stay with his grandparents for a while, he is painfully forced to emancipate himself. He hangs on to her rotten tooth which fell out, to have a part of her with him all the time, and one night inadvertently swallows it, literally incorporating his mother. By the end of the novel, however, Jack has learned to accept that there is Jack's Room and Ma's Room, although he is still nervous when his mother is anywhere else in their new apartment.

He is diagnosed by his psychiatrist as being "like a newborn in many ways, despite his remarkably accelerated literacy and numeracy" (2010, 226). At age five he has an astounding range of vocabulary, including such terms as *omnivores* and *equinox*, he confidently uses various tenses and has no problem to tell stories. He is not only able to read, but also understands (and dislikes) sarcasm, and recognizes when the doctor is quoting poetry by the special inflexion of his voice. The fact that nonetheless he still makes occasional grammatical mistakes typical of the language acquisition of children (using the wrong past tense forms, for instance, or a wrong word order in questions) lends authenticity to his mind-style. On the other hand, he cannot tell the police his mother's name or address, nor can he describe the house where they live – abilities generally expected of a child his age, though the readers of course know that his ignorance and awkwardness are only natural, given his history. His world knowledge is completely false, since he originally believes that everything he ever learned from books or television is entirely fictional. As long as he stayed in Room, his schemas were capable of explaining what he perceived around him, but outside there is a disequilibrium for him, an unpleasant and frightening cognitive imbalance. As Meadows (1993, 70) argues, much of cognition and learning depends on our ability of employing relevant knowledge we already have in existing memory to explain new phenomena; having a starting point from which he sets off in the wrong direction necessarily hampers his ability to orient himself in the world and answer questions meaningfully. So it is no wonder that the police officers questioning him originally take him for a "disturbed juvenile" (Donoghue 2010, 183), while Jack, ironically, regards them as slow-witted in turn: "Outsiders don't understand anything" (2010, 189).

His cognitive development, obviously, has been extremely uneven, very advanced in some fields and retarded in others. A certain discrepancy in the development of children is not unusual. "There is evidence that infants rarely pass all items associated with stage n [...] before passing any items associated with n+1 according to Piaget's stages" (Harris 1983, 753). Yet for his interlocutors Jack's extreme cognitive discrepancies are disconcerting: "Knows more math than me but can't go down a slide" (Donoghue 2010, 348), his grandmother grumbles. He has never worn shoes, cannot climb stairs, does not know that flowers grow in the ground, is afraid of rain. However, by the end of the novel Jack has adapted. His spatial perception has also improved, he can gauge distances better and no longer keeps bumping into furniture. He has slowly ceased to hang on slavishly to the old rules established in the time of their detention, which gave him a small sense of control in the new and alien world. He has also learned to deal with the sensory overload overwhelming him in the first few days of freedom, when the wealth of new stimuli made it difficult for him to decide what to choose, try, and look at next, though he continues to view the excess supply of goods with a healthy scepticism. "Outsiders are not like us, they've got a million of things and different kinds of each thing. [...] In Room we knowed [sic!] what everything was called but in the world there's so much, persons don't even know the names" (2010, 328; 333).

As the psychiatrist predicts, social adjustment is naturally problematic for Jack. He has had no contact with other people, except his mother. But peers and relatives, neighbors and teachers help with a child's socialization and intellectual development, and they give advice and emotional and material support to parents (Siegel 2011, 53) – something mother and son have been deprived of. His only friends were the cartoon figures on TV, and the objects in Room. Now he slowly needs to enlarge "the circle of trust" (Donoghue 2010, 227), but must also learn to respect people's wish for privacy and become aware of social taboos and rules of behavior. It is easy to adopt the 'polite' phrase of saying that something tastes "interesting" instead of "yucky" (2010, 254), but more difficult to know why he should not hug a kid he has just met, why his grandmother wants to wear a swimsuit when he insists on her bathing with him ("In Room we were sometimes naked and sometimes dressed, we never minded" [2010, 353]), or why his aunt is angry when he touches his baby cousin's pudenda – he himself talks about his mother's vagina or his own penis without any bashfulness or sense of embarrassment. Gender norms are also something he will have to come to terms with. In Room, his mother let his hair grow, so outside everybody takes him for a girl, and to his Uncle's dismay he prefers a pink 'Dora the Explorer' bag to the Spiderman design supposedly more appropriate for a boy. Also, at the end of the novel, he still has not confronted the traumatic question of who is his father – he still seems to be unaware that everyone has a father.

Jack is aided in the necessary adjustments by his high degree of emotional intelligence and his positive self-image, which bode well for his future development of social competence (Petermann 2002, 176). Thus, although he has never interacted with other children, he finds a role model for his relation to his little cousin in John the Baptist, whom he has seen in a painting of the Madonna and

Child in the lap of St. Anna his mother showed him. Of course he can also be childishly naive, for instance, when he fails to realize that his mother merely pretends not to be hungry to give him a larger share of the scarce food in Room. A study by van Vliet and Wohlwill has shown that children growing up in comparative isolation – on lonely farms, islands, or in sparsely populated areas – may have deficits in verbal and social-role aspects of cognitive development, but may also become more exploratory than their peers and are used to taking over household chores (van Vliet and Wohlwill 1985, 205). Of course these cases of relative isolation cannot be compared to Jack's fate, but it is noteworthy that Jack indeed has problems with social roles, since he refuses to accept that Ma may have roles beyond being 'the mother' – which is why we never get to know her real name. He notes with wonder that in her job as a saleswoman "Grandma doesn't seem like Grandma. Ma says everybody's got a few different selves" (Donoghue 2010, 388). But he is also used to helping his mother with the household, he provides his own meals, and quietly occupies himself when his mother lies in bed unresponsive and thoughtfully puts a glass of water beside her bed. Later, he even saves her life a second time when he realizes she has taken an overdose of pills and calls the nurse for help.

So he is anything but "a freak, or an idiot savant" (2010, 291) with "developmental retardation" (2010, 269), which the sensation-mongering yellow press make him out to be, nor is he in a "borderline catatonic state" even on the night of the flight, "lashing out convulsively" (2010, 205) at his rescuers when he merely tries to shake off the blanket over his head. Neither does the round of self-styled experts discussing his case on TV do justice to him, who loquaciously regard him as a signifier for the condition of modernity, as a symbolic child sacrifice, or as a new Kaspar Hauser (2010, 366–367).

While Jack at his age is plastic enough to survive the prison experience without serious harm, the results of seven years of false imprisonment are more baleful for his mother, who has endured an ordeal of enforced passivity, humiliation, and frequent sexual violation. She tells her son that she suffered from severe depression and cognitive distortions in the first two years of her incarceration:

> I used to be scared to go to sleep, in case he came back [...] but when I was asleep was the only time I wasn't crying, so I slept about sixteen hours a day. [...] I drove myself crazy looking at my watch and counting the seconds. Things spooked me, they seemed to get bigger or smaller while I was watching them, but if I looked away they started sliding. [...] Sometimes I heard voices from the TV telling me things. (2010, 118)

Indeed, perceptual disturbances and hallucinations, such as hearing voices, and paranoia are among the typical results of solitary confinement (Grassian, 2006,

335–337). When Ma bore the child, she gained a new meaning in life, which saved her from becoming insane or suicidal, and possibly also from developing Stockholm syndrome. While she bore up well most of the time in prison, her helplessness vis-à-vis the rapist and the feeling of being at his complete mercy must have taken their toll, because occasionally she fell into a catatonic state, unresponsive even to Jack. Not surprisingly, after their release, to erase all memories of her ordeal, she throws into the trash all their old and frayed clothes – to Jack's consternation at such wastefulness – and is horrified that he wants to keep their old rug: "'This is a fresh start, remember?' She says *remember* but she don't [sic!] want to remember Room" (Donoghue 2010, 381), Jack complains, but after some argument, she finally allows him to hide the old rug in his new wardrobe. After her release, she, too, has to learn social reintegration, but cannot deal with her trauma. She finds it difficult to reconcile her wish to renew old contacts and follow up new interests with Jack's intense clinging. She has to come to terms with her parents' divorce and her father's inability to accept Jack, the product of her rape. Trailed by paparazzi and goaded by an insensitive interviewer who suggests she might have acted selfishly when she did not give up Jack for adoption but kept him with her during her captivity, she blames herself for her mothering and attempts to commit suicide.

At the end of the novel, she seems to be better, which is evinced also by her hesitant agreement to Jack's keen wish to visit Room once more. This brief return forces her to face her trauma. To be sure, so great is her physical revulsion that she vomits when she sees the place, but she does go inside the shed with her son. In this final scene, the focus, however, is on Jack and his reaction to his old home: it all seems "wrong. Smaller than Room and emptier. [...] Nothing says anything to me. 'I don't think this is it,' I whisper to Ma. [...] 'Has it got shrunk?'" (Donoghue 2010, 399–400). Feeling that this is no longer where he belongs, he can say goodbye to Room. From now on, he will no longer hanker after this prison but move on.

4 Prison Metaphors and Metaphors of Imprisonment in *Room*[10]

A few words must finally be said about the metaphors and metonymies of carcerality (Fludernik 2005b) in this unusual prison novel. It is remarkable that throughout the first part of the novel, which Jack and Ma spend in captivity, few explicit metaphors alluding to the prison appear, which is only logical as the narrator does not perceive their room as a jail. Rather, he once thinks, absurdly, that people on a TV channel doing the same gymnastics workout again and again might be locked in and forced drearily to keep going; he himself does not experience the sense of "insipidity, boredom [and] monotony" (Fludernik 2008, 71) we generally associate with prisons. To be sure, the stereotypical equation of prison with hell (Fludernik 2005a, 3; 2005b, 230) is suggested by the nick-name the two victims give to the kidnapper. Jack, however, is unaware that Old Nick is a common designation for the devil; he discovered this name for a spooky creature turning up at night in a book. In fact, we never learn the criminal's real name. Another conventional conception, namely of imprisonment as live burial (Fludernik 2005a, 5; 2005b, 234) or a living death is modified by Donoghue in so far as Jack has to die metaphorically, i.e., he has to pretend to be dead and to be wrapped in Rug as in a winding sheet, to escape from jail into a new life in the outside world. The Christian imagery of resurrection (significantly, the last chapter set in prison is entitled 'dying,' the ultimate chapter in the novel, 'living') and the biblical stories Ma tells the boy add a metaphysical component to the description of prison. Although prison metaphors are rare in these first chapters, there are intertextual references to imprisonment: Ma tells Jack the legend of St. Paul, who is said to have been freed from prison by an angel; and she narrates to him Alexander Dumas's story of *The Count of Monte Cristo*, from whence she also draws the idea for their escape.

Paradoxically, the situation is different in the second part of the novel, i.e., after their jailbreak: in these later chapters many more prison metaphors appear, partly because the journalists reporting on the case fling about stock phrases, and

---

[10] Fludernik distinguishes between prison metaphors, in which prison is the target domain and life in prison is explained by a comparison to other areas of human experience involving experiences like confinement, torture, despair, or infinite boredom; and metaphors of imprisonment, in which the prison serves as a source domain, and the "emotional impact of imprisonment" is projected on to other situations experienced as constraining, oppressive, and hopelessly tedious (2005a, 3–4). See also Fludernik 2005b.

partly because Donoghue uses metaphors and metonymies to link Jack and Ma's prison experience to their new lives in freedom. As far as narrative technique is concerned, the story continues to be narrated through the eyes of Jack, who listens to snippets of the newscasts about his fate and insists on accompanying his mother everywhere, repeating the half-understood buzzwords he overhears and thereby giving us brief access to the opinions and diction of various adults.

As might be expected, the sensation press delight in describing the place of detention with such lurid and clichéd phrases as "an impregnable twenty-first-century dungeon" (Donoghue 2010, 205) or "hellhole," where the mother "eked out" her "precious youth" and had to give birth to a child "under medieval conditions" (2010, 291); they speak melodramatically about "the long nightmare of their incarceration" (2010, 205) and insist on talking about "solitary confinement" (2010, 292) although Ma protests that they were never alone but always together. They want to know about the victims' "days of boredom" (2010, 293) and comment on their "eery pallor" (2010, 205) – all of these phrases correspond to hackneyed metaphorical and metonymic conceptualizations of the prison experience common in our culture. Their designation of Old Nick as a "Garden-shed Ogre" (2010, 269) is merely corny – as opposed to the narrator's naive dread of the criminal as a giant coming to tear him apart –, as is their extolling of Jack as a "pint-sized hero" and "Little Prince" (2010, 269), while in the same breath they compare him to a "monkey" (2010, 269) climbing the stairs on all fours. They are eager to worm out of Ma whether she felt "emotionally dependent on [her] captor" (2010, 290) and misses "being behind a locked door" (2010, 296). Even the kind nurse insensitively asks whether Ma is homesick for Room, to which the latter furiously replies: "it wasn't a *home*, it was a soundproofed cell" (2010, 258).

Jack, who is familiar with the concept of imprisonment as a punitive measure from TV crime series but never felt that the term applied to him, becomes fascinated with the idea of jailing after his escape. He wonders whether the dog which bit him during his escape went to prison for the crime ("No, no [...] it was an honest mistake" (2010, 186) the policewoman assures him). He is obviously relieved when Old Nick is arrested and studies the mug shots, wondering whether the man's pick-up truck, which he used to entrap the mother and to transport the supposedly dead child off, will also be jailed. And he is confident, with a view to St. Paul's miraculous rescue from prison, that "the angel won't burst him [i.e. Old Nick] out because he's a bad guy" (2010, 310). Even more interesting is the way in which Jack draws on his limited world experience and employs metaphors of imprisonment to his new impressions, forcing readers to view their own familiar reality from an estranged angle. Thus he uses the prison as a source domain when in the police station he sees a vending machine for the first time and thinks of the candies inside as being imprisoned in a jail, wishing he knew the code to let them out (2010, 200–201). The fence surrounding the children's playground for him conjures up memories of his mother's description of the chain fence surrounding the shed, making it impossible for her to dig a tunnel (2010, 325) – which for a moment invites readers to view the construction of play areas as prisons for toddlers. In a reversal of normal expectations, Jack asserts at one point: "In Room I was safe and Outside is the scary" (2010, 273).

Especially fascinating are the ironic and thought-provoking parallels that Donoghue establishes between the state of imprisonment in the garden shed and their supposed freedom after their escape. It is indicative of Ma's trauma that she asks the police officer not to close the door of the room where he questions her right after her rescue – being behind closed doors is insufferable for her at that stage. Even at the end of the novel she cannot bring herself to take Jack to the zoo, because she cannot bear the sight of cages. Metonymically, the animals in this passage are likened to prisoners, but also vice versa Ma and Jack to animals that were penned up in a shed; the reference also recalls modern American prison cells, which look like cages (Fludernik 2004, 150). Furthermore, while Ma assures her son that they are not confined in the psychiatric clinic they are first taken to, but free to come and go, after her suicide attempt she is not allowed to leave the hospital for some time. "Ma said we'd be free but this doesn't feel like free" (Donoghue 2010, 320), Jack pertinently comments. The psychiatrist did not even want to let the boy go to his grandparents, pleading the need for "*continuity* and *therapeutic isolation,*" until "Grandma shouted that he wasn't allowed keep [sic!] me like a prisoner when I do have a family" (2010, 315). Later, after the mother's discharge, they move to a new independent living facility with a doorman who does not lock them in, as Jack suspects, but other people out; and in their new apartment the mother draws the bolt so that nobody can open the door from the outside, thereby practically shutting herself in. Although in prisons solitary confinement is regarded as a kind of torture with harmful psychic effects, in the world Jack has to learn that being solitary can also be a relief ("people don't always want to be with people. [...] It gets tiring" [2010, 329]), and that his mother craves some privacy and a room of her own for her psychic health and "to do [her] thinking in" (2010, 380) – a conscious reference to Virginia Woolf's famous text. The basic ambivalence of isolation is directly addressed here, by contrasting voluntary seclusion as a site "of refuge, peace and creativity" and enforced imprisonment, which "is experienced as threatening and alienating. Whoever has the key has the power" (Fludernik 2005a, 15). In an interview, Ma also tries to put her own fate of abuse and incarceration into a larger context, voicing a social criticism Jack does not really understand, but dutifully reports. Slavery, his mother reminds an interviewer, is "not a new invention" (Donoghue 2010, 295), and twenty-five thousand prisoners in the United States are kept in isolation cells, some for decades, without gaining the attention of the media. Physical and mental liberty do not necessarily coincide. "People are locked up in all sorts of ways" (2010, 295), also in their traumas and routines, as the novel shows. Such social criticism ties in with Jack's own childlike critical remarks about the lack of time for anything people 'in the world' seem to have, and their hypocritical treatment of children, whom they like to photograph but do not really want to play with. *Room* also castigates the ruthless media exploitation of crime cases and the "greedy interpreting gaze" (Tonkin 2010) of journalists, psychiatrists, and self-styled experts. Yet Donoghue adds a dose of humor, mainly through Jack's tendency to take idioms literally and his funny misunderstandings of quite ordinary things, such as his belief that a clothes shop with the inscription *Men, Women, Children* is actually selling people (Donoghue 2010, 386) – a comic counterpoint to Ma's reference to slavery.

A tour de force tracing the cognitive development of a child born in captivity who has to refresh all his cognitive schemas[11] to adjust to a new world of liberty, a narrative blending horror and hope, and leavening social criticism with humor – *Room* subverts conventional expectations and transgresses borders of genre. A secluded room may indeed be an "overdetermined" (Tonkin 2010) site in literature, having been widely used to symbolize anything from the mind and the self to the womb, a safe haven, a prison, a tomb, a place of creativity, or even the universe, but Donoghue's novel "bursts free of every preset category" (Tonkin 2010). In an interview with Boyd Tonkin, Donoghue said that when composing the text she was aware of memorable child narrators in books like *The Go-Between* (1953), *Paddy Clarke Ha Ha* (1993), and *A Portrait of the Artist as a Young Man* (1916); but if there are any echoes to these novels, they are faint and only generally pertain to the successful sustaining of a child's mind-style. She also looked to *The Collector* as a model, but obviously chose to narrate the gruesome story of a woman's confinement from a different angle. Interestingly, she confesses that when describing how, "from his own perspective of normality, the boy gapes at all the exotica beyond" (Donoghue in Tonkin 2010), she also thought about eighteenth-century adventure stories like *Robinson Crusoe* (1719) and *Gulliver's Travels* (1726), whose protagonists are also confronted with alien worlds, which force them to readjust their cognitive scripts. In this paper, I have interpreted *Room* mainly as a prison novel, and in this context of a child in prison,

---

11 The term schema refreshment was coined by Guy Cook and is now widely used in cognitive poetics.

deluded by a parent as to the actual danger of the situation, the film *La Vita è Bella*, directed by Roberto Benigni in 1997, comes to mind as the closest parallel, in which a father pretends to his son that their confinement in a Nazi concentration camp is a mere game. Except for remote affinities, however, *Room* is an entirely original text, "sophisticated in outlook and execution" (Maslin 2010), haunting and deeply moving.

References

Barr, Nicola. 2010. "Room by Emma Donoghue." *Observer*, 1 August. Accessed 2 January 2017. Web.
Bender, Aimee. 2010. "Separation Anxiety." *New York Times*, 16 September. Accessed 15 April 2016. Web.
Bortolussi, Marisa, and Peter Dixon. 2003. *Psychonarratology: Foundations for the Empirical Study of Literary Response*. Cambridge: Cambridge University Press.
Brombert Victor. 1978. *The Romantic Prison: The French Tradition*. Princeton: Princeton University Press.
Caracciolo, Marco. 2014. "Two Child Narrators: Defamiliarization, Empathy, and Reader-Response in Mark Haddon's *The Curious Incident* and Emma Donoghue's *Room*." *Semiotica* 202: 183–205.
Charles, Ron. 2010. "Emma Donoghue's 'Room,' reviewed by Ron Charles." *Washington Post*, 15 September. Accessed 15 April 2016. Web.
Cook, Guy. 1990. *A Theory of Discourse Deviation: The Application of Schema Theory to the Analysis of Literary Discourse*. PhD thesis, University of Leeds. Accessed 3 January 2017. Web.
Culler, Jonathan. 1975. *Structuralist Poetics: Structuralism, Linguistics and the Study of Literature*. London: Routledge.
Donoghue, Emma. 2010. *Room*. London: Picador.
Fludernik, Monika. 2004. "Prison Metaphors – The Carceral Imaginary?" In *In the Grip of the Law: Trials, Prisons and the Space Between*, edited by Monika Fludernik and Greta Olson, 145–167. Frankfurt am Main: Peter Lang.
---. 2005a. "Metaphoric (Im)prison(ment) and the Constitution of a Carceral Imaginary." *Anglia* 123.1: 1–25.
---. 2005b. "The Metaphorics and Metonymics of Carcerality: Reflections on Imprisonment as Source and Target Domain in Literary Texts." *English Studies* 86.3: 226–244.
---. 2008. "Carceral Topography: Spatiality, Liminality and Corporality in the Literary Prison." *Textual Practice* 13.1: 43–47.
Gibbs, Jonathan. 2010. "Room by Emma Donoghue: review." *The Telegraph*, 30 July. Accessed 15 April 2016. Web.
Goshin, Lorie S., Byrne, Mary W., and Barbara Blanchard-Lewis. 2014. "Preschool Outcomes of Children Who Lived as Infants in a Prison Nursery." *The Prison Journal* 94.2: 139–158.
Grassian, Stuart. 2006. "Psychiatric Effects of Solitary Confinement." *Washington University Journal of Law & Policy* 22: 325–383. Accessed 20 May 2016. Web.

Harris, P. 1983. "Infant Cognition." In *Handbook of Child Psychology. Vol 2: Infancy and Developmental Psychobiology*, edited by Marshall M. Haith and Joseph M. Haith, 4th ed. 689–783. New York: John Wiley & Sons.
Jeon, Hyun-Joo, Peterson, Carla A., and Jamie DeCoster. 2013. "Parent-Child Interaction, Task-Oriented Regulation, and Cognitive Development in Toddlers Facing Developmental Risks." *Journal of Applied Developmental Psychology* 34.6: 257–267.
Meadows, Sara. 1993. *The Child As Thinker: The Development and Acquisition of Cognition in Childhood*. London: Routledge.
Maccoby, Eleanor E., and John A. Martin. 1983. "Socialization in the Context of the Family: Parent-Child Interaction." In *Handbook of Child Psychology. Vol. 4: Socialization, Personality and Social Development*, edited by Mavis Hetherington, 1–101. New York: John Wiley & Sons.
Maslin, Janet. 2010. "A Captive's View of Life, and He's 5." *New York Times*, 12 September. Accessed 20 May 2016. Web.
Nünning, Ansgar. 2005. "Reconceptualizing Unreliable Narration: Synthesizing Cognitive and Rhetorical Approaches." *A Companion to Narrative Theory*, edited by James Phelan and Peter J. Rabinowitz, 89–107. Oxford: Blackwell.
Palmer, Alan. 2010. *Social Minds in the Novel*. Columbus: Ohio State University Press.
Perry, Menakhem. 1979. "Literary Dynamics: How the Order of a Text Creates its Meaning." *Poetics Today* 1.1–2: 35–64, 311–61.
Petermann, Franz. 2002. "Klinische Kinderpsychologie: Das Konzept der Sozialen Kompetenz." *Zeitschrift für Psychologie* 210.4: 175–185.
Phelan, James. 2005. *Living to Tell about It. A Rhetoric and Ethics of Character Narration*. Ithaca and London: Cornell University Press.
---. 2007. "Estranging Unreliability, Bonding Unreliability, and the Ethics of *Lolita*." *Narrative* 15.2: 222–238.
Olson, Greta. 2003. "Reconsidering Unreliability: Fallible and Untrustworthy Narrators." *Narrative* 11.1: 93–109.
Siegel, Jane A. 2011. *Disrupted Childhoods: Children of Women in Prison*. Piscataway: Rutgers University Press.
Tonkin, Boyd. 2010. "Room with a Panoramic View: How Emma Donoghue's Latest Novel Aims to Tell a Universal Story." *Independent*, 6. August. Accessed 15 April 2016. Web.
Van Vliet, Willem, and Joachim F. Wohlwill. 1985. "Habitats for Children: The State of Evidence." In *Habitats for Children. The Impacts of Density*, edited by Joachim F. Wohlwill and Willem van Vliet, 201–229. Hillsdale: Lawrence Erlbaum Associates.

Franz K. Stanzel
Epilogue: Notes on a Possible History of Reception – From Stanzel to Fludernik[1]

The eternal silence of these infinite spaces terrifies me.
Blaise Pascal

It is terrifying for an author when, after laboring over a book for a very long time, he releases it into the world, but it is met only with profound silence. I personally experienced such terror: many years had passed before I learnt that my *Typische Erzählsituationen* (1955) had not, as I had initially feared, disappeared into a black hole from which no echo could escape. Towards the end of my career as a literary critic and literary theorist, it calms, even satisfies me, to note that some prominent narratologists have entered into a dialogue with my thoughts on narration over the years: Käte Hamburger, Wolfgang Kayser, Robert Weimann, Wolfgang Iser, Wayne C. Booth, Dorrit Cohn, Roy Pascal, Gérard Genette, Seymour Chatman, Mieke Bal, Gerald Prince, Ulrich Broich, Dieter Meindl, Jochen Vogt, Helmut Bonheim, Werner Wolf, Ansgar Nünning, and many others.

After years of researching in various fields, I am pleasantly surprised to see that the discussion of my *Theorie* (1979) is still ongoing. This is evidenced by the inclusion of my concepts in recent handbooks and introductions and new translations of *Theorie*, for instance, a modern Greek version (1999), and an attempt to list only the most important critical or approving scholarly comments would go beyond the scope of this essay. In what follows, I will therefore concentrate on the contributions of my "successor" – I hope she is not displeased with this appellative term – who did not only engage with my narrative theory in more detail than anybody else, but critically developed a number of its aspects: Monika Fludernik.

Monika Fludernik began her academic career, which soon became extremely successful, at the University of Graz with her dissertation "Erzähler- und Figurensprache in James Joyce's *Ulysses*" (1982), a topic which effectively foreshadowed one of the essential questions of her later publications. From among her many works, I would like to single out one piece to briefly exemplify how Fludernik grapples with my theory, namely the comprehensive essay "Second

---

[1] This epilogue is a partial translation of Franz K. Stanzel's "Fingerzeige für eine allfällige Rezeptionsgeschichte," first published in *Unterwegs: Erzähltheorie für Leser*. The translation of the epigraph is taken from Pascal (1995, 73).

DOI 10.1515/9783110569957-015

Person Fiction: Narrative *You* as Addressee and/or Protagonist" (1993a). While I only mentioned second-person narration *en passant* with regard to Michel Butor's novel *Modification* in my *Theorie*, Fludernik establishes this narrative mode as a discrete form. This previously understudied narrative form, Fludernik shows, can be employed productively not only to elucidate the complexity of the shift from the teller to the reflector mode, but also to make visible the issues involved in Genette's distinction between homodiegetic and heterodiegetic narration (1993a, 219; 222). This essay exemplifies how Fludernik expands and diversifies certain postulates of my narrative theory, and eventually relates them to approaches by other theorists, especially Genette. She successfully makes use of this procedure in her substantive monographs.

Fludernik describes *The Fictions of Language and the Languages of Fiction* as "a kind of handbook on free indirect discourse and related phenomena" (1993b, XII). The phenomenon of free indirect discourse has proven to be challenging from a perspective focused on grammar as well as for literary critics who had been on it for over a century. In *The Fictions of Language*, Fludernik brings this discussion to fruition. She uses free indirect discourse as a crucial "discovery tool" for understanding the subtle fusion of the voices constituting a narrative text – a "tool" like no other in narrative theory. With an eye to the history of the field of narrative theory, the way in which Fludernik approaches certain problems and works on their solutions is particularly interesting. In the case of free indirect discourse, Ann Banfield's monograph, provocatively entitled *Unspeakable Sentences: Narration and Representation in the Language of Fiction* (1982), gave her the impulse to reevaluate an old problem.

From a disciplinary and ethological perspective, it is instructive to see that two concepts in narrative theory in particular sparked a great amount of debate and, in turn, proved consequential for the development of the field: the first was Käte Hamburger's concept of the timelessness of the epic preterite and, second, Banfield's theory of free indirect discourse as "unspeakable sentences." These concepts were not intensely debated because they were wrong, but because their range of validity was significantly overstated. The faring of these two theories demonstrates, once again, how some disagreements in narratology – as well as in literary studies in general – are not, in fact, substantive disagreements but are rooted in a far too inclusive demarcation of the textual range that they are applicable to.

In the case of Banfield, it is obvious that her "unspeakable" sentences are exclusively written in the reflector mode, as I already noted in a comment in the second edition of *Theorie* with regard to an earlier study by Banfield entitled "Reflective and Non-Reflective Consciousness in the Language of Fiction" (1981).

The ensuing debates on Banfield's *Unspeakable Sentences* have shown that her thesis can only be accepted if its application is limited to texts written in the reflector mode. Fludernik provides ample evidence for the limited applicability of Benfield's thesis, yet in so doing, she develops areas of narrative theory that extend far beyond the problem of free indirect discourse: "Stanzel's typology [...] anticipates Banfield's linguistic distinction between the speaker text and narration in his teller/reflector mode opposition" (1993b, 64). Consequently, Fludernik equates Banfield's "speakerless" sentences with sentences in the reflector mode in which the narrative voice cannot be heard. She goes on to make my distinction between the teller and reflector mode a central pillar of her argument. She also needs to be credited with far-reaching observations concerning several other questions that are addressed in my *Theorie*, such as those dealing with "referentless pronoun[s]" (1993b, 135), "familiarizing article[s]" (1993b, 145), the present tense as narrative time (1993b, 193) and others. Finally, the model of the typological circle is taken up by Fludernik. Discussion of the model suggested the blending of narrative situations. Fludernik, by contrast, insists on arranging narrative situations on a scale rather than sorting them into rigid categories (1993b, 283; 290 and elsewhere).

Fludernik's development of my theory is especially productive when she takes up my concept of *Personalisierung* (Stanzel 1979, 221), which I initially developed while working on James Joyce and subsequently elaborated on in my discussions of narrative texts by Thomas Mann, Katherine Mansfield, and others. At first, the term *Personalisierung* was translated as *figuralization* in English. Following the introduction of the term *reflector mode*, it was later on translated as *reflectorization*. Fludernik uses two terms, which appear synonymous at first glance, to achieve some sort of monosemy. The terms *figuralization* and *reflectorization* become key terms in her monograph *Towards a 'Natural' Narratology* (1996). She devotes the entire fifth chapter to a discussion of their differentiation. This demonstrates, once again, how Fludernik infuses old terms with new relevance, in this case by integrating my original reader-oriented notion of the term with more recent contributions on the topic. In so doing, she draws on the distinction between a mimetic (a personalized narrator speaks to the reader) and a non-mimetic (narrative function, "itness," "voiced by the narrative itself") conception of the narrative act, which had not yet been established when I published by monograph. She conceptualizes the monosemic disambiguation of the terms *figuralization* and *reflectorization* as follows:

> The distinguishing criterion has been the presence or absence of a character 'on stage' to whom linguistic signals of consciousness can be attributed. If no such character is available, and there is also no narrator persona to whom these signals could be attributed, then

the passage is one of *figuralization*. The text evokes a perceiving consciousness, whether of a mere observer or of a complete 'voice' on the story level. *Reflectorization*, on the other hand, can be defined as the *ironic* echoing of figural discourse well beyond free indirect discourse into the very opinions voiced by the narrative itself. (Fludernik 1996, 217)

I quote this passage at length to show which nuances of a narrative text can be brought to the fore with the help of both terms – nuances which would otherwise go unnoticed. Admittedly, such a level of analysis is challenging to the reader. Personally, it is not always easy for me to follow all of my "successor's" arguments. But I am thankful and satisfied that my work, amongst others, serves as a starting point for an ever more complex and differentiated description of narrative texts.

Translated and adapted for this publication by
Lea Gorski and Karoline Rauschen, with Birte Christ

References

Banfield, Ann. 1981. "Reflective and Non-Reflective Consciousness in the Language of Fiction." *Poetics Today* 2.2: 61–76.
---. 1982. *Unspeakable Sentences: Narration and Representation in the Languages of Fiction*. Abingdon: Routledge.
Fludernik, Monika. 1982. "Erzähler- und Figurensprache in James Joyce Ulysses." PhD diss., University of Graz, Austria.
---. 1993a. "Second Person Fiction: Narrative You as Addressee and/or Protagonist." *Arbeiten aus Anglistik und Amerikanistik* 18: 217–247.
---. 1993b. *The Fictions of Language and the Languages of Fiction*. London: Routledge.
---. 1996. *Towards a 'Natural' Narratology*. London: Routledge.
Pascal, Blaise. 1995. *Pensées and Other Writings*. Translated by Honor Levi. Oxford: Oxford World Classics.
Stanzel, Franz K. 1955. *Die typischen Erzählsituationen im Roman*. Wien: Braumüller.
---. 1979. *Theorie des Erzählens*. Göttingen: Vandenhoeck & Ruprecht.
---. 1999. *Θεωρία της αφήγησης*. Translated by Kyriaki Chryssomalli-Henrich. Thessaloniki: University Studio Press.
---. 2002. "Fingerzeige für eine allfällige Rezeptionsgeschichte." In *Unterwegs: Erzähltheorie für Leser*, 101–104. Göttingen: Vandenhoeck & Ruprecht.

Contributors

Jan Alber is Professor of English Literature and Cognitive Studies at RWTH Aachen University and President of the International Society for the Study of Narrative (ISSN). He is the author of *Narrating the Prison* (2007) and *Unnatural Narrative: Impossible Worlds in Fiction and Drama* (2016). Jan Alber received fellowships and research grants from the British Academy, the German Research Foundation, and the Humboldt Foundation. In 2013, the German Association of University Teachers of English awarded him the prize for the best *Habilitation* written between 2011 and 2013. Between 2014 and 2016, he was a COFUND Marie-Curie Fellow at the Aarhus Institute of Advanced Studies. Jan Alber worked as Monika Fludernik's assistant for several years, and has learned many things from her. He admires her knowledge and persistence very much, and believes that he could not have had a better mentor.

Dorothee Birke is Marie Curie Research Fellow at the Aarhus Institute for Advanced Studies, Denmark. Her monograph *Writing the Reader: Configurations of a Cultural Practice in the English Novel* came out in 2016; further book publications include *Memory's Fragile Power: Crises of Memory, Identity and Narrative in Contemporary British Novels* and the edited volume *Realisms in Contemporary Culture: Theories, Politics and Medial Configurations* (with Stella Butter). Her main research interests are reception theory, narrative theory, history of reading and the novel as well as political theatre. Monika Fludernik has been a long-term source of inspiration, mentor, and advisor of her habilitation at the University of Freiburg.

Philippe Carrard is Emeritus Professor of French at the University of Vermont and currently a Visiting Scholar in the Program of Comparative Literature at Dartmouth College. His research bears mostly on conventions of writing in factual discourse. In this area, he has recently published *History as a Kind of Writing: Textual Strategies in Contemporary French Historiography* (2017) and *L'Histoire s'écrit*, a translation of selected essays by Hayden White (2017). He knows Monika through conferences and a both scholarly and social visit to Freiburg.

Marco Caracciolo is Assistant Professor of English and Literary Theory at Ghent University in Belgium, where he leads the ERC Starting Grant project "Narrating the Mesh." He is the author of three books: *The Experientiality of Narrative* (2014); *Strange Narrators in Contemporary Fiction* (2016); and *A Passion for Specificity* (co-authored with psychologist Russell Hurlburt, 2016). Marco's work explores the phenomenology of narrative, or the structure of the experiences afforded by literary fiction and other narrative media. Before coming to Ghent, Marco spent two years at the University of Freiburg on a post-doctoral fellowship from the Alexander von Humboldt Foundation; Monika Fludernik was his host professor.

Birte Christ is Assistant Professor of American Literary and Cultural Studies at Justus-Liebig-University Gießen. Birte's most important publication in the field of narratology is "Paratext and Digitized Narrative: Mapping the Field" (2013), with Dorothee Birke. She is interested mostly in using concepts and insights of narratology for ideological analysis, which is the case in her monograph *Modern Domestic Fiction* (2012). Birte did not know what she was about to get into when she attended a seminar on *Ulysses* with Monika Fludernik in the year 2000 – writing a PhD thesis under her tutelage, being taken along to *Narrative* conferences, and continuing to be the recipient of much-needed academic advice would only be a very small part of what it means to be a member of the "family."

Eva von Contzen is Assistant Professor of English Literature at the University of Freiburg and the principal investigator of the ERC-funded project "Lists in Literature and Culture: Towards a Listology." She is the author of *The Scottish Legendary: Towards a Poetics of Hagiographic Narration* (2016) and has published on narrative theory and medieval literature, sanctity in the Middle Ages, Neo-Latin epic, and lists in literature. She is the co-editor of a handbook of historical narratology (together with Stefan Tilg; forthcoming). Currently, her main project is devoted to lists and enumerations in literary texts from Antiquity to postmodernism. Monika Fludernik's work on diachronic narratology has inspired her to become a narratologist.

Hilary Duffield is Professor of English Literature at the University of Trier. Her current research interests include narratives of environmental crisis and the Anthropocene, cognitive approaches to television and film narrative, fantastic journeys in space and time – representations in fiction and film. Her book *Coincidence and Counterfactuality: Plotting Time and Space in Narrative Fiction* (2008; published as Hilary Dannenberg) won the George and Barbara Perkins award for the most significant contribution to the study of narrative in 2010. She worked as Assistant Professor to Monika Fludernik at the University of Freiburg from 1995 to 2002.

Kerstin Fest is Assistant Professor of English Literature at the University of Freiburg. Her monograph *And All Women Mere Players? Performance and Identity in*

Dorothy Richardson, Jean Rhys and Radclyffe Hall appeared in 2009. She contributed a chapter on idleness and the comedy of manners to *Idleness, Indolence and Leisure in English Literature* edited by Monika Fludernik and Miriam Nandi (2016) and published articles on queer theory, chick lit, and art in *German Life and Letters* and *The Journal of Popular Culture*. She is now working on a Habilitationsschrift on eighteenth-century English theatre under the supervision of Monika Fludernik, who was also her PhD supervisor.

Benjamin Kohlmann is Assistant Professor of English Literature at the University of Freiburg. His first monograph *Committed Styles: Modernism, Politics, and Left-Wing Literature* was published by Oxford UP in 2014. He specialises in the politics of writing, contemporary literary theory, and the links between literature and political economy. Even though Benjamin is not a narratologist, he got the chance to rejoin Monika's team in Freiburg when he returned from doing his doctoral work in the UK. As an 'Assistent' at Monika's chair, Benjamin has always admired her ability to take a genuine interest in (and her willingness to engage with) work that falls outside the field of narratology. It is hard to imagine a more brilliant – or a more supportive – mentor.

Susan S. Lanser is Professor Emerita of Comparative Literature, English, and Women's, Gender, and Sexuality Studies at Brandeis University. She is the author of *The Narrative Act: Point of View in Prose Fiction* (1981), *Fictions of Authority: Women Writers and Narrative Voice* (1992), and *The Sexuality of History: Modernity and the Sapphic, 1565-1830* (2014) and co-editor with Robyn Warhol of *Narrative Theory Unbound: Queer and Feminist Interventions* (2015). Her current research interests encompass narrative theory, eighteenth-century literature and culture, and narratives of the Israeli-Palestinian conflict. She has long admired and benefited from the work of Monika Fludernik, not least because of their shared commitments to both eighteenth-century studies and narratology.

Wolfgang G. Müller is retired Professor of English Literature at the Friedrich-Schiller-University of Jena. His book-length publications include *Die politische Rede bei Shakespeare* (1979), *Topik des Stilbegriffs* (1981), and an edition of Shakespeare's *Hamlet* (2006). His research interests cover the theory and practice of poetry analysis, meter, style and rhetoric, Shakespeare's drama, narratology, the tradition of *Don Quijote* in European literature, the literary flâneur and the relation of literature and philosophy. He first met Monika Fludernik at a conference in Salzburg in the 1980s and shares many scholarly concerns with her, especially the conviction that there is a necessary bond between linguistics and literary studies.

Miriam Nandi is Assistant Professor of English Literature at the University of Freiburg. Her work focusses on the various ways in which cultural and historical alterity are mediated in narrative. She wrote her first monograph *M/Other India/s* (2007) under Monika Fludernik's tutelage and has benefited from her tremendous support ever since. Without Monika Fludernik's enthusiastic reference letters Miriam would hardly have been accepted into Cornell's *School of Criticism and Theory* in 2005, nor would she have acquired the Margarete von Wrangell research grant for her Habilitation on forms and functions of the early modern diary. Most likely, she would not have completed the Habilitation process had it not been for Monika Fludernik's insistence to get her act together. Miriam continues to admire her mentor's unshakable loyalty, academic brilliance, and honesty.

Ansgar Nünning is Professor of English and American Literature and Cultural Studies and founding director of the "Giessener Graduiertenzentrum Kulturwissenschaften" (GGK) and the "International Graduate Centre for the Study of Culture" (GCSC), funded by the Excellence Initiative, at Justus-Liebig-University in Giessen. His most recent publications include *Cultural Ways of Worldmaking: Media and Narratives* (ed. with Vera Nünning and Birgit Neumann, 2010), *Metzler Lexikon Literatur- und Kulturtheorie: Ansätze – Personen – Grundbegriffe* (ed., 5th ed. 2013) and *Emergent Forms of Life in Anglophone Literature: Conceptual Frameworks and Critical Analyses* (ed. with Michael Basseler and Daniel Hartley, 2015). In addition to narrative theory, English and American literature, cultures of memory, and literary and cultural theory, his recent research interests include forms of life and notions of a good life, narratives of slow change (e.g. climate change, mind change, stories of health and illness) and the interfaces between narratives/narrative studies and medicine/salutogenesis. He has collaborated with Monika Fludernik in various capacities since 1995, while also contributing to some of the lecture series organized, and volumes edited, by Monika in Freiburg.

Vera Nünning has been Professor of English Philology at Heidelberg University since 2002, and she also served as Vice-Rector for International Affairs from 2006-2009 and as one of the Vice-Presidents of the German consortium of the Turkish-German University in Istanbul. Among her most recent works are *New Approaches to Narrative: Cognition – Culture – History* (ed., 2013), *Ritual and Narrative* (ed. with Jan Rupp and Gregor Ahn, 2013), *Changing Fictions, Changing Minds*

(2014), and *Unreliable Narration and Trustworthiness: Intermedial and Interdisciplinary Perspectives* (ed., 2015). Besides British literature from the eighteenth to the twenty-first century and cultural history from the sixteenth to the nineteenth century, her main research interests have recently been contemporary literature, postclassical narrative theory, and the interfaces between narrative studies and psychology. She has known Monika and (like Ansgar) been an avid reader of her works for twenty years.

Greta Olson is Professor of English and American Literary and Cultural Studies at the University of Giessen, general editor of the *European Journal of English Studies*, and co-founder of the "European Network for Law and Literature Research." Publications include "Law's Pluralities: Arguments for Cultural Approaches to Law," *German Law Journal* 18.2. (2017), "The Politics of Form," *EJES* 20.3, with Sarah Copland (2016), *Criminals as Animals from Shakespeare to Lombroso* (2013), and *Current Trends in Narratology* (2011). She works on cultural approaches to law, the politics of narrative, critical media and American studies, and feminism and sexuality. She initially tried to impress Monika Fludernik by doing research on narrative unreliability, yet soon found that her own thinking and approach to texts had been radically altered by this narratologist's scrupulous attention to form. This scrupulousness is also expressed in Monika's care for her students and mentees as well as her friends.

Margarete Rubik is Emerita Professor of English Literature at the University of Vienna. She has published widely in the fields of Restoration and eighteenth-century literature and modern fiction and drama, for instance the study *Early Women Dramatists: Women Playwrights in England 1550 – 1800*, a special issue on *Aphra Behn*, edited for the journal *Women's Writing*, or the paper "Navigating through Fantasy Worlds: Cognition and the Intricacies of Reader Response in Jasper Fforde's *The Eyre Affair*," which appeared in the volume *Cognition and Literary Interpretation*. Her research interests are wide, ranging from seventeenth-century to contemporary literature and cognitive poetics. She was a colleague of Monika Fludernik's at the University of Vienna and has been a friend of hers ever since.

Wolf Schmid is Professor Emeritus of Slavic Literatures at the University of Hamburg. He has founded the Hamburg "Research Group of Narratology," the "Interdisciplinary Center for Narratology," and, with his Hamburg colleagues, the "European Narratology Network." He has authored *Elemente der Narratologie* (Russian 2003, 2008; German 2005, 2008, 2014; English 2010, Chinese and Brazilian translations in preparation) and *Mentale Ereignisse* (2017). He is executive editor of the series *Narratologia*. He has admired Monika's work for many years, sharing with her the interest in speech and mind representation in fiction.

During a quarter of a century as Emeritus Professor of English at the University of Graz, **Franz K. Stanzel** has seen his *Theory of Narrative* through its 8th edition (2008), and translations into several languages including Japanese. Together with M. Löschnigg he edited a comparative study of the presentation of the Great War in English and German literature, *Intimate Enemies* (second ed. 1994). Much time was also devoted to organizing symposia and exhibitions concerning the history of national images and stereotypes in literature, *Europäer: Ein imagologischer Vergleich* (second ed. 1998), and *Europäischer Völkerspiegel* (1999). Finally, he traced the motif of telegony, the belief in the effect the imagination can have on a child in the act of its begetting from antiquity to modern times in *Telegonie – Fernzeugung* (2008). He was one of the founder-members of the Anglistenverband in 1966/67 as well as of the Association for Canadian Studies in the German Speaking Countries.

Robyn Warhol is Arts and Sciences Professor and Chair of the English Department at the Ohio State University, where she is also a core faculty member of Project Narrative. She is co-author of *Narrative Theory: Core Concepts and Critical Debates* (2012) and of *Love Among the Archives: Writing the Lives of Sir George Scharf, Victorian Bachelor* (2015), and co-editor with Susan S. Lanser of *Narrative Theory Unbound: Queer and Feminist Interventions* (2015). Recently she has been studying the narrative structures of seriality in Victorian novels and contemporary TV shows. In the mid-1980s, she and Monika Fludernik met on an MLA panel about narratorial direct address in fiction; since Warhol's time at the Freiburg Institute for Advanced Study in the summers of 2011 and 2012, the two have been good friends.

www.ingramcontent.com/pod-product-compliance
Lightning Source LLC
Chambersburg PA
CBHW030617230426
43661CB00053B/2029